ACCA

PAPER F5

PERFORMANCE MANAGEMENT

BPP Learning Media is an **ACCA Approved Content Provider** for the ACCA qualification. This means we work closely with ACCA to ensure our products fully prepare you for your ACCA exams.

In this Practice & Revision Kit, which has been reviewed by the **ACCA examination team,** we:

- Discuss the **best strategies** for revising and taking your ACCA exams
- Ensure you are well **prepared** for your exam
- Provide you with **lots of great guidance** on tackling questions
- Provide you with **three** mock exams
- Provide **ACCA exam answers** as well as our own for selected questions

Our **Passcard** product also supports this paper.

FOR EXAMS FROM IN SEPTEMBER 2016, DECEMBER 2016, MARCH 2017 AND JUNE 2017

PRACTICE & REVISION KIT

First edition 2008

Tenth edition February 2016

ISBN 9781 4727 4437 1
(previous ISBN 9781 4727 2688 9)
e-ISBN 9781 4727 4652 8

British Library Cataloguing-in-Publication Data
A catalogue record for this book
is available from the British Library

Published by
BPP Learning Media Ltd
BPP House, Aldine Place
London W12 8AA

www.bpp.com/learningmedia

Printed in the United Kingdom by RICOH UK Limited
Unit 2
Wells Place
Merstham
RH1 3LG

We are grateful to the Association of Chartered Certified
Accountants for permission to reproduce past examination
questions. The suggested solutions in the Practice & Revision Kit
have been prepared by BPP Learning Media Ltd, except where
otherwise stated.

BPP
LEARNING MEDIA

About this Practice & Revision Kit

ACCA will start to transition F5–F9 to computer based examination (CBE), beginning with a pilot in limited markets in September 2016. Students will initially have the choice of CBE or paper exams and as a result, changes will be made to BPP's learning materials to ensure that we fully support students through this transition.

This Practice & Revision Kit is valid for exams from the September 2016 sitting through to the June 2017 sitting and in this Practice & Revision Kit you will find questions in both multiple choice question (MCQ) and objective testing question (OTQ) format. OTQs include a wider variety of questions types including MCQ as well as number entry, multiple response and drag and drop. More information on these question types will be available on the ACCA website.

OTQ's will only appear in computer based exams but these questions will still provide valuable practice for all students whichever version of the exam is taken. These are clearly marked on the contents page as either CBE style OTQ bank or CBE style OT case.

In addition please note that the specimen paper based exam paper has been included as Mock Exam 3 in this Practice & Revision Kit. The questions in Sections A and B are MCQ only whereas in the computer based exam these sections will contain OTQs.

At the time of going to print, ACCA had not yet announced the proposed duration of the computer-based exam and so all timings given throughout this Practice & Revision Kit are based on the paper-based exam which is 3 hours and 15 minutes long. Time management is a key skill for success in this exam and so we recommend you use these indicative timings when attempting questions.

ACCA are recommending that all students consult the ACCA website on a regular basis for updates on the launch of the new CBEs.

Contents

BPP
LEARNING MEDIA

Question index

The headings in this checklist/index indicate the main topics of questions, but questions often cover several different topics.

Questions set under the old syllabus *Financial Management and Control* and *Performance Management* papers are included because their style and content are similar to those which appear in the F5 exam. The questions have been amended to reflect the current exam format.

BPP LEARNING MEDIA

Mock exam 1

Mock exam 2 (CBE style)

Mock exam 3 (Specimen exam)

Topic index

Listed below are the key Paper F5 syllabus topics and the numbers of the questions in this Kit covering those topics.

If you need to concentrate your practice and revision on certain topics or if you want to attempt all available questions that refer to a particular subject, you will find this index useful.

Syllabus topic	Question numbers
Activity based costing	31-35, 36-40, 41-45, ME1 16-20.
Balanced Scorecard	250-254, 260-264, ME2 32.
Budgetary systems and types	199, 200, 201 288, ME1 31, ME2 31,
Cost volume profit (CVP) analysis	133
Decision rules	96-100, 101-105, ME1 21-25,
Learning curve	164-168, 169-173, ME1 26-30, ME2 26-30
Limiting factor	46-50, 51-55 111-115, ME2 16-20
Linear programming	126-130, 132,
Make-or-buy decisions	116-120
Management information systems	281
Mix and yield variances	174-178, 202
Non-financial performance indicators	285
Performance measurement	255-259, 284, 286, 287, ME1 32
Planning and operational variances	179-183, 184-18, 189-193, 194-198, 202
Pricing decisions	131
Relevant costs	106-110, 121-125
Return on investment and residual income	265-269, 270-274, 275-279, 280, ME2 21-25
Standard costs	203, 204, ME1 26-30, ME2 26-30
Target costing	56-60
Throughput accounting	46-50, 51-55 111-115, ME2 16-20
Transfer pricing	245-249, 282.

Helping you with your revision

BPP Learning Media – Approved Content Provider

As an ACCA **Approved Content Provider**, BPP Learning Media gives you the **opportunity** to use revision materials reviewed by the ACCA examination team. By incorporating the ACCA examination team's comments and suggestions regarding the depth and breadth of syllabus coverage, the BPP Learning Media Practice & Revision Kit provides excellent, **ACCA-approved** support for your revision.

Tackling revision and the exam

Using feedback obtained from the ACCA examination team review:

- We look at the dos and don'ts of revising for, and taking, ACCA exams
- We focus on Paper F5; we discuss revising the syllabus, what to do (and what not to do) in the exam, how to approach different types of question and ways of obtaining easy marks

Selecting questions

We provide signposts to help you plan your revision.

- A full **question index**
- A **topic index** listing all the questions that cover key topics, so that you can locate the questions that provide practice on these topics, and see the different ways in which they might be examined

Making the most of question practice

At BPP Learning Media we realise that you need more than just questions and model answers to get the most from your question practice.

- Our **top tips** included for certain questions provide essential advice on tackling questions, presenting answers and the key points that answers need to include.
- We show you how you can pick up **easy marks** on some questions, as we know that picking up all readily available marks often can make the difference between passing and failing.
- We include **marking guides** to show you what the examination team rewards.
- We include **comments from the examination team** to show you where students struggled or performed well in the actual exam.
- We refer to the **BPP Study Text for exams in September 2016, December 2016, March 2017 and June 2017** for detailed coverage of the topics covered in questions.

Attempting mock exams

There are three mock exams that provide practice at coping with the pressures of the exam day. We strongly recommend that you attempt them under exam conditions. **Mock exams 1 and 2** reflect the question styles and syllabus coverage of the paper-based and computer-based exams respectively; **Mock exam 3** is the Specimen exam paper.

Revising F5

All questions are compulsory so you must revise the **whole** syllabus. Since the exam includes 15 multiple choice questions, you should expect questions to cover a large part of the syllabus. Selective revision **will limit** the number of questions you can answer and hence reduce your chances of passing. It is better to go into the exam knowing a reasonable amount about most of the syllabus rather than concentrating on a few topics to the exclusion of the rest.

Practising as many exam-style questions as possible will be the key to passing this exam. You must do questions under **timed conditions** and ensure you write full answers to the discussion parts as well as doing the calculations.

Make sure you practise written sections as well as the calculations.

Avoid looking at the answer until you have finished a question. Your biggest problem with F5 questions may be knowing how to start, and this needs practice.

Also ensure that you attempt all three mock exams under exam conditions.

Passing the F5 exam

Displaying the right qualities

- You are expected to have a core of management accounting knowledge from your previous studies of F2.

- You will be required to identify the requirements of multiple choice questions quickly, so that you can make your answers confidently within the available time.

- You will be required to carry out calculations, with clear workings and a logical structure.

- You will be required to interpret data.

- You will be required to explain management accounting techniques and discuss whether they are appropriate for a particular organisation.

- You must be able to apply your skills in a practical context.

- You must understand what numbers tell you about the performance of a business.

Avoiding weaknesses

- There is no choice in this paper, all questions have to be answered. You must therefore study the entire syllabus, there are no short-cuts.

- Ability to answer multiple choice questions and cases improves with practice. Try to get as much practice with these questions as you can.

- The longer questions will be based on simple scenarios and answers must be focused and specific to the organisation.

- Answer plans for the longer questions will help you to focus on the requirements of the question and enable you to manage your time effectively – but there will not be much time.

- Answer all parts of the longer questions. Even if you cannot do all the calculation elements, you will still be able to gain marks in the discussion parts.

Gaining the easy marks

Easy marks in this paper tend to fall into three categories.

Multiple choice questions

Some MCQs are easier than others. Answer those that you feel fairly confident about as quickly as you can. Come back later to those you find more difficult. This could be a way of making use of the time in the examination most efficiently and effectively.

Many MCQs will not involve calculations. Make sure that you understand the wording of 'written' MCQs before selecting your answer.

Calculations in Section C questions

There will be some relatively straightforward calculations at the start of the question and they will then probably get progressively more difficult. If you get stuck, make an assumption, state it and move on.

A Section C question may separate discussion requirements from calculations, so that you do not need to do the calculations first in order to answer the discussion part. This means that you should be able to gain marks from making sensible, practical comments without having to complete the calculations.

Discussions that are focused on the specific organisation in the question will gain more marks than regurgitation of knowledge. Read the question carefully and more than once, to ensure you are actually answering the specific requirements.

Pick out key words such as 'describe', 'evaluate' and 'discuss'. These all mean something specific.

- 'Describe' means to communicate the key features of
- 'Evaluate' means to assess the value of
- 'Discuss' means to examine in detail by argument

Clearly label the points you make in discussions so that the marker can identify them all rather than getting lost in the detail.

Provide answers in the form requested. Use a report format if asked for and give recommendations if required.

Tackling Objective Test Case Questions

First, read the whole case scenario. Make a note of any specific instructions or assumptions such as ignore inflation.

Then skim through the requirements of the five questions. The questions are independent of each other and can be answered in any order.

Some of the OTs will be easier than others. For example, you may be asked to identify the advantages of ABC costing compared with traditional absorption costing. Answer these OTs quickly.

Other OTs will be more difficult and/or complex. There are two types of OT that may take you longer to answer.

The first more time-consuming OT will involve doing a computation. For example, you may be asked to calculate the throughput accounting ratio of a product. You will probably need to jot down a quick proforma to answer a computational question like this. If the OT is a multiple choice question, remember that the wrong answers will usually involve common errors so don't assume that because you have the same answer as one of the options that your answer is necessarily correct! Double check to make sure you haven't made any silly mistakes. If you haven't got the same answer as any of the options, rework your computation, thinking carefully about what errors you could have made. If you still haven't got one of the options, choose the one which is nearest to your answer.

The second more time-consuming OT is one where you are asked to consider a number of statements and identify which one (or more) of them is correct. Make sure that you read each statement at least twice before making your selection. Be careful to follow the requirements of the OT exactly, for example if you are asked to identify **two** correct statements.

Exam formulae

Set out below are the formulae **which you will be given in the exam** in a formulae sheet. You should learn to use them. If you are not sure what the symbols mean, or how the formulae are used, you should refer to the appropriate chapter in the Study Text.

Exam formulae

Chapter in Study Text

Demand curve

5

$P = a - bQ$

$b = \dfrac{\text{Change in price}}{\text{Change in quantity}}$

a = price when $Q = 0$

$MR = a - 2bQ$

Learning curve

9

$Y = ax^b$

Where Y = the cumulative average time per unit to produce X units

a = the time taken for the first unit of output

x = the cumulative number of units

b = the index of learning (log LR/log 2)

LR = the learning rate as a decimal

BPP LEARNING MEDIA

Exam formulae   xiii

Exam information

Computer-based Exams

ACCA have announced that they intend to commence the launch of computer based exams (CBE's) for F5–F9. They will be piloting computer based exams in limited markets in September 2016 with the aim of rolling out into all markets internationally over a five year period. Paper based examinations will be run in parallel while the CBE's are phased in and BPP materials have been designed to support you, whichever exam option you choose.

Format of the exam

The exam format is the same irrespective of the mode of delivery and will comprise three exam sections

Section	Style of question type	Description	Proportion of exam, %
A	Objective test (OT)	15 questions × 2 marks	30
B	Objective test (OT) case	3 questions × 10 marks Each question will contain 5 subparts each worth 2 marks	30
C	Constructed Response (Long questions)	2 questions × 20 marks	40
Total			100

Section A and B questions will be selected from the entire syllabus. The paper version of these objective test questions contain multiple choice only and the computer based versions will contain a variety. The responses to each question or subpart in the case of OT cases are marked automatically as either correct or incorrect by computer.

Section C questions will mainly focus on the following syllabus areas but a minority of marks can be drawn from any other area of the syllabus:

- Decision-making techniques (syllabus area B)
- Budgeting and control (syllabus area C)
- Performance measurement and control (syllabus area D)

The responses to these questions are human marked.

Additional information

The Study Guide provides more detailed guidance on the syllabus.

Useful websites

The websites below provide additional sources of information of relevance to your studies for *Performance Management*.

- www.accaglobal.com

  ACCA's website. The students' section of the website is invaluable for detailed information about the qualification, past issues of Student Accountant (including technical articles) and a free downloadable Student Planner App.

- www.bpp.com

  Our website provides information about BPP products and services, with a link to the ACCA website.

Questions

PART A: SPECIALIST COST AND MANAGEMENT ACCOUNTING TECHNIQUES

Questions 1 to 60 cover Specialist cost and management accounting techniques, the subject of Part A of the BPP Study Text for Paper F5.

Section A questions

MCQ bank – Specialist cost and management accounting techniques
59 mins

1   The following costs have arisen in relation to the production of a product:

    (i)   Planning and concept design costs
    (ii)   Testing costs
    (iii)   Production costs
    (iv)   Distribution and customer service costs

In calculating the life cycle costs of a product, which of the above items would be included?

    A   (iii) only
    B   (i), (ii) and (iii) only
    C   (i), (ii) and (iv) only
    D   All of the above   **(2 marks)**

2   In which of the following ways might financial returns be improved over the life cycle of a product?

    (1)   Maximising the breakeven time
    (2)   Minimising the time to market
    (3)   Minimising the length of the life cycle

    A   1 and 2 only
    B   1 and 3 only
    C   2 only
    D   2 and 3 only   **(2 marks)**

3   One of the products manufactured by a company is Product X, which sells for $40 per unit and has a material cost of $10 per unit and a direct labour cost of $7 per unit. The total direct labour budget for the year is 50,000 hours of labour time at a cost of $12 per hour. Factory overheads are $2,920,000 per year.

The company is considering the introduction of a system of throughput accounting. It has identified that machine time as the bottleneck in production. Product X needs 0.01 hours of machine time per unit produced. The maximum capacity for machine time is 4,000 hours per year.

What is the throughput accounting ratio for Product X?

    A $3,41
    B $2.80
    C $2.10
    D $1.90   **(2 marks)**

4   The following statements have been made about material flow cost accounting.

(1)   In material flow cost accounting, waste is treated as a negative product and given a cost.

(2)   Material flow cost accounting should encourage management to focus on ways of achieving the same amount of finished output with less material input.

Which of the above statements is/are true?

A   1 only
B   2 only
C   Neither 1 nor 2
D   Both 1 and 2   **(2 marks)**

5   Which of the following statements about activity based costing are true?

A   The cost driver for quality inspection is likely to be batch size.

B   The cost driver for materials handling and despatch costs is likely to be the number of orders handled.

C   In the short run, all the overhead costs for an activity vary with the amount of the cost driver for the activity.

D   A cost driver is an activity based cost.   **(2 marks)**

6   The following information relates to the expected cost of a new product over its expected three-year life.

	Year 0	Year 1	Year 2	Year 3
Units made and sold		25,000	100,000	75,000
R&D costs	$850,000	$90,000		
Production costs				
Variable per unit		$30	$25	$20
Fixed costs		$500,000	$500,000	$500,000
Selling and distribution costs				
Variable per unit		$6	$5	$4
Fixed costs		$700,000	$500,000	$300,000
Customer service costs				
Variable per unit		$4	$3	$2

What is the expected average life cycle cost per unit?

A $35.95
B $46.25
C $48.00
D $50.95   **(2 marks)**

7   The following statements have been made about throughput accounting.

(1)   Inventory has no value and should be valued at $0.
(2)   Efficiency is maximised by utilising direct labour time and machine time to full capacity.

Which of the above statements is/are true?

A   1 only
B   2 only
C   Neither 1 nor 2
D   Both 1 and 2   **(2 marks)**

8   In environmental costing, the future cost of cleaning up operations for a product or activity may be classified as which of the following?

A   Carbon footprint
B   Contingent cost
C   Hidden cost
D   Relationship cost   **(2 marks)**

9   The following statements have been made about throughput accounting.

(1)   Direct labour should always be treated as a factory cost when measuring throughput.

(2)   If machine time is the bottleneck resource, there is no value in taking measures to improve direct labour efficiency.

Which of the above statements is/are true?

A   1 only
B   2 only
C   Neither 1 nor 2
D   Both 1 and 2   **(2 marks)**

10   The following statements have been made about traditional absorption costing and activity based costing.

(1)   Traditional absorption costing may be used to set prices for products, but activity based costing may not.

(2)   Traditional absorption costing tends to allocate too many overhead costs to low-volume products and not enough overheads to high-volume products.

(3)   Implementing ABC is expensive and time consuming

Which of the above statements is/are true?

A   1 only
B   2 only
C   3 only
D   1 and 2 only   **(2 marks)**

11   The following data refers to a soft drinks manufacturing company that passes its product through four processes and is currently operating at optimal capacity.

Process	Washing	Filling	Capping	Labelling
Time per dozen units	6 mins	3 mins	1.5 mins	2 mins
Machine hours available	1,200	700	250	450

Product data	$ per unit
Selling price	0.60
Direct material	0.18
Direct labour	0.02
Factory fixed cost	$4,120

Which process is the bottleneck?

A   Washing
B   Filling
C   Capping
D   Labelling   **(2 marks)**

12   In which of the following ways might financial returns be improved over the life cycle of a product?

1.   Maximising the time to market
2.   Minimising the breakeven time
3.   Maximising the length of the life cycle

A   (1) and (2) only
B   (1) and (3) only
C   (2) only
D   (2) and (3) only   **(2 marks)**

13   In material flow cost accounting (MFCA), input manufacturing costs are categorised into material costs, waste treatment costs and which of the following?

A   System costs and energy costs
B   Positive product costs
C   Negative product costs
D   Positive products costs and negative product costs   **(2 marks)**

14   In the theory of constraints and throughput accounting, which of the following methods may be used to elevate the performance of a binding constraint?

(Method 1) Acquire more of the resource that is the binding constraint

(Method 2)   Improve the efficiency of usage of the resource that is the binding constraint

A   Method 1 only
B   Method 2 only
C   Method 1 and Method 2
D   Neither method would be effective   **(2 marks)**

15   ABC Company uses throughput accounting. Machine time is the current binding constraint on production output, and management are looking for ways to increase the throughput accounting (TA) ratio for a product that the machine is used to manufacture.

Which of the following will have NO effect on the TA ratio?

A   Increasing the selling price of the product

B   Obtaining a lower purchase price for materials for the product

C   Reducing factory costs

D   Reducing the machine time per unit to make the product   **(2 marks)**

                                                                          (Total = 30 marks)

CBE style OTQ bank – Specialist cost and management accounting techniques   **59 mins**

16   The following statements have been made about environmental management accounting.

                                                                          True   False

(1)   A system of environmental management accounting provides environmental information for internal use by management, but not for external reporting.   ☐   ☐

(2)   Environmental management accounting systems typically make use of life cycle costing.   ☐   ☐

                                                                          (2 marks)

17   Which **two** of following statements about throughput accounting and the theory of constraints are true?

☐   A principle of throughput accounting is that a buffer inventory should be built up for output from the bottleneck resource.

☐   Unless output capacity is greater than sales demand, there will always be a binding constraint.

☐   The production capacity of a bottleneck resource should determine the production schedule for the organisation as a whole.

☐   Idle time should be avoided in areas of production that are not a bottleneck resource.   **(2 marks)**

18   Which of the following statements about target costing is **not** true?

☐   Target costing is better suited to assembly orientated industries than service industries that have a large fixed cost base.

☐   Costs may be reduced in target costing by removing product features that do not add value.

☐   A target cost gap is the difference between the target cost for a product and its projected cost.

☐   Products should be discontinued if there is a target cost gap.   **(2 marks)**

19   Which **two** of the following statements about activity based costing are true?

☐   Implementation of ABC is unlikely to be cost effective when variable production costs are a low proportion of total production costs.

☐   In a system of ABC, for costs that vary with production levels, the most suitable cost driver is likely to be direct labour hours or machine hours.

☐   Activity based costs are the same as relevant costs for the purpose of short-run decision making.

☐   Activity based costing is a form of absorption costing.   **(2 marks)**

20   Are the following statements about target costing true or false?

	True	False
A risk with target costing is that cost reductions may affect the perceived value of the product.	☐	☐
An effective way of reducing the projected cost of a new product is to simplify the design.	☐	☐
The value of target costing depends on having reliable estimates of sales demand.	☐	☐
Target costing may be applied to services that are provided free of charge to customers, such as costs of call centre handling.	☐	☐

(2 marks)

21   Which **two** of the following statements about life cycle costing are true?

☐   A product is usually most profitable during the growth phase of its life cycle.

☐   Life cycle costing is useful for deciding the selling price for a product.

☐   An important use of life cycle costing is to decide whether to go ahead with the development of a new product.

☐   Life cycle costing encourages management to find a suitable balance between investment costs and operating expenses.   **(2 marks)**

22   The selling price of Product X is set at $550 for each unit and sales for the coming year are expected to be 800 units.

A return of 30% on the investment of $500,000 in Product X will be required in the coming year.

What is the target cost for each unit of Product X?

$ ☐   **(2 marks)**

23 Are the following statements about environmental cost accounting true or false?

	True	False
The majority of environmental costs are already captured within a typical organisation's accounting system. The difficulty lies in identifying them	☐	☐
Input/output analysis divides material flows within an organisation into three categories: material flows; system flows; and delivery and disposal flows	☐	☐

(2 marks)

24 Budget information relating to a company that manufactures four products is as follows.

Product	Maximum sales demand	Machine hours per unit	Maximum machine hours required	Sales price per unit	Material cost per unit
	Units			$	$
A	1,000	0.1	100	15	6
B	500	0.2	100	21	10
C	2,000	0.3	600	18	9
D	1,000	0.2	200	25	16
			1,000		

Only 750 machine hours are available during the period. Applying the principles of throughput accounting, how many units of Product B should be made if the company produces output to maximise throughput and profit?

$ [   ] units

(2 marks)

25 The following estimates have been produced for a new product with an expected life of four years.

	Year 1	Year 2	Year 3	Year 4
Units made and sold	5,000	10,000	25,000	10,000
	$	$	$	$
R&D costs	0.9 million	0.3 million		
Marketing costs	0.3 million	0.3 million	0.1 million	0.1 million
Production cost per unit	80	40	30	30
Customer service cost per unit	20	15	10	5
Disposal costs				0.2 million

What is the expected life cycle cost per unit?

$ [   ]

(2 marks)

26 Product YZ2 is made in a production process where machine time is a bottleneck resource. Production of one unit of Product YZ2 takes 0.25 machine hours. The costs and selling price of Product YZ2 are as follows:

	$
Materials	10
Labour (0.5 hours)	7
Other factory costs	7
	24
Sales price	30
Profit	6

In a system of throughput accounting, what is the return per factory hour?

$ [   ]

(2 marks)

27   A company manufactures Product Q, which sells for $50 per unit and has a material cost of $14 per unit and a direct labour cost of $10 per unit. The total direct labour budget for the year is 18,000 hours of labour time at a cost of $10 per hour. Factory overheads are $1,620,000 per year. The company has identified machine time as the bottleneck in production. Product Q needs 0.05 hours of machine time per unit produced. The maximum capacity for machine time is 6,000 hours per year.

What is the throughput accounting ratio for Product Q (to 1 dp)?

(2 marks)

28   Which **two** of the following statements about activity based costing are true?

☐   ABC recognises the complexity of modern manufacturing by the use of multiple cost drivers

☐   ABC establishes separate cost pools for support activities

☐   ABC reapportions support activity costs

☐   BC is an appropriate costing system when overheads vary with time spent on production   (2 marks)

29   ABC is felt to give a more useful product cost than classic absorption costing (with overheads absorbed on labour hours) if which of the following **two** apply?

☐   Labour costs are a relatively minor proportion of total costs

☐   Overheads vary with many different measures of activity

☐   Overheads are difficult to predict

☐   Cost drivers are difficult to identify   (2 marks)

30   Which **two** of the following costs are likely to rise when just in time (JIT) manufacturing is introduced?

☐   Set-up costs

☐   Raw material handling costs

☐   Raw material storage costs

☐   Customer order costs   (2 marks)

(Total = 30 marks)

Section B CBE OT case questions

Triple

20 mins

The following scenario relates to questions 31 – 35.

Triple Co makes three types of gold watch – the Diva (D), the Classic (C) and the Poser (P). A traditional product costing system is used at present; although an activity based costing (ABC) system is being considered. Details of the product lines for a typical period are:

	Hours per unit		Materials	Production
	Labour hours	Machine hours	Cost per unit $	Units
Product D	½	1½	20	750
Product C	1½	1	15	1,250
Product P	1	3	10	7,000

Direct labour costs $6 per hour and production overheads are absorbed on a machine hour basis. The overhead absorption rate for the period is $28 per machine hour.

Total production overheads are $654,500 and further analysis shows that the total production overheads can be divided as follows:

	%
Costs relating to machinery	20
Costs relating to materials handling	15

The following total activity volumes are associated with each product line for the period as a whole:

	Number of movements of materials
Product D	12
Product C	21
Product P	87
	120

Required

31 Calculate the cost per unit for product D using traditional methods, absorbing overheads on the basis of machine hours.

D $ [   ] per unit

(2 marks)

32 Calculate the total amount of machining overhead that would be allocated to Product C for the period. *using ABC*

$ [   ]

(2 marks)

33 Calculate the overhead assigned to Product D in respect of materials handling.

$ [   ] ~~per unit~~

(2 marks)

34 Triple Co is attempting to identify the correct cost driver for a cost pool called quality control.

Which of the following would be the correct figure to use?

- [ ] Number of units produced
- [✓] Number of inspections
- [ ] Labour hours
- [ ] Number of machine set ups

(2 marks)

35   If Triple Co decide to adopt ABC, which of the following is a disadvantage that Triple Co may encounter as a result of this decision.

- ☐ ABC can only be applied to production overheads
- ☐ The cost per unit may not be as accurate as it was under traditional absorption costing.
- ☑ The benefits obtained from ABC might not justify the costs.
- ☐ It will not provide much insight into what drives overhead costs.

    (2 marks)

(Total = 10 marks)

Brick by Brick   20 mins

The following scenario relates to questions 36 – 40.

Brick by Brick (BBB) is a building business that provides a range of building services to the public. Recently they have been asked to quote for garage conversions (GC) and extensions to properties (EX) and have found that they are winning fewer GC contracts than expected. In addition, BBB also produces and sells different types of brick to the construction industry. The three types of brick produced are clay, concrete, and reclaimed bricks.

BBB has a policy to price all jobs at budgeted total cost plus 50%. Overheads are currently absorbed on a labour hour basis. BBB thinks that a switch to activity based costing (ABC) to absorb overheads would reduce the costs associated with GC and hence make them more competitive.

You are provided with the following data:

Overhead category	Annual overheads $	Activity driver	Total number of activities per year
Supervisors	90,000	Site visits	500
Planners	70,000	Planning documents	250
Property related	240,000	Labour hours	40,000
Total	400,000		

A typical GC takes 300 labour hours to complete. A GC requires only one site visit by a supervisor and needs only one planning document to be raised. An EX requires six site visits and five planning documents.

36   Calculate the total overheads assigned to a GC using labour hours to absorb the overheads.

    GC $ ☐   **(2 marks)**

37   Calculate the total overheads assigned to a GC using ABC principles in respect of supervisors costs.

    GC $ ☐   **(2 marks)**

38   Calculate the total overheads assigned to a EX using ABC principles in respect of planning costs.

    EX $ ☐   **(2 marks)**

39   The absorption cost and ABC cost per service have now been correctly calculated as follows:

	GC	EX
Absorption cost	$11,000	$20,500
ABC cost	$10,260	$20,980

Which of the following statements are true?

(1)   Changing to a system of ABC costing should lead to a more competitive price being charged for the GC.

(2)   Using ABC would cause total overhead costs to increase

☐   1 only

☐   2 only

☐   Neither 1 nor 2

☐   Both 1 and 2   (2 marks)

40   Which of the following statements about Brick by Brick and the use of ABC is true?

☐   The traditional absorption approach gives a better indication of where cost savings can be made

☐   ABC is a cheaper system for BBB than absorption costing

☐   ABC eliminates the need for cost apportionment

☐   ABC improves pricing decisions   (2 marks)

                                                                          (Total = 10 marks)

Jola Publishing Co   20 mins

The following scenario relates to questions 41 – 45.

Jola Publishing Co publishes two forms of book.

The company publishes a children's book (CB), which is sold in large quantities to government controlled schools. The book is produced in four large production runs. The second book is a comprehensive technical journal (TJ). It is produced in monthly production runs, 12 times a year.

The directors are concerned about the performance of the two books and are wondering what the impact would be of a switch to an activity based costing (ABC) approach to accounting for overheads. They currently use absorption costing, based on number of books produced for all overhead calculations. Overheads amount to $2,880,000.

The CB will be inspected on 180 occasions next year, whereas the TJ will be inspected just 20 times.

Machine time per unit is 6 minutes for the CB and 10 minutes for the TJ.

Jola Publishing will produce its annual output of 1,000,000 CBs in four production runs and approximately 10,000 TJs per month in each of 12 production runs.

Required

41   Calculate the overhead cost per unit of the CB using the current system of absorption costing.

$ [   ] per unit   (2 marks)

42 Jola Publishing Co has decided to adopt ABC. Management has put together a list of steps. Please put this list in the order it should be carried out.

1   Calculate the overhead cost per unit of CB and TJ
2   Calculate the absorption rate for each 'cost driver'
3   Determine what causes the cost of each activity – the 'cost driver'
4   Identify major activities within each department which create cost
5   Create a cost centre/cost pool for each activity – 'the activity cost pool'

- [ ] 4, 5, 3, 2, 1.
- [ ] 5, 3, 2, 1, 4.
- [ ] 4, 2, 1, 3, 5.
- [ ] 4, 1, 2, 3, 5.   **(2 marks)**

43 The overheads involved have been analysed as follows:

Overhead	$	Activity driver
Production costs	2,160,000	Machine hours
Quality control	668,000	Number of inspections
Production set up costs	52,000	Number of set ups
	2,880,000	

Calculate the total activity based allocation of production overheads for production of the CB.

[   ]   **(2 marks)**

44 Calculate the total activity based allocation of quality control overheads for production of the TJ.

[   ]   **(2 marks)**

45 If Jola Publishing Co decides to introduce an ABC costing system, which of the following is an advantage of ABC that they can expect to benefit from?

- [ ] A reduction in overhead costs
- [ ] Cost savings compared to absorption costing
- [ ] Simplification of the costing process
- [ ] More accurate costs per unit   **(2 marks)**

     (Total = 10 marks)

Corrie   20 mins

The following scenario relates to questions 46 – 50.

Corrie produces three products, X, Y and Z. The capacity of Corrie's plant is restricted by process alpha. Process alpha is expected to be operational for eight hours per day and can produce 1,200 units of X per hour, 1,500 units of Y per hour, and 600 units of Z per hour.

Selling prices and material costs for each product are as follows.

Product	Selling price $ per unit	Material cost $ per unit	Throughput contribution $ per unit
X	150	70	80
Y	120	40	80
Z	300	100	200

Conversion costs are $720,000 per day.

Required

46   Calculate the profit per day if daily output achieved is 6,000 units of X, 4,500 units of Y and 1,200 units of Z.

$ [   ]   **(2 marks)**

47   Determine the efficiency of the bottleneck process given the output achieved is 6,000 units of X, 4,500 units of Y and 1,200 units of Z.

[   ] %   **(2 marks)**

48   Calculate the conversion costs per factory hour.

$ [   ]   **(2 marks)**

49   A change in factory cost arose, giving a new figure for conversion costs per factory hour of $80,000. Calculate the revised TA ratio for each product.

X [   ]

Y [   ]

Z [   ]   **(2 marks)**

50   Which **two** of the following statements about using throughput accounting (TA) are true?

☐ Corrie Co's priority, using TA, should be given to products with the highest throughput contribution per unit

☐ TA assumes that labour costs are largely fixed

☐ The TA ratio for each product should be less than 1

☐ TA assumes that material costs can be controlled in the short term   **(2 marks)**

(Total = 10 marks)

A Co   **20 mins**

The following scenario relates to questions 51 – 55.

A Co makes two products, B1 and B2. Its machines can only work on one product at a time. The two products are worked on in two departments by differing grades of labour. The labour requirements for the two products are as follows:

| | *Minutes per unit of product* | |
	B1	*B2*
Department 1	12	16
Department 2	20	15

There is currently a shortage of labour and the maximum times available each day in Departments 1 and 2 are 480 minutes and 840 minutes, respectively. The bottleneck or limiting factor is labour in Department 1. The current selling prices and costs for the two products are shown below:

	B1 $ per unit	B2 $ per unit
Selling price	50.00	65.00
Direct materials	10.00	15.00
Direct labour	10.40	6.20
Variable overheads	6.40	9.20
Fixed overheads	12.80	18.40
Profit per unit	10.40	16.20

As part of the budget-setting process, A Co needs to know the optimum output levels. All output is sold.

Required

51   Calculate the maximum number of each product that could be produced each day.

B1 Department 1 [   ] units

B1 Department 2 [   ] units

B2 Department 1 [   ] units

B2 Department 2 [   ] units   **(2 marks)**

52   Using traditional contribution analysis, calculate the contribution per unit of limiting factor of B1 (answer to two decimal points).

$ [   ]   **(2 marks)**

53   Calculate the throughput per minute of bottleneck resource of B2 (answer to two decimal points).

$ [   ]   **(2 marks)**

54   A Co need to decide whether to base their decisions about optimum levels of production using a throughput accounting approach, or a limiting factor approach. Which of the following is an example of an advantage of choosing a throughput accounting approach?

[ ] The throughput accounting approach eliminates employee idle time

[ ] The throughput accounting approach eliminates bottlenecks in manufacturing

[ ] The throughput accounting approach eliminates the cost of holding inventory

[ ] The throughput accounting approach is more suitable for short term decision making than limiting factor analysis   **(2 marks)**

55   If A Co decides to apply the theory of constraints, in what order will the following steps be carried out? (Insert nos. 1-4 in the boxes opposite each sentence)

[ ] Subordinate everything else to the decisions made about exploiting the bottlenecks

[ ] Elevate the system's bottlenecks

[ ] Identify A Co's bottlenecks

[ ] Decide how to exploit the system's bottlenecks   **(2 marks)**

(Total = 10 marks)

Cam Co

20 mins

The following scenario relates to questions 56 – 60.

Cam Co manufactures webcams, devices which can provide live video and audio streams via personal computers. It has recently been suffering from liquidity problems and hopes that these will be eased by the launch of its new webcam, which has revolutionary audio sound and visual quality.

The webcam is expected to have a product life cycle of two years. Market research has already been carried out to establish a target selling price and projected lifetime sales volumes for the product. Cost estimates have also been prepared, based on the current proposed product specification. Cam Co uses life cycle costing to work out the target costs for its products. You are provided with the following relevant information for the webcam:

Projected lifetime sales volume	50,000 units
Target selling price per unit	$200
Target profit margin — % of sales	35%

Note. Estimated lifetime cost per unit:

	$	$
Manufacturing costs		
Direct material (bought in parts)	40	
Direct labour	26	
Machine costs	24	
Quality control costs	10	
		100
Non-manufacturing costs		60
Estimated lifetime cost per unit		160

The following information has been identified as relevant:

(1)   Direct material cost: all of the parts currently proposed for the webcam are bespoke parts. However, most of these can actually be replaced with standard parts costing 55% less. However, three of the bespoke parts, which currently account for 20% of the estimated direct material cost, cannot be replaced, although an alternative supplier charging 10% less has been sourced for these parts.

(2)   Direct labour cost: the webcam uses 45 minutes of direct labour, which costs $34.67 per hour. The use of more standard parts, however, will mean that whilst the first unit would still be expected to take 45 minutes, there will now be an expected rate of learning of 90% (where 'b' = – 0.152). This will end after the first 100 units have been completed.

Required

56   Identify the target cost.   — selling price less: profit x target cost

$ [   ]   **(2 marks)**

57   Calculate the direct material cost per unit in light of the new information in point (1).

$ [   ]   **(2 marks)**

58   Calculate the average direct labour cost per unit in light of the new information in point (2).

$ [   ]   = total cost / total unit   **(2 marks)**

59   The following statements have been made about Cam Co's target costing system.

(1)   Target costing ensures that new product development costs are recovered in the target price for the webcam. ✗ lifecycle costing   ✗ estimated

(2)   A cost gap is the difference between the target price and the target cost of the webcam.

Which of the above statements is/are true?

☐   1 only

☐   2 only

☑   Neither 1 nor 2

☐   Both 1 and 2   **(2 marks)**

60   Which of the following represents a possible method for closing the target cost gap for the webcam?

☐   Increase its selling price

☐   Employ more specialist staff in its production

☑   Redesign the webcam

☐   Increase the number of bespoke components   **(2 marks)**

(Total = 10 marks)

PART B: DECISION-MAKING TECHNIQUES

Questions 61 to 133 cover Decision-making techniques, the subject of Part B of the BPP Study Text for Paper F5.

Section A questions

MCQ bank – Decision-making techniques   78 mins

61   A decision tree is a way of representing decision choices in the form of a diagram. It is usual for decision trees to include probabilities of different outcomes.

The following statements have been made about decision trees.

(1)   Each possible outcome from a decision is given an expected value.
(2)   Each possible outcome is shown as a branch on a decision tree.

Which of the above statements is/are true?

A   1 only
B   2 only
C   Neither 1 nor 2
D   Both 1 and 2   (2 marks)

62   The following statements have been made about price elasticity of demand.

(1)   When sales demand is inelastic, a company can increase profits by raising the selling price of its product.

(2)   Price elasticity of demand is measured as the amount of change in sales price (measured as a percentage of the current sales price) divided by the amount of change in quantity demanded (measured as a percentage of the current sales volume)

Which of the above statements is/are true?

A   1 only
B   2 only
C   Neither 1 nor 2
D   Both 1 and 2   (2 marks)

63   The following statements have been made about cost plus pricing.

(1)   A price in excess of full cost per unit will ensure that a company will cover all its costs and make a profit.

(2)   Cost plus pricing is an appropriate pricing strategy when jobs are carried out to customer specifications.

Which of the above statements is/are true?

A   1 only
B   2 only
C   Neither 1 nor 2
D   Both 1 and 2   (2 marks)

64   The following statements have been made about solving linear programming problems for budgeting purposes.

    (1)   Slack occurs when less than the maximum available of a limited resource is required.

    (2)   When the linear programming problem includes a constraint for minimum sales demand for a product, there may be a surplus for sales demand in the optimal solution.

    Which of the above statements is/are true?

    A   1 only
    B   2 only
    C   Neither 1 nor 2
    D   Both 1 and 2   **(2 marks)**

65   The following statements have been made about decision making under conditions of uncertainty.

    (1)   Expected value is a more reliable basis for decision making where the situation and outcome will occur many times than for a one-off decision.

    (2)   A risk-averse decision maker avoids all risks in decision making.

    Which of the above statements is/are true?

    A   1 only
    B   2 only
    C   Neither 1 nor 2
    D   Both 1 and 2   **(2 marks)**

66   Which method of pricing is most easily applied when two or more markets for the product or service can be kept entirely separate from each other?

    A   Price discrimination
    B   Product line pricing
    C   Skimming
    D   Volume discounting   **(2 marks)**

67   A company has fixed costs of $1.3 million. Variable costs are 55% of sales up to a sales level of $1.5 million, but at higher volumes of production and sales, the variable cost for incremental production units falls to 52% of sales.

    What is the breakeven point in sales revenue, to the nearest $1,000?

    A $1,977,000
    B $2,027,000
    C $2,708,000
    D $2,802,000   **(2 marks)**

68   A company wishes to go ahead with one of three mutually exclusive projects, but the profit outcome from each project will depend on the strength of sales demand, as follows.

	Strong demand Profit/(Loss)	Moderate demand Profit	Weak demand Profit/(Loss)
	$	$	$
Project 1	70,000	10,000	(7,000)
Project 2	25,000	12,000	5,000
Project 3	50,000	20,000	(6,000)
Probability of demand	0.1	0.4	0.5

What is the value to the company of obtaining this perfect market research information, ignoring the cost of obtaining the information?

A $3,000
B $5,500
C $6,000
D $7,500   **(2 marks)**

69   The price elasticity of demand for a product at its current price level is inelastic. What will happen if the price of the product is reduced?

A   Total revenue will fall and profit will fall
B   Total revenue will fall and profit may either increase or fall
C   Total revenue will increase and profit will increase
D   Total revenue will increase and profit may either increase or fall   **(2 marks)**

70   A manufacturing company makes two joint products, CP1 and CP2, in a common process. These products can be sold at the split-off point in an external market, or processed further in separate processes to produce products FP1 and FP2. Details of these processes are shown in the diagram.

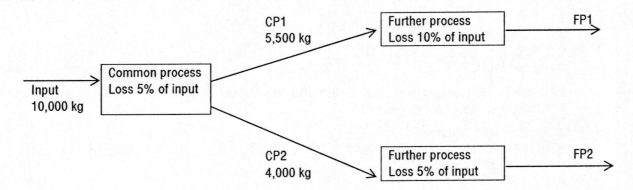

CP1 has a market price of $6 per kg and CP2 has a market price of $5 per kg. Relevant further processing costs are $2 per input kg in the process to make FP1 and $3 per input kg in the process to make FP2. Both FP1 and FP2 sell for $9 per kg.

For each 10,000 kg input to the common process, how much additional profit is obtained by further processing each of the joint products instead of selling them at the split-off point?

A $2,750
B $4,450
C $8,750
D $9,500   **(2 marks)**

71   A company makes and sells four products. Direct labour hours are a scarce resource, but the company is able to sub-contract production of any products to external suppliers. The following information is relevant.

Product	W	X	Y	Z
	$ per unit	$ per unit	$ per unit	$ per unit
Sales price	10	8	12	14
Variable cost	8	5	8	12
Cost of external purchase	9	7.1	10	13
Direct labour hours per unit	0.1	0.3	0.25	0.2

In what order of priority should the company make these products in-house, rather than purchase them externally?

A   W, Y, X then Z
B   W, Z, X then Y
C   X, Z, W then Y
D   Z, X, Y then W   **(2 marks)**

72   A company is selling a product at a price of $120 per unit. At this price it is selling 200,000 units per period. It has been estimated that for every $5 increase or reduction in price, sales demand will fall or increase by 10,000 units.

At what selling price will total sales revenue per period be maximised?

A $80
B $90
C $100
D $110   **(2 marks)**

73   A company makes and sells a single product. When sales per month are $6.8 million, total costs are $6.56 million. When sales per month are $5.2 million, total costs are $5.44 million. There is a step cost increase of $400,000 in fixed costs when sales are $6.0 million, but variable unit costs are constant at all levels of output and sales.

What is the breakeven point for sales revenue per month?

A $6.0 million
B   There are two breakeven points: $5.64 million and $6.36 million
C $5.64 million only
D $6.36 million only   **(2 marks)**

74   Analysing the range of different possible outcomes from a particular situation, with a computer model that uses random numbers is known as:

A   Probability analysis
B   Sensitivity analysis
C   Simulation modelling
D   Stress testing   **(2 marks)**

75   What method of uncertainty or risk analysis is also called 'What if?' analysis?

A   Decision tree analysis
B   Sensitivity analysis
C   Simulation modelling
D   Stress testing   **(2 marks)**

76   A company produces and sells a single product. Budgeted sales are $2.4 million, budgeted fixed costs are $360,000 and the margin of safety is $400,000. What are budgeted variable costs?

A $1.640 million
B $1.728 million
C $1.968 million
D $2.040 million   **(2 marks)**

77 A company uses linear programming to decide on the production and sales budget that will maximise total contribution and profit for a financial period. The optimal solution involves using all available direct labour hours, for which the shadow price is $4.50 per hour, and machine hours, for which the shadow price is $3 per machine hour. Direct labour is paid $8 per hour.

If the objective of the company is to maximise total contribution and profit in each period, how much should the company be willing to pay per hour to obtain additional direct labour hours of production capacity?

A   Up to but not including $4.50
B   Up to but not including $9.50
C   Up to but not including $12.50
D   Up to but not including $15.50   (2 marks)

78 The demand for a product at its current price has a price elasticity greater than 1.0 (ignoring the minus sign). Which of the following statements must be correct?

(1)   A reduction in the sales price will increase total revenue.

(2)   A reduction in the sales price by x% will result in a percentage increase in sales demand which is greater than x%.

(3)   An increase in the selling price will increase total profit.

A   Statements 1 and 2 only must be correct
B   Statements 1 and 3 only must be correct
C   Statements 2 and 3 only must be correct
D   All three statements must be correct   (2 marks)

79 A company makes two products, X and Y, on the same type of direct labour and production capacity per period is restricted to 60,000 direct labour hours. The contribution per unit is $8 for Product X and $6 for Product Y. The following constraints apply to production and sales:

x   ≤ 10,000   (Sales demand for Product X)
y   ≤ 12,000   (Sales demand for Product Y)
5x + 4y   ≤ 60,000   (Direct labour hours)

The contribution-maximising output is to produce and sell 10,000 units of Product X and 2,500 units of Product Y.

What is the shadow price per direct labour hour and for how many additional hours of labour does this shadow price per hour apply?

A $1.50 per hour for the next 38,000 direct labour hours
B $1.50 per hour for the next 47,500 direct labour hours
C $1.60 per hour for the next 38,000 direct labour hours
D $1.60 per hour for the next 47,500 direct labour hours   (2 marks)

80 In a linear programming problem to determine the contribution-maximising production and sales volumes for two products, X and Y, the following information is available.

	Product X per unit	Product Y per unit	Total available per period
Direct labour hours	2 hours	4 hours	10,000 hours
Material X	4 kg	2 kg	14,000 kg
Contribution per unit	$12	$18	

The profit-maximising level of output and sales is 3,000 units of Product X and 1,000 units of Product Y.

What is the shadow price of a direct labour hour?

A $1.00
B $2.40
C $4.00
D $4.50   (2 marks)

(Total = 40 marks)

CBE style OTQ bank – Decision-making techniques   59 mins

81   To calculate and use expected values in decision-making, we must be able to do which **two** of the following?

☐   Identify all possible outcomes and their probabilities

☐   Assume the investor is risk neutral

☐   Assume the decision will often be repeated

☐   Assume the decision is a 'one-off'   **(2 marks)**

82   A benefit sacrificed by taking one course of action instead of the most profitable alternative course of action is known as which of the following?

☐   Opportunity cost

☐   Incremental cost

☐   Relevant cost

☐   Sunk cost   **(2 marks)**

83   A special job for a customer will required 8 tonnes of a Material M. The company no longer uses this material regularly although it holds 3 tonnes in inventory. These originally cost $44 per tonne, and could be resold to a supplier for $35 per tonne. Alternatively these materials could be used to complete another job instead of using other materials that would cost $126 to purchase. The current market price of Material M is $50 per tonne.

The company must decide whether to agree to the customer's request for the work, and to set a price. What would be the relevant cost of Material M for this job?

$ [   ]   **(2 marks)**

84   A company wishes to decide on a selling price for a new product. Weekly sales of each product will depend on the price charge and also on customers' response to the new product. The following pay-off table has been prepared.

	Probability	Price P1 $	Price P2 $	Price P3 $	Price P4 $
Price		5.00	5.50	6.00	6.50
Unit contribution		3.00	3.50	4.00	4.50
Weekly demand		units	units	units	units
Best possible	0.3	10,000	9,000	8,000	7,000
Most likely	0.5	8,000	7,500	7,000	6,000
Worst possible	0.2	6,000	5,000	4,000	3,000

If the choice of selling price is based on a maximin decision rule, which price would be selected?

P [   ]   **(2 marks)**

85 The following decision tree shows four decision options: 1, 2, 3 and 4

	Probability	Benefit $
1	1.0	9,500
2	0.3	14,000
	0.3	10,000
	0.4	5,000
3	0.4	10,000
	0.6	9,000
4	0.7	8,000
	0.3	14,000

Using the expected value rule, which choice should be made so as to optimise the expected benefit?

Choice [   ]

(2 marks)

86 A company wants to decide whether to make its materials in-house or whether to sub-contract production to an external supplier. In the past it has made four materials in-house, but demand in the next year will exceed in-house production capacity of 8,000 units. All four materials are made on the same machines and require the same machine time per unit: machine time is the limiting production factor.
The following information is available.

Material	W	X	Y	Z
Units required	4,000	2,000	3,000	4,000
Variable cost of in-house manufacture	$8 per unit	$12 per unit	$9 per unit	$10 per unit
Directly attributable fixed cost expenditure	$5,000	$8,000	$6,000	$7,000
Cost of external purchase	$9 per unit	$18 per unit	$12 per unit	$12 per unit

Directly attributable fixed costs are fixed cash expenditures that would be saved if production of the material in-house is stopped entirely.

If a decision is made solely on the basis of short-term cost considerations, what materials should the company purchase externally?

☐ 4,000 units of W and 1,000 units of Z

☐ 4,000 units of W and 4,000 units of Z

☐ 3,000 units of Y and 2,000 units of Z

☐ 1,000 units of Y and 4,000 units of Z (2 marks)

87 If the price elasticity of demand is zero, which **two** of the following are true?

☐ Demand is 'perfectly inelastic'.

☐ There is no change in price regardless of the quantity demanded

☐ The demand curve is a horizontal straight line

☐ There is no change in the quantity demanded, regardless of any change in price (2 marks)

88   A company wishes to decide on a selling price for a new product. Weekly sales of each product will depend on the price charge and also on customers' response to the new product. The following pay-off table has been prepared.

	Probability	Price P1 $	Price P2 $	Price P3 $	Price P4 $
Price		5.00	5.50	6.00	6.50
Unit contribution		3.00	3.50	4.00	4.50
Weekly demand		Units	Units	Units	Units
Best possible	0.3	10,000	9,000	8,000	7,000
Most likely	0.5	8,000	7,500	7,000	6,000
Worst possible	0.2	6,000	5,000	4,000	3,000

If the choice of selling price is based on a minimax regret decision rule, which price would be selected?

P [   ]   **(2 marks)**

89   A company wishes to go ahead with one of two mutually exclusive projects, but the profit outcome from each project will depend on the strength of sales demand, as follows.

	Strong demand Profit $	Moderate demand Profit $	Weak demand Profit/(Loss) $
Project 1	80,000	50,000	(5,000)
Project 2	60,000	25,000	10,000
Probability of demand	0.2	0.4	0.4

The company could purchase market research information, at a cost of $4,500. This would predict demand conditions with perfect accuracy.

What is the value to the company of obtaining this perfect market research information?

☐ $1,500

☐ $3,500

☐ $4,500

☐ $6,000   **(2 marks)**

90   A company budgets to sells its three products A, B and C in the ratio 2:3:5 respectively, measured in units of sales. Unit sales prices and variable costs are as follows.

Product	A $ per unit	B $ per unit	C $ per unit
Sales price	20	18	24
Variable cost	11	12	18

Budgeted fixed costs are $1.2 million. What sales will be needed to achieve a target profit of $400,000 for the period, to the nearest $1,000?

$ [   ]   **(2 marks)**

91   What is the main purpose of sensitivity analysis?

☐   To calculate the expected value of an outcome that is uncertain

☐   To predict the future outcome from an uncertain situation

☐   To gain insight into which assumptions or variables in a situation are critical

☐   To determine the outcome from a situation in the event of the worst possible outcome   **(2 marks)**

92   Market research into demand for a product indicates that when the selling price per unit is $145, demand in each period will be 5,000 units and if the price is $120, demand will be 11,250 units. It is assumed that the demand function for this product is linear. The variable cost per unit is $27.

What selling price should be charged in order to maximise the monthly profit?

$ [   ]   **(2 marks)**

93   A company makes and sells three products. The budget for the next period is as follows:

Product	A	B	C
	$ per unit	$ per unit	$ per unit
Sales price	12	18	20
Variable cost	3	6	11
	9	12	9
Fixed cost	6	9	6
Profit	3	3	3
Number of units	30,000	40,000	10,000

What is the breakeven point in sales, to the nearest $1,000?

$ [   ]   **(2 marks)**

94   Which **two** pieces of information are required when deciding, purely on financial grounds, whether or not to process a joint product further?

☐   The final sales value of the joint product

☐   The further processing cost of the joint product

☐   The value of the common process costs.

☐   The method of apportioning the common costs between the joint products   **(2 marks)**

95   Which **two** statements are true when using linear programming to solve production problems?

☐   If the aim is to minimise costs, the solution is where the total cost line touching the feasible area at a tangent is as far away from the origin as possible.

☐   If the aim is to minimise costs, the solution is where the total cost line touching the feasible area at a tangent is as close to the origin as possible.

☐   If the aim is to maximise profit, the solution is where the total cost line touching the feasible area at a tangent is as far away from the origin as

☐   If the aim is to maximise profit, the solution is where the total contribution line is touching the feasible area at a tangent is as close to the origin as possible

☐   If the aim is to maximise profit, the solution is where the total contribution line touching the feasible area at a tangent is as far away from the origin as possible   **(2 marks)**

(Total = 30 marks)

Section B questions

MCQ case questions

BDU Co   **20 mins**

The following scenario relates to questions 96 – 100.

BDU Co is a manufacturer of baby equipment and is planning to launch a revolutionary new style of sporty pushchair. The company has commissioned market research to establish possible demand for the pushchair and the following information has been obtained.

If the price is set at $425, demand is expected to be 1,000 pushchairs, at $500 it will be 730 pushchairs and at $600 it will be 420 pushchairs. Variable costs are estimated at either $170, $210 or $260.

A decision needs to be made on what price to charge.

The following contribution table has been produced showing the possible outcomes.

Price

		$425	$500	$600
Variable cost	$170	255,000	240,900	180,600
	$210	215,000	211,700	163,800
	$260	165,000	175,200	142,800

96   What price would be set if BDU were to use a maximax decision criterion?

A $425
B $500
C $600
D   Not possible to determine from the available information   **(2 marks)**

97   What price would be set if BDU were to use a maximin decision criterion?

A $425
B $500
C $600
D   Not possible to determine from the available information   **(2 marks)**

98 What price would be set if BDU were to use a minimax regret decision criterion?

 A $425
 B $500
 C $600
 D Not possible to determine from the available information (2 marks)

99 If the probabilities of the variable costs are $170: 0.4, $210: 0.25 and $260: 0.35, which price would the risk-neutral decision maker choose?

 A $425
 B $500
 C $600
 D Not possible to determine from the available information (2 marks)

100 Which one of the following techniques, used by BDU Co, reduces uncertainty in decision making?

 A Expected value analysis
 B Market research
 C Sensitivity analysis
 D Relevant costing (2 marks)

(Total = 10 marks)

Cement Co

20 mins

The following scenario relates to questions 101 – 105.

Cement Co is a company specialising in the manufacture of cement, a product used in the building industry. The company has found that when weather conditions are good, the demand for cement increases since more building work is able to take place. Cement Co is now trying to work out the level of cement production for the coming year in order to maximise profits. The company doesn't want to miss out on the opportunity to earn large profits by running out of cement. However, it doesn't want to be left with large quantities of the product unsold at the end of the year, since it deteriorates quickly and then has to be disposed of. Cement Co has decided to produce at one of the three levels of production to match forecast demand.

Pay-off table

			SUPPLY (number of bags)		
		Probability *	350,000	280,000	200,000
	Weather		$'000	$'000	$'000
	Good	0.25	1,750	1,400	1,000
DEMAND	Average	0.45	1,085	1,400	1,000
	Poor	0.30	325	640	1,000

Required

101 What is the level of cement production that the company should choose based on the maximin decision rule?

 A 350,000 bags
 B 280,000 bags
 C 200,000 bags
 D 280,000 bags and 350,000 bags give the same result (2 marks)

102 What is the level of cement production that the company should choose based on the maximax decision rule?

 A 350,000 bags
 B 280,000 bags
 C 200,000 bags
 D 200,000 bags and 350,000 bags give the same result (2 marks)

103 What is the level of cement production that the company should choose based on the minimax regret decision rule?

    A   350,000 bags
    B   280,000 bags
    C   200,000 bags
    D   200,000 bags and 280,000 bags give the same result   **(2 marks)**

104 What is the level of cement production that the company should choose based on expected values?

    A   350,000 bags
    B   280,000 bags
    C   200,000 bags
    D   200,000 bags and 280,000 bags give the same result   **(2 marks)**

105 The following statements have been made about Cement Co's use of expected value analysis:

    (1)   Expected value analysis is suitable for risk averse decision makers, as all likely outcomes are presented

    (2)   The average profit calculated will correspond to one of the possible outcomes

Which of the above statements is/are true?

    A   1 only
    B   2 only
    C   Neither 1 nor 2
    D   Both 1 and 2   **(2 marks)**

(Total = 10 marks)

Ennerdale   **20 mins**

The following scenario relates to questions 106 – 110.

Ennerdale has been asked to quote a price for a one-off contract. The company's management accountant has asked for your advice on the relevant costs for the contract. The following information is available:

Materials

The contract requires 3,000 kg of material K, which is a material used regularly by the company in other production. The company has 2,000 kg of material K currently in inventory which had been purchased last month for a total cost of $19,600. Since then the price per kilogram for material K has increased by 5%.

The contract also requires 200 kg of material L. There are 250 kg of material L in inventory which are not required for normal production. This material originally cost a total of $3,125. If not used on this contract, the inventory of material L would be sold for $11 per kg.

Labour

The contract requires 800 hours of skilled labour. Skilled labour is paid $9.50 per hour. There is a shortage of skilled labour and all the available skilled labour is fully employed in the company in the manufacture of product P. The following information relates to product P:

	$ per unit	$ per unit
Selling price		100
Less:		
Skilled labour ʉʰᵒᵘʳˢ	38	
Other variable costs	22	
		(60)
		40

Finance costs

In order to complete the contract, a member of the finance team will be required to work 8 hours overtime. The individual's annual salary is $25,000, and they work a 37.5 hour week. Overtime is paid at a rate of $15 per hour. Alternatively, an experienced contract accountant can be hired to administer the project in 75% of the time it would take the internal finance department member to complete. The contractor's rate is $25 per hour. It took the member of the finance team three hours to put together the information for this quote and no overtime was required.

Required

106   What is the relevant cost of material K which should be included in the contract?

     A $29,400
     B $29,890
     C $30,870
     D $30,380   **(2 marks)**

107   What is the relevant cost of material L which should be included in the contract?

     A $2,200
     B $2,500
     C $3,125
     D   NIL   **(2 marks)**

108   What is the relevant cost of skilled labour which should be included in the contract?

     A $8,000
     B $15,600
     C $7,600
     D $12,400   **(2 marks)**

109   What is the relevant cost of finance which should be included in the contract?

     A   Nil
     B $120
     C $150
     D $158,46   **(2 marks)**

110   The following statements have been made about Ennerdale's relevant costing system.

     (1)   Sunk costs can never be a relevant cost for the purpose of decision making.

     (2)   If Ennerdale charges the minimum price for a product or service, based on relevant costs, it will not improve its overall profitability.

     Which of the above statements is/are true?

     A   1 only
     B   2 only
     C   Neither 1 nor 2
     (D)   Both 1 and 2   **(2 marks)**

                                                       (Total = 10 marks)

March 2017

Metallica Co

20 mins

The following scenario relates to questions 111 – 115.

Metallica Co is an engineering company that manufactures a number of products, using a team of highly skilled workers and a variety of different metals. A supplier has informed Metallica Co that the amount of M1, one of the materials used in production, will be limited for the next three-month period.

The only items manufactured using M1 and their production costs and selling prices (where applicable) are shown below.

	Product P4 $/unit	Product P6 $/unit
Selling price	125	175
Direct materials:		
M1*	15	10
M2	10	20
Direct labour	20	30
Variable overhead	10	15
Fixed overhead	20	30
Total cost	75	105

*   Material M1 is expected to be limited in supply during the next three months. These costs are based on M1 continuing to be available at a price of $20 per square metre. The price of M2 is $10 per square metre.

Required

111   Calculate the contribution per unit for each product.

    A   P4 $100, P6 $70
    B   P4 $50, P6 $70
    C   P4 $70, P6 $100
    D   P4 $70, P6 $50

                (2 marks)

112   Metallica Co carried out some market research which suggested that a change should be made to the selling price of both Product P4 and P6. As a result, the new contribution per unit for P4 is $85 and for P6 it is $95. Which of the following answers is correct?

    A   The contribution per limiting factor of P4 and P6 is $85 and $47.50 respectively, therefore P4 should be produced first.

    B   The contribution per limiting factor of P4 and P6 is $113.33 and $190 respectively, therefore P6 should be produced first.

    C   The contribution per limiting factor of P4 and P6 is $85 and $47.50 respectively, therefore P6 should be produced first.

    D   The contribution per limiting factor of P4 and P6 is $113.33 and $190 respectively, therefore P4 should be produced first.

                (2 marks)

113   If Metallica Co operated in a throughput accounting environment, which of the following costs would **not** be included in the calculation for throughput contribution?

    A   Selling price
    B   Direct materials
    C   Direct labour
    D   None of the above

                (2 marks)

114   Which of the following constraints would necessitate the performance of limiting factor analysis by Metallica Co?

    A   Limited demand for P4 or P6
    B   Limited M1 or M2
    C   Limited labour
    D   All of the above

                (2 marks)

115 Once a scarce resource is identified, Metallica Co carries out a limiting factor analysis using 4 steps. What is the correct order for carrying out these steps?

A   Step 1: Rank the products in order of the contribution per unit of the scarce resource
      Step 2: Allocate resources using the ranking
      Step 3: Calculate the contribution per unit of the scarce resource for each product
      Step 4: Calculate the contribution per unit for each product

B   Step 1: Calculate the contribution per unit of the scarce resource for each product
      Step 2: Rank the products in order of the contribution per unit of the scarce   resource
      Step 3: Allocate resources using the ranking
      Step 4: Calculate the contribution per unit for each product

C   Step 1: Calculate the contribution per unit of the scarce resource for each product
      Step 2: Calculate the contribution per unit for each product
      Step 3: Rank the products in order of the contribution per unit of the scarce resource
      Step 4: Allocate resources using the ranking

D   Step 1: Calculate the contribution per unit for each product
      Step 2: Calculate the contribution per unit of the scarce resource for each product
      Step 3: Rank the products in order of the contribution per unit of the scarce resource
      Step 4: Allocate resources using the ranking   (2 marks)

(Total = 10 marks)

Pixie Pharmaceuticals   20 mins

The following scenario relates to questions 116 – 120.

Pixie Pharmaceuticals is a research-based company which manufactures a wide variety of drugs for use in hospitals. The purchasing manager has recently been approached by a new manufacturer based in a newly industrialised country who have offered to produce three of the drugs at their factory. The following cost and price information has been provided.

Drug	Fairyoxide	Spriteolite	Goblinex
Production (units)	20,000	40,000	80,000
	$	$	$
Direct material cost, per unit	0.80	1.00	0.40
Direct labour cost, per unit	1.60	1.80	0.80
Direct expense cost, per unit	0.40	0.60	0.20
Fixed cost per unit	0.80	1.00	0.40
Selling price each	4.00	5.00	2.00
Imported price	2.75	4.20	2.00

Required

116 Calculate the profit figure the company will make by producing all the drugs itself.

A $96,000
B $136,000
C $48,000
D $216,000   (2 marks)

117 What saving/(increased cost) per unit would be made/(incurred) if Fairyoxide was purchased from the overseas producer?

A $0.85
B $0.05
C $0.45
D $(0.05)   (2 marks)

118   What saving/(increased cost) would be made/(incurred) per unit if Spriteolite was purchased from the overseas producer?

      A $(0.80)
      B $0.20
      C $0.80
      D $(0.20)   **(2 marks)**

119   What saving/(increased cost) would be made/(incurred) if Goblinex was purchased from the overseas producer?

      A $0.60
      B $(0.20)
      C $0.20
      D $(0.60)   **(2 marks)**

120   The following two statements have been made about the decision Pixie Pharmaceuticals has to make about producing the products in house or purchasing from the overseas producer:

      (1)   In a make or buy decision with no limiting factors, the relevant costs are the differential costs between the make and buy options.

      (2)   Cost is the only relevant factor in Pixie Pharmaceutical's make or buy decision.

      Which of the above statements is/are true?

      A   1 only
      B   2 only
      C   Both 1 and 2
      D   Neither 1 nor 2   **(2 marks)**

(Total = 10 marks)

T Co

20 mins

The following scenario relates to questions 121 – 125.

The Telephone Co (T Co) is a company specialising in the provision of telephone systems for commercial clients.

T Co has been approached by a potential customer, Push Co, who wants to install a telephone system in new offices it is opening. Whilst the job is not a particularly large one, T Co is hopeful of future business in the form of replacement systems and support contracts for Push Co. T Co is therefore keen to quote a competitive price for the job. The following information should be considered:

(i)   One of the company's salesmen has already been to visit Push Co, to give them a demonstration of the new system, together with a complimentary lunch, the costs of which totalled $400.

(ii)   The installation is expected to take one week to complete and would require three engineers, each of whom is paid a monthly salary of $4,000. The engineers have just had their annually renewable contract renewed with T Co. One of the three engineers has spare capacity to complete the work, but the other two would have to be moved from contract X in order to complete this one. Contract X generates a contribution of $200 per engineer per week. There are no other engineers available to continue with Contract X if these two engineers are taken off the job. It would mean that T Co would miss its contractual completion deadline on Contract X by one week. As a result, T Co would have to pay a one-off penalty of $500. Since there is no other work scheduled for their engineers in one week's time, it will not be a problem for them to complete Contract X at this point.

(iii) 120 telephone handsets would need to be supplied to Push Co. The current cost of these is $18.20 each, although T Co already has 80 handsets in inventory. These were bought at a price of $16.80 each. The handsets are the most popular model on the market and frequently requested by T Co's customers.

(iv)   Push Co would also need a computerised control system called 'Swipe 2'. The current market price of Swipe 2 is $10,800, although T Co has an older version of the system, 'Swipe 1', in inventory, which could be modified at a cost of $4,600. T Co paid $5,400 for Swipe 1 when it ordered it in error two months ago and has no other use for it. The current market price of Swipe 1 is $5,450, although if Push Co tried to sell the one they have, it would be deemed to be 'used' and therefore only worth $3,000.

Required

121   What figure should be included in the relevant cost statement for engineers costs?

A $5,538.46
B $3,392.31
C $1,300
D $500   **(2 marks)**

122   What figure should be included in the relevant cost statement for telephone handsets?

A $2,072
B $2,184
C $2,016
D $2,128   **(2 marks)**

123   What figure should be included in the relevant cost statement for the computerised control system?

A $7,600
B $10,800
C $10,050
D $10,000   **(2 marks)**

124   Which of the following statements about T Co's decision to quote for the contract is/are correct?

(1)   The opportunity cost is defined as the relevant cost of taking a business opportunity to install the telephone system for Push Co.

(2)   The decision to install the telephone system should be taken on the basis of whether it improves profit or reduces costs for T Co.

A   1 only is correct
B   2 only is correct
C   Neither 1 nor 2 is correct
D   Both 1 and 2 are correct   **(2 marks)**

125   What type of cost is the $400, detailed in point (i)?

A   Sunk cost
B   Historic cost
C   Relevant cost
D   Committed cost   **(2 marks)**

(Total = 10 marks)

CBE OT case questions

Rotanola Co

The following scenario relates to questions 126 – 130.

Rotanola Co manufactures mobile phones. It has been extremely successful in the past but the market has become extremely competitive. The company is considering a number of different strategies to improve its profitability.

The most successful product is the RTN99 which is sold for $110. Weekly demand is currently 20,000 phones. Market research has revealed that if Rotanola Co reduced the price of the RTN99 by $10, demand would increase by 2,000 phones.

Each time the phone is produced, Rotanola Co incurs extra costs of $30 for materials, $18 for labour, $14 for variable overheads and $23 for fixed costs, based on expected weekly output of 20,000 phones. The most expensive component in the phone is the battery which costs $15. Rotanola has been offered a discounted price of $12 by the supplier if it buys 22,000 batteries per week.

The company needs to come up with innovative new products as the technology moves very fast and what is useful today becomes obsolete tomorrow. The latest idea is to produce a phone incorporating virtual touch technology which makes the phone vibrate in a number of ways.

The following estimates for this phone (the RTNBZ) have been produced.

		$	$
Sales	(25,000 units @ $150)		3,750,000
Materials	(@ $50)	1,250,000	
Labour	(@ $18)	450,000	
Variable overheads	(@ $16)	400,000	
			2,100,000
Attributable fixed overheads			575,000
Profit			1,075,000

There is some doubt as to the likely cost of materials. The probability of it being $50 as expected is 0.6, the probability of it rising it to $60 is 0.3 and the probability of it falling to $40 is 0.1.

Forecast sales units are also subject to economic conditions. There is a 50% chance that sales will be as expected, a 40% chance that sales will be 10% lower than expected and a 10% chance that sales will be 5% higher than expected.

Required

126 Derive the straight line demand equation for the RTN99.

$P = \boxed{} - \boxed{} Q$

(2 marks)

127 Derive the total cost function for the RTN99 before the volume discount.

$TC = \boxed{} + \boxed{} Q$

(2 marks)

128 Derive the total cost function for the RTN99 after the volume discount.

$TC = \boxed{} + \boxed{} Q$

(2 marks)

129 Calculate the expected profit on the RTNBZ.

$\boxed{\$ }$

(2 marks)

130 The following statements have been made about Rotanola Co.

(1) Rotanola Co can use market research to reduce uncertainty and monitor performance.

(2) Rotanola Co could use market research to estimate by how much costs and revenues would need to differ from their estimated values before the decision would change.

Which of the above statements is/are true?

☐ 1 only
☐ 2 only
☐ Neither 1 nor 2
☐ Both 1 and 2   (2 marks)

(Total = 10 marks)

Section C questions

131 RB Co   39 mins

Just over two years ago, RB Co was the first company to produce a specific 'off-the-shelf' accounting software package. The pricing strategy, decided on by the managing director, for the packages was to add a 50% mark-up to the budgeted full cost of the packages. The company achieved and maintained a significant market share and high profits for the first two years.

Budgeted information for the current year (Year 3) was as follows.

Production and sales   15,000 packages
Full cost $400 per package

At a recent board meeting, the finance director reported that although costs were in line with the budget for the current year, profits were declining. He explained that the full cost included $80 for fixed overheads. This figure had been calculated by using an overhead absorption rate based on labour hours and the budgeted level of production of 15,000 packages. He pointed out that this was much lower than the current capacity of 25,000 packages.

The marketing director stated that competitors were beginning to increase their market share. He also reported the results of a recent competitor analysis which showed that when RB Co announced its prices for the current year, the competitors responded by undercutting them by 15%. Consequently, he commissioned an investigation of the market. He informed the board that the market research showed that at a price of $750 there would be no demand for the packages but for every $10 reduction in price the demand would increase by 1,000 packages.

The managing director appeared to be unconcerned about the loss of market share and argued that profits could be restored to their former level by increasing the mark-up.

Required

(a) Discuss the managing director's pricing strategy in the circumstances described above.   (5 marks)

(b) Suggest and explain two alternative strategies that could have been implemented at the launch of the packages.   (4 marks)

(c) Based on the data supplied by the market research, derive a straight line demand equation for the packages.   (3 marks)

(d) RB's total costs (TC) can be modelled by the equation $TC = 1{,}200{,}000 + 320Q$. Explain the meaning of this equation.   (3 marks)

(e) Explain what is meant by price elasticity of demand and explain the implications of elasticity for RB's pricing strategy.   (5 marks)

(Total = 20 marks)

132 The Cosmetic Co (12/10 amended)

The Cosmetic Co is a company producing a variety of cosmetic creams and lotions. The creams and lotions are sold to a variety of retailers at a price of $23.20 for each jar of face cream and $16.80 for each bottle of body lotion. Each of the products has a variety of ingredients, with the key ones being silk powder, silk amino acids and aloe vera. Six months ago, silk worms were attacked by disease causing a huge reduction in the availability of silk powder and silk amino acids. The Cosmetic Co had to dramatically reduce production and make part of its workforce, which it had trained over a number of years, redundant.

The company now wants to increase production again by ensuring that it uses the limited ingredients available to maximise profits by selling the optimum mix of creams and lotions. Due to the redundancies made earlier in the year, supply of skilled labour is now limited in the short term to 160 hours (9,600 minutes) per week, although unskilled labour is unlimited. The purchasing manager is confident that they can obtain 5,000 grams of silk powder and 1,600 grams of silk amino acids per week. All other ingredients are unlimited. The following information is available for the two products:

	Cream	Lotion
Materials required: silk powder (at $2.20 per gram)	3 grams	2 grams
– Silk amino acids (at $0.80 per gram)	1 gram	0.5 grams
– Aloe vera (at $1.40 per gram)	4 grams	2 grams
Labour required: skilled ($12 per hour)	4 minutes	5 minutes
– Unskilled (at $8 per hour)	3 minutes	1.5 minutes

Each jar of cream sold generates a contribution of $9 per unit, whilst each bottle of lotion generates a contribution of $8 per unit. The maximum demand for lotions is 2,000 bottles per week, although demand for creams is unlimited. Fixed costs total $1,800 per week. The company does not keep inventory although if a product is partially complete at the end of one week, its production will be completed in the following week.

Required

(a)   On the graph paper provided, use linear programming to calculate the optimum number of each product that the Cosmetic Co should make per week, assuming that it wishes to maximise contribution. Calculate the total contribution per week for the new production plan. All workings MUST be rounded to 2 decimal places.

(14 marks)

(b)   Calculate the shadow price for silk powder and the slack for silk amino acids. All workings MUST be rounded to 2 decimal places.

(6 marks)

(Total = 20 marks)

133 Bits and Pieces (6/09 amended)

Bits and Pieces (B&P) operates a retail store selling spares and accessories for the car market. The store has previously only opened for six days per week for the 50 working weeks in the year, but B&P is now considering also opening on Sundays.

The sales of the business on Monday through to Saturday averages at $10,000 per day with average gross profit of 70% earned.

B&P expects that the gross profit % earned on a Sunday will be 20 percentage points lower than the average earned on the other days in the week. This is because they plan to offer substantial discounts and promotions on a Sunday to attract customers. Given the price reduction, Sunday sales revenues are expected to be 60% **more than** the average daily sales revenues for the other days. These Sunday sales estimates are for new customers only, with no allowance being made for those customers that may transfer from other days.

B&P buys all its goods from one supplier. This supplier gives a 5% discount on **all** purchases if annual spend exceeds $1,000,000.

It has been agreed to pay time and a half to sales assistants that work on Sundays. The normal hourly rate is $20 per hour. In total five sales assistants will be needed for the six hours that the store will be open on a Sunday. They will also be able to take a half-day off (four hours) during the week. Staffing levels will be allowed to reduce slightly during the week to avoid extra costs being incurred.

The staff will have to be supervised by a manager, currently employed by the company and paid an annual salary of $80,000. If he works on a Sunday he will take the equivalent time off during the week when the assistant manager is available to cover for him at no extra cost to B&P. He will also be paid a bonus of 1% of the extra sales generated on the Sunday project.

The store will have to be lit at a cost of $30 per hour and heated at a cost of $45 per hour. The heating will come on two hours before the store opens in the 25 'winter' weeks to make sure it is warm enough for customers to come in at opening time. The store is not heated in the other weeks.

The rent of the store amounts to $420,000 per annum.

Required

(a)   Calculate whether the Sunday opening incremental revenue exceeds the incremental costs over a year (ignore inventory movements) and on this basis reach a conclusion as to whether Sunday opening is financially justifiable.   **(12 marks)**

(b)   Discuss whether the manager's pay deal (time off and bonus) is likely to motivate him.   **(4 marks)**

(c)   Briefly discuss whether offering substantial price discounts and promotions on Sunday is a good suggestion.   **(4 marks)**

(Total = 20 marks)

PART C: BUDGETING AND CONTROL

Questions 134 to 204 cover Budgeting and control, the subject of Part C of the BPP Study Text for Paper F5.

Section A questions

MCQ bank – Budgeting and control
59 mins

134 Which one of the following is the **least** likely reason why standard costs might not easily be applied to road haulage and distribution services.

    A   It is difficult to measure labour times reliably
    B   Variable costs are negligible
    C   It is difficult to identify a standard item for costing
    D   Standard costing applies to manufacturing industries only   **(2 marks)**

135 For which one of the following variances should a production manager usually be held responsible?

    A   Material price planning variance
    B   Material price operational variance
    C   Material usage planning variance
    D   Material usage operational variance   **(2 marks)**

136 The following statements have been made about standard mix and yield variances.

    (1)   Mix variances should be calculated whenever a standard product contains two or more direct materials.
    (2)   When a favourable mix variance is achieved, there may be a counterbalancing adverse yield variance.

    Which of the above statements is/are true?

    A   1 only
    B   2 only
    C   Neither 1 nor 2
    D   Both 1 and 2   **(2 marks)**

137 The following statements have been made about flexible budgets.

    (1)   Flexible budgets enable proper comparisons to be made between actual and expected revenues and costs.

    (2)   In every variance reporting system with flexible budgets that compares budgeted and actual profit, there must be a sales volume variance.

    Which of the above statements is/are true?

    A   1 only
    B   2 only
    C   Neither 1 nor 2
    D   Both 1 and 2   **(2 marks)**

138 A company sells two products X and Y. Product X sells for $30 per unit and achieves a standard contribution of $12 per unit, which is 40% of the selling price. Product Y, a new product, sells for $80 per unit and achieves a standard contribution of just $10 per unit, which is 12.5% of the selling price. Budgeted sales are 5,000 units of X and 3,000 units of Y.

However the sudden cancellation of an advertising campaign for Product Y has meant that sales for the product will be well below budget, and there has been some price discounting in an attempt to obtain sales for the product. Sales of X were in line with the budget.

Which one of the following sales variances, if calculated, would you expect to show a favourable variance for the period?

A   Sales mix variance
B   Sales price variance
C   Sales quantity variance
D   Sales volume variance   **(2 marks)**

139   Which of the following provides the most suitable definition of the controllability principle in business?

A   A fundamental principle of management is the responsibility to control the organisation

B   Managers should be held accountable only for costs and revenues over which they have some influence or control

C   Organisations should be divided into budget centres for the purpose of operational control

D   Performance measures should be reported to managers to enable them to control operations   **(2 marks)**

140   The following statements have been made about standard mix and yield variances.

(1)   Mix and yield variances enable management to resolve problems with the quality of production output.

(2)   Persistent adverse mix variances may have an adverse effect on sales volume variances and direct labour efficiency variances.

Which of the above statements is/are true?

A   1 only
B   2 only
C   Neither 1 nor 2
D   Both 1 and 2   **(2 marks)**

141   The following statements have been made about the application of standard costing systems.

(1)   Standard costing systems are compatible with a Total Quality Management approach to operations.

(2)   Standard costing systems are less commonly used in an industry that operates in a rapidly changing environment.

Which of the above statements is/are true?

A   1 only
B   2 only
C   Neither 1 nor 2
D   Both 1 and 2   **(2 marks)**

142   The following statements have been made about learning curves.

(1)   Learning curves are easier to apply in companies with a high labour turnover than those with a lower rate of staff turnover.

(2)   Learning rates are not affected by time gaps between the production of additional units of a product.

Which of the above statements is/are true?

A   1 only
B   2 only
C   Neither 1 nor 2
D   Both 1 and 2   **(2 marks)**

143   The following statements have been made about the use of expected values in budgeting.

(1)   Expected values may not be expected to occur, which means that probabilistic budgets are of limited value for budgetary control.

(2)   The use of expected values and probabilities in budgeting is most useful when there is a high level of uncertainty about the future.

Which of the above statements is/are true?

- A   1 only
- B   2 only
- C   Neither 1 nor 2
- D   Both 1 and 2   (2 marks)

144   What are the three building blocks in Fitzgerald and Moon's performance model for a service business?

- A   Objectives, standards and rewards
- B   Dimensions, standards and rewards
- C   Objectives, standards and measures
- D   Dimensions, rewards and measures   (2 marks)

145   For which one of the following reasons is zero based budgeting (ZBB) often considered more suitable for public sector service organisations than for private sector companies?

- A   ZBB is more suited to costs where there is little discretionary spending, as in the public sector services

- B   The public sector is better able to afford the high cost of ZBB

- C   ZBB is used in a top-down approach to budgeting, which is more common in the public sector than the private sector

- D   It is easier to put public sector activities into decision packages because they are more easily definable than in the private sector   (2 marks)

146   The following statements have been made about the use of spreadsheets for budgeting.

(1)   Spreadsheets greatly assist sensitivity analysis during the planning process.

(2)   Spreadsheets greatly assist the budgeting process by facilitating the preparation of alternative draft budgets.

Which of the above statements is/are true?

- A   1 only
- B   2 only
- C   Neither 1 nor 2
- D   Both 1 and 2   (2 marks)

147   A company operates in export and import markets, and its operational cash flows are affected by movements in exchange rates, which are highly volatile. As a result, the company has great difficulty in establishing a budgeting system that is reliable for more than three months ahead.

Which of the following approaches to budgeting would be most appropriate for this company's situation?

- A   Flexible budget
- B   Incremental budget
- C   Rolling budget
- D   Zero based budget   (2 marks)

148   Tech World is a company which manufactures mobile phone handsets. From its past experiences, Tech World has realised that whenever a new design engineer is employed, there is a learning curve with a 75% learning rate which exists for the first 15 jobs.

A new design engineer has just completed his first job in five hours.

Note. At the learning rate of 75%, the learning factor (b) is equal to -0.415.

How long would it take the design engineer to complete the sixth job?

- A   2.377 hours
- B   1.442 hours
- C   2.564 hours
- D   5 hours   (2 marks)

(Total = 30 marks)

CBE style OTQ bank – Budgeting and control 59 mins

149 The following cost information relates to product XY, which is produced in a continuous process from several different materials.

	$
Actual quantity of materials at standard price	19,960
Actual quantity of materials at actual price	23,120
Actual yield at standard materials cost	20,800
Standard yield from actual input of materials at standard cost	19,552

What is the materials yield variance for the period?

Note. Use minus sign to denote adverse variance.

$ [   ]   **(2 marks)**

150 Which **two** of the following statements correctly describe an attainable standard?

☐ This standard is the least useful and most rarely used type of standard.

☐ This standard makes allowances for expected wastage and inefficiencies.

☐ This standard is based on perfect operating conditions.

☐ This standard should give employees a realistic, but challenging target of efficiency   **(2 marks)**

151 The first item of a new product took 2,000 hours to manufacture (at a labour cost of $15 per hour). A 90% learning curve was expected to apply, and it was decided to establish a standard time as the time required to manufacture the 50th item of the product, rounded to the nearest hour. The 50th item actually took 980 hours.

What was the labour efficiency variance for the 50th unit produced?

☐ $645 (A)

☐ $43 (A)

☐ $1,860 (F)

☐ $1,905 (F)   **(2 marks)**

152 The following information is given about standard and actual material costs during one month for a production process.

Material	Standard cost per kg	Actual cost per kg	Standard mix	Actual mix kg
P	3.00	3.50	10%	820
Q	2.50	2.75	20%	1,740
R	4.00	3.50	30%	2,300
S	5.25	5.00	40%	2,640
				7,500

What was the materials mix variance?

Note. Use minus sign to denote adverse variance.

$ [   ]   **(2 marks)**

153 A company makes and sells three products. Budgeted and actual results for the period just ended were as follows.

Product	Budgeted sales	Budgeted profit per unit	Actual sales	Actual profit per unit
	Units	$	Units	$
X	800	10	700	8
Y	1,000	6	1,200	6
Z	600	12	350	16
	2,400		2,250	

What was the sales mix variance?

Note. Use minus sign to denote adverse variance.

$ [   ] **(2 marks)**

154 Why might it be argued that, in a total quality environment, variance analysis from a standard costing system is redundant (select **two** answers)?

☐ For standard costing to be useful for control purposes, it requires a reasonably stable environment.

☐ The ethos behind a system of standard costing is that performance is satisfactory if it meets predetermined standards.

☐ The control aspect of standard costing systems is achieved by making individual managers responsible for the variances relating to their part of the organisation's activities.

☐ Standard costs are set based on ideal standards rather than attainable ones. **(2 marks)**

155 A standard product uses 3 kilograms of direct material costing $4 per kg. During the most recent month, 120 units of the product were manufactured. These required 410 kilograms of material costing $4.50 per kg. It is decided in retrospect that the standard usage quantity of the material should have been 3.5 kg, not 3 kg.

What is the materials operational usage variance, if it is chosen to use planning and operational variances for reporting performance?

Note. Use minus sign to denote adverse variance.

$ [   ] **(2 marks)**

156 A company makes and sells three products. Budgeted and actual results for the period just ended were as follows.

Product	Budgeted sales	Budgeted profit per unit	Actual sales	Actual profit per unit
	Units	$	Units	$
X	800	10	700	8
Y	1,000	6	1,200	6
Z	600	12	350	16
	2,400		2,250	

What was the sales quantity variance?

Note. Use minus sign to denote adverse variance.

$ [   ] **(2 marks)**

157   In which THREE of the following ways might a budgetary control be a disincentive to management to achieve targeted performance?

☐   Control reports are provided too late

☐   Targets are too easy

☐   Targets are not communicated

☐   Budgets are imposed by senior management   **(2 marks)**

158   Which THREE of the following statements are true in the context of a just in time (JIT) inventory system?

☐   It is dependent upon a close and mutually beneficial working relationship with suppliers.

☐   It can result in much reduced inventory holding costs

☐   It inevitably increases the need for safety inventories

☐   It requires suppliers to operate sound quality control procedures

☐   It works best if supplies are obtained from a number of different suppliers   **(2 marks)**

159   Which **two** of the following points state why it is generally regarded to be more difficult to set standards for service function costs than for manufacturing costs?

☐   There is often no measurable output from service functions

☐   The activities of many service functions are of a non-standard nature

☐   The costs of many service functions are predominantly variable

☐   Tasks in many service industries are usually quick and simple   **(2 marks)**

160   Which of the following correctly describes a standard hour?

☐   An hour during which only standard units are made

☐   An hour during which no machine breakdowns occur

☐   The quantity of work achievable at standard performance in an hour

☐   An hour for which standard labour rates are paid   **(2 marks)**

161   A company operates in the energy market, and its operational cash flows are affected by movements in the price of oil, which is highly volatile. As a result, the company has great difficulty in establishing a budgeting system that is reliable for more than two or three months ahead.

Which of the following approaches to budgeting would be most appropriate for this company's situation?

☐   Flexible budget

☐   Incremental budget

☐   Rolling budget

☐   Zero based budget   **(2 marks)**

162   What is an attainable standard?

☐   A standard which is based on currently attainable working conditions.

☐   A standard which is established for use over a long period, which is used to show trends.

☐   A standard which can be attained under perfect operating conditions, and which includes no allowance for wastage, spoilage, machine breakdowns and other inefficiencies

☐   A standard which can be attained if production is carried out efficiently, machines are operated properly and/or materials are used properly. Some allowance is made for waste and inefficiencies

(2 marks)

163   Capacity levels used in setting standard absorption rates for production overheads are often related to performance standards.

☐   To which performance standard is budgeted capacity often associated?
☐   Basic standard
☐   Attainable standard
☐   Ideal standard
☐   Current standard

(2 marks)

(Total = 30 marks)

Section B questions

MCQ case questions

Crush Co   20 mins

The following scenario relates to questions 164 – 168

Crush Co has developed a new product. The first batch of 100 units will take 1,500 labour hours to produce. Crush Co has estimated that there will be an 85% learning curve that will continue until 6,400 units have been produced. Batches after this level will each take the same amount of time as the 64th batch. The batch size will always be 100 units.

Note: The learning index for an 85% learning curve is -0.2345

Ignore the time value of money.

164   Calculate the cumulative average time per batch for the first 64 batches.

A   567.7 hours
B   565.6 hours
C   433.3 hours
D   570 hours

(2 marks)

165   The total time for the first 16 batches of 100 units was 9,000 hours. What was the actual learning rate closest to (to the nearest %)?

A   80%
B   75%
C   78%
D   73%   (2 marks)

166   The following statements have been made about Crush Co and the learning curve:

(1)   Decisions about allocating resources and costing the new product should be based on the time taken to produce the 64th batch.

(2)   The learning process does not start until the second batch comes off the production line.

Which of the above statements is/are true?

A   1 only
B   2 only
C   Neither 1 nor 2
D   Both 1 and 2   (2 marks)

167   The following statements have been made about learning curve:

(1)   The learning curve must assume a certain degree of motivation among employees of Crush Co
(2)   The learning curve phenomenon is not always present

Which of the above statements is/are true?

A   1 only
B   2 only
C   Neither 1 nor 2
D   Both 1 and 2   (2 marks)

168   Which of the following conditions, if present in Crush Co would allow the learning curve to flourish?

A   The process is a repetitive one
B   There is a continuity of workers
C   There are no prolonged breaks during the production process
D   All of the above   (2 marks)

(Total = 10 marks)

BBB Co   **20 mins**

The following scenario relates to questions 169 – 173.

BBB Co has developed a new product. The first batch of 50 units will take 750 labour hours to produce. There will be an 90% learning curve that will continue until 3,550 units have been produced. Batches after this level will each take the same amount of time as the 71st batch. The batch size will always be 50 units.

Note: The learning index for an 90% learning curve is -0.152

Ignore the time value of money.

169   Calculate the time taken for the 71st batch.

A   392.35 hours
B   330.75 hours
C   393.23 hours
D   345.65 hours   (2 marks)

170 The total time for the first 16 batches of units was 8,500 hours. What was the actual learning rate closest to (to the nearest %)?

    A   92%
    B   89%
    C   78%
    D   85%   **(2 marks)**

171 The following statements have been made about BBB Co and the learning curve:

(1) The learning effect comes to an end in BBB Co after the 71st unit, however, some learning effects can continue indefinitely.

(2) The learning curve is restricted to the manufacturing industry.

Which of the above statements is/are true?

    A   1 only
    B   2 only
    C   Neither 1 nor 2
    D   Both 1 and 2   **(2 marks)**

172 The costs of producing more units in BBB Co has been reduced due to the following factors. Which factor from the below is due to the learning curve effect?

    A   Bulk quantity discounts received from the supplier
    B   Lower labour costs
    C   A reduction in materials price
    D   Economies of scale achieved in energy costs   **(2 marks)**

173 The learning curve effect in BBB Co could be extended by which of the following?

    A   Increasing staff turnover
    B   Increasing the level of staff training
    C   Allowing extended breaks in production
    D   Introducing a new mechanised process   **(2 marks)**

(Total = 10 marks)

Ash Co   **20 mins**

The following scenario relates to questions 174 – 178.

Ash Co makes product X by mixing together two ingredients, A and B. The standard cost card for one unit of X is as follows:

Material	Kgs per unit	$ per kg	$ per unit
A	2	1.50	3.00
B	5	1.75	8.75
			11.75

The budgeted output for the March was 60 units. After one month of production, 50 units of X were produced from 110 kg of A and 225 kg of B.

174 Calculate the materials usage variance.

    A $28.75 (F)
    B $146.25 (F)
    C $146.25 (A)
    D $28.75 (A)   **(2 marks)**

175 Calculate the material mix variance.

    A $14.29 (A)
    B $3.57 (A)
    C $3.57 (F)
    D $14.29 (F)   **(2 marks)**

176 Calculate the material yield variance.

    A $160.54 (F)
    B $25.15 (F)
    C $131.96 (F)
    D $25.15 (A)   **(2 marks)**

177 Which of the following factors would result in an adverse material usage variance in Ash Co?

    (1)   Using an inferior quality of material A or B
    (2)   Making changes to the production process
    (3)   Introducing increased quality controls resulting in more items of Product X being rejected. *would affect the yield*

    A   1 and 3 only
    (B)   1 and 2 only
    C   2 and 3 only
    D   1, 2 and 3   **(2 marks)**

178 Which of the following factors would result in a material mix variance in Ash Co?

    A   The cost of materials A or B changes
    B   The production manager in Ash Co deviates from the standard mix
    C   The selling price of Product X changes
    D   An inferior quality of material A or B is used   **(2 marks)**

            (Total = 10 marks)

Birch Co   **20 mins**

The following scenario relates to questions 179 – 183.

Birch Co budgeted to make and sell 20,000 units of Product X in a four-week period, as follows:

	$
Budgeted sales ($4 per unit per week)	80,000
Variable costs ($2.50 per unit)	50,000
Contribution	30,000
Fixed costs	3,000
Profit	27,000

The actual results for the period were as follows.

	$
Budgeted sales ($4 per unit)	64,000
Variable costs ($2.50 per unit)	40,000
Contribution	24,000
Fixed costs	3,000
Profit	21,000

In retrospect, it is decided that the optimum budget, would have been to sell only 17,500 units in the period.

179 Calculate the sales volume planning variance.

    A $3,750 (F)
    B $2,250 (F)
    C $3,750 (A)
    D $2,250 (A)   **(2 marks)**

180   Calculate the sales volume operational variance.

    A $3,750 (A)
    B $2,250 (A)
    C $2,250 (F)
    D $3,750 (F)   **(2 marks)**

181   In a subsequent 4 week period, Birch Co's actual fixed costs were $3,500. There were 18,000 units produced. The budgeted fixed costs was $3,000 based on budgeted production of 17,500 units. Calculate the fixed production overhead total variance.

    A $440 (A)
    B $525 (A)
    C $500 (F)
    D $500 (A)   **(2 marks)**

182   Which of the following factors would contribute to a planning variance in Birch Co?

    A   A better negotiation of the material price with the supplier
    B   An increase in wage costs due to unplanned overtime worked
    C   An improvement in technology that led to an international reduction in sales price of Product X
    D   A break in production due to a machine breakdown, which was caused by human error   **(2 marks)**

183   A manager in Birch Co asked for the market share variance. Which of the following variances was she looking for?

    A   The sales volume planning variance
    B   The sales volume operational variance
    C   The sales price planning variance
    D   The sales price operational variance   **(2 marks)**

                                                        (Total = 10 marks)

CBE OT case questions

Elm Co   20 mins

The following scenario relates to questions 184 – 188.

Elm Co is a company which operates in Sealand. Elm Co budgeted to sell 25,000 units of a new product during the year. The budgeted sales price was $8 per unit, and the variable cost $4 per unit.

Actual sales during the year were 22,000 units and variable costs of sales were $88,000. Sales revenue was only $9 per unit. With the benefit of hindsight, it is realised that the budgeted sales price of $8 was too low, and a price of $10 per unit would have been much more realistic.

Required

184   Calculate the favourable sales price planning variance.

                                                                 (2 marks)

185   Calculate the adverse sales price operational variance.

                                                                   (2 marks)

186   In a subsequent year, the cost of labour was $73,000. 4,000 hours were worked. The budgeted cost of labour was $15 per labour hour. Calculate the adverse labour rate variance for this subsequent year.

                                                                   (2 marks)

187 The following statements have been made about Elm Co.

(1) The sales manager of Elm Co should be held responsible if an unfavourable planning sales price variance is found.

(2) It is possible for the revised price to be manipulated and revised to a level whereby a favourable operational sales price could be found.

Which of the above statements is/are true?

☐ 1 only
☐ 2 only
☐ Neither 1 nor 2
☐ Both 1 and 2 (2 marks)

188 The following statements have been made about Elm Co.

(1) The operational manager of Elm Co should examine each variance in isolation only.
(2) A change in economic conditions in Sealand will result in operational variances

Which of the above statements is/are true?

☐ 1 only
☐ 2 only
☐ Neither 1 nor 2
☐ Both 1 and 2 (2 marks)

(Total = 10 marks)

Maple Co 20 mins

The following scenario relates to questions 189 – 193.

A company made a product called Bark. Bark had a standard direct material cost in the budget of:

2.5 kg of Material X at $4 per kg = $10 per unit.

The average market price for Material X during the period was $5 per kg, and it was decided to revise the material standard cost to allow for this.

During the period, 8,000 units of Bark were manufactured. They required 22,000 kg of Material X, which cost $123,000.

Required

189 Calculate the adverse material price planning variance.

[   ] (2 marks)

190 Calculate the adverse material price operational variance.

[   ] (2 marks)

191 Calculate the adverse material usage operational variance.

[   ] (2 marks)

192   The following possible reasons have been given for a material price planning variance.

   (1)   Maple Co failed to order a sufficient amount of material X for production from the main supplier. They sourced the rest of the material from another supplier at a higher price to make up for this.

   (2)   There was a disruption to the supply of material X to the market

   Which of the above statements is/are valid reasons?

   ☐   1 only
   ☐   2 only
   ☐   Neither 1 nor 2
   ☐   Both 1 and 2   (2 marks)

193   The following statements have been made about variances in Maple Co.

   (1)   Any operational variances arising should be a realistic measure of what the causes of the variances have cost Maple Co.

   (2)   The causes of the planning variances should not be investigated immediately by the operational manager in Maple Co.

   Which of the above statements is/are true?

   ☐   1 only
   ☐   2 only
   ☐   Neither 1 nor 2
   ☐   Both 1 and 2   (2 marks)

                                                                     (Total = 10 marks)

Pine Co   20 mins

The following scenario relates to questions 194 – 198.

Pine Co makes a single product. At the beginning of the budget year, the standard labour cost was established as $45 per unit, and each unit should take 3 hours to make.

However, during the year, the standard labour cost was revised. The labour rate was reduced to $14 per hour, and the revised labour time was 4.5 hours per unit.

In the first month after revision of the standard cost, budgeted production was 10,000 units but only 8,000 units were actually produced. These took 24,300 hours of labour time, which cost $352,350.

Required

194   Calculate the favourable labour rate planning variance.

   ┌─────────────────┐
   │   │
   └─────────────────┘   (2 marks)

195   Calculate the adverse labour efficiency planning variance.

   ┌─────────────────┐
   │   │
   └─────────────────┘   (2 marks)

196   Calculate the adverse labour rate operational variance.

   ┌─────────────────┐
   │   │
   └─────────────────┘   (2 marks)

197   Calculate the favourable labour efficiency operational variance.

   ┌─────────────────┐
   │   │
   └─────────────────┘   (2 marks)

198 The following statements have been made about labour variances in Pine Co.

(1) Production management's motivation is likely to increase if they know they will not be held responsible for poor planning and faulty standard setting.

(2) Planning variances will provide a more realistic and fair reflection of actual performance.

Which of the above statements is/are true?

☐ 1 only
☐ 2 only
☐ Neither 1 nor 2
☐ Both 1 and 2   (2 marks)

(Total = 10 marks)

Section C questions

199 Mic Co (12/13 amended)   39 mins

Mic Co produces microphones for mobile phones and operates a standard costing system. Before production commenced, the standard labour time per batch for its latest microphone was estimated to be 200 hours. The standard labour cost per hour is $12 and resource allocation and cost data were therefore initially prepared on this basis.

Production of the microphone started in July and the number of batches assembled and sold each month was as follows:

Month	No of batches assembled and sold
July	1
August	1
September	2
October	4
November	8

The first batch took 200 hours to make, as anticipated, but, during the first four months of production, a learning effect of 88% was observed, although this finished at the end of October. The learning formula is shown on the formula sheet and at the 88% learning rate the value of b is −0.1844245.

Mic Co uses 'cost plus' pricing to establish selling prices for all its products. Sales of its new microphone in the first five months have been disappointing. The sales manager has blamed the production department for getting the labour cost so wrong, as this, in turn, caused the price to be too high. The production manager has disclaimed all responsibility, saying that, 'as usual, the managing director prepared the budgets alone and didn't consult me and, had he bothered to do so, I would have told him that a learning curve was expected.'

Required

(a) Calculate the actual total monthly labour costs for producing the microphones for each of the five months from July to November.   (9 marks)

(b) Discuss the implications of the learning effect coming to an end for Mic Co, with regard to costing, budgeting and production.   (4 marks)

(c) Discuss the potential advantages and disadvantages of involving senior staff at Mic Co in the budget setting process, rather than the managing director simply imposing budgets on them.   (7 marks)

(Total = 20 marks)

200 ZBB (12/10 amended)

39 mins

Some commentators argue that: 'With continuing pressure to control costs and maintain efficiency, the time has come for all public sector organisations to embrace zero-based budgeting. There is no longer a place for incremental budgeting in any organisation, particularly public sector ones, where zero-based budgeting is far more suitable anyway.'

Required

(a) Discuss the particular difficulties encountered when budgeting in public sector organisations compared with budgeting in private sector organisations, drawing comparisons between the two types of organisations.

(5 marks)

(b) Explain the terms 'incremental budgeting' and 'zero-based budgeting'.

(4 marks)

(c) State the main stages involved in preparing zero-based budgets.

(3 marks)

(d) Discuss the view that 'there is no longer a place for incremental budgeting in any organisation, particularly public sector ones,' highlighting any drawbacks of zero-based budgeting that need to be considered.

(8 marks)

(Total = 20 marks)

201 Designit (12/12 amended)

39 mins

Designit is a small company providing design consultancy to a limited number of large clients. The business is mature and fairly stable year on year. It has 30 employees and is privately owned by its founder. Designit prepares an annual fixed budget. The company's accounts department consists of one part-qualified accountant who has a heavy workload. He prepares the budget using spreadsheets. The company has a November year end.

Designit pays each of its three sales managers an annual salary of $150,000, plus an individual bonus based on sales targets set at the beginning of the year. There are always two levels of bonus that can be earned, based on a lower and an upper level of fee income. For the year ended 30 November 20X2, for example, each of the sales managers was given a lower target of securing $1.5m of fee income each, to be rewarded by an individual bonus equating to 20% of salary. If any of the managers secured a further $1.5m of fee income, their bonus would increase by 5% to the upper target of 25%. None of the managers achieved the upper target but all of them achieved the lower one.

This is the same every year and Designit finds that often the managers secure work from several major clients early in the year and reach the $1.5m target well before the year has ended. They then make little effort to secure extra fees for the company, knowing that it would be almost impossible to hit the second target. This, together with a few other problems that have arisen, has made the company consider whether its current budgeting process could be improved and whether the bonus scheme should also be changed.

Designit is now considering replacing the fixed budget with a monthly rolling budget, which Designit believes will make the budgeting process more relevant and timely and encourage managers to focus on the future rather than the past. It would also prevent the problem of targets being met too early on in the year by the sales managers because the targets would be set for monthly performance rather than annual performance. For example, a manager could be given a target of securing $200,000 fee income in the first month for a reward of 2% of salary. Then, depending on what is happening both within the business and in the economy as a whole, at the end of the first month, a different target fee income could be set for the second month.

Required

(a) Explain what a monthly rolling budget is and how it would operate at Designit.   **(4 marks)**

(b) Discuss the problems that may be encountered if Designit decides to introduce monthly rolling budgets together with a new bonus scheme, such as the one outlined above.   **(6 marks)**

(c) Discuss the problems with the current bonus scheme and, assuming that the company decides against introducing rolling budgets, describe and justify an alternative, more effective bonus scheme that could be introduced.   **(6 marks)**

(d) Discuss the risk of using the company accountant's own spreadsheets for budgeting.   **(4 marks)**

(Total = 20 marks)

202 Crumbly Cakes (6/09 amended)   39 mins

Crumbly Cakes make cakes, which are sold directly to the public. The new production manager (a celebrity chef) has argued that the business should use only organic ingredients in its cake production. Organic ingredients are more expensive but should produce a product with an improved flavour and give health benefits for the customers. It was hoped that this would stimulate demand and enable an immediate price increase for the cakes.

Crumbly Cakes operates a responsibility based standard costing system which allocates variances to specific individuals. The individual managers are paid a bonus only when net favourable variances are allocated to them.

The new organic cake production approach was adopted at the start of March 20X9, following a decision by the new production manager. No change was made at that time to the standard costs card. The variance reports for February and March are shown below (Fav = Favourable and Adv = Adverse).

Manager responsible	Allocated variances	February variance $	March variance $
Production manager	Material price (total for all ingredients)	25 Fav	2,100 Adv
	Material mix	0	600 Adv
	Material yield	20 Fav	400 Fav
Sales manager	Sales price	40 Adv	7,000 Fav
	Sales contribution volume	35 Adv	3,000 Fav

The production manager is upset that he seems to have lost all hope of a bonus under the new system. The sales manager thinks the new organic cakes are excellent and is very pleased with the progress made.

Crumbly Cakes operate a JIT inventory system and holds virtually no inventory.

Required

(a) Assess the performance of the production manager and the sales manager and indicate whether the current bonus scheme is fair to those concerned.   **(7 marks)**

In April 20X9 the following data applied:

Standard cost card for one cake (not adjusted for the organic ingredient change)

Ingredients	Kg	$
Flour	0.10	0.12 per kg
Eggs	0.10	0.70 per kg
Butter	0.10	1.70 per kg
Sugar	0.10	0.50 per kg
Total input	0.40	
Normal loss (10%)	(0.04)	
Standard weight of a cake	0.36	

The budget for production and sales in April was 50,000 cakes. Actual production and sales was 60,000 cakes in the month, during which the following occurred:

Ingredients used	Kg	$
Flour	5,700	$741
Eggs	6,600	$5,610
Butter	6,600	$11,880
Sugar	4,578	$2,747
Total input	23,478	$20,978
Actual loss	(1,878)	
Actual output of cake mixture	21,600	

All cakes produced must weigh 0.36 kg as this is what is advertised.

Required

(b)   Calculate the material price, mix and yield variances for April. You are not required to make any comment on the performance of the managers.   **(9 marks)**

With the benefit of hindsight the management of Crumbly Cakes realises that a more realistic standard cost for current conditions would be $0.40 per cake. The planned standard cost is unrealistically low.

Required

(c)   Calculate the total cost planning and operational variances for April. Briefly comment on each variance.

(4 marks)

(Total = 20 marks)

203 Secure Net (12/09 amended)   39 mins

Secure Net (SN) manufacture security cards that restrict access to government owned buildings around the world.

The standard cost for the plastic that goes into making a card is $4 per kg and each card uses 40 g of plastic after an allowance for waste. In November 100,000 cards were produced and sold by SN and this was well above the budgeted sales of 60,000 cards.

The actual cost of the plastic was $5.25 per kg and the production manager (who is responsible for all buying and production issues) was asked to explain the increase. He said 'World oil price increases pushed up plastic prices by 20% compared to our budget and I also decided to use a different supplier who promised better quality and increased reliability for a slightly higher price. I know we have overspent but not all the increase in plastic prices is my fault. The actual usage of plastic per card was 35 g per card and again the production manager had an explanation. He said 'The world-wide standard size for security cards increased by 5% due to a change in the card reader technology, however, our new supplier provided much better quality of plastic and this helped to cut down on the waste.'

SN operates a just in time (JIT) system and hence carries very little inventory.

Required

(a)   Discuss the behavioural problems that can arise from using standard costs and ways to prevent them.

(4 marks)

(b)   Analyse the above total variances into component parts for planning and operational variances in as much detail as the information allows.   **(8 marks)**

(c)   Assess the performance of the production manager.   **(8 marks)**

(Total = 20 marks)

204 Noble (6/11 amended)

Noble is a restaurant that is only open in the evenings, on **six** days of the week. It has eight restaurant and kitchen staff, each paid a wage of $8 per hour on the basis of hours actually worked. It also has a restaurant manager and a head chef, each of whom is paid a monthly salary of $4,300. Noble's budget and actual figures for the month of May was as follows:

	Budget	$	Actual	$
Number of meals	1,200		1,560	
	$		$	
Revenue: Food	48,000s		60,840	
Drinks	12,000		11,700	
		60,000		72,540
Variable costs:				
Staff wages	(9,216)		(13,248)	
Food costs	(6,000)		(7,180)	
Drink costs	(2,400)		(5,280)	
Energy costs	(3,387)		(3,500)	
		(21,003)		(29,208)
Contribution		38,997		43,332
Fixed costs:				
Manager's and chef's pay	(8,600)		(8,600)	
Rent, rates and depreciation	(4,500)	(13,100)	(4,500)	(13,100)
Operating profit		25,897		30,232

The budget above is based on the following assumptions:

(1) The restaurant is only open six days a week and there are four weeks in a month. The average number of orders each day is 50 and demand is evenly spread across all the days in the month.

(2) The restaurant offers two meals: Meal A, which costs $35 per meal and Meal B, which costs $45 per meal. In addition to this, irrespective of which meal the customer orders, the average customer consumes four drinks each at $2.50 per drink. Therefore, the average spend per customer is either $45 or $55 including drinks, depending on the type of meal selected. The May budget is based on 50% of customers ordering Meal A and 50% of customers ordering Meal B.

(3) Food costs represent 12.5% of revenue from food sales.

(4) Drink costs represent 20% of revenue from drinks sales.

(5) When the number of orders per day does not exceed 50, each member of hourly paid staff is required to work exactly six hours per day. For every incremental increase of five in the average number of orders per day, each member of staff has to work 0·5 hours of overtime for which they are paid at the increased rate of $12 per hour. You should assume that all costs for hourly paid staff are treated wholly as variable costs.

(6) Energy costs are deemed to be related to the total number of hours worked by each of the hourly paid staff, and are absorbed at the rate of $2.94 per hour worked by each of the eight staff.

Required

(a) Prepare a flexed budget for the month of May, assuming that the standard mix of customers remains the same as budgeted.
(12 marks)

(b) After preparation of the flexed budget, you are informed that the following variances have arisen in relation to total food and drink sales:

Sales mix contribution variance	$1,014 Adverse
Sales quantity contribution variance	$11,700 Favourable

BRIEFLY describe the sales mix contribution variance and the sales quantity contribution variance. Identify why each of them has arisen in Noble's case.
(4 marks)

(c)   Noble's owner told the restaurant manager to run a half-price drinks promotion at Noble for the month of May on all drinks. Actual results showed that customers ordered an average of six drinks each instead of the usual four but, because of the promotion, they only paid half of the usual cost for each drink. You have calculated the sales margin price variance for drink sales alone and found it to be a worrying $11,700 adverse. The restaurant manager is worried and concerned that this makes his performance for drink sales look very bad.

Required

Briefly discuss **two** other variances that could be calculated for drinks sales or food sales in order to ensure that the assessment of the restaurant manager's performance is fair. These should be variances that COULD be calculated from the information provided above although no further calculations are required here.

(4 marks)

(Total = 20 marks)

PART D: PERFORMANCE MEASUREMENT AND CONTROL

Questions 205 to 289 cover Performance measurement and control, the subject of Part D of the BPP Study Text for Paper F5.

Section A questions

MCQ bank – Performance measurement and control   117 mins

205   The following statements have been made about a transfer pricing system where Division A transfers output to Division B.

  (1)   Internal transfers should be preferred when there is an external market for the transferred item, because there will be more control over quality and delivery.

  (2)   The transfer price will determine how profits will be shared between the two divisions.

  Which of the above statements is/are true?

  A   1 only
  B   2 only
  C   Neither 1 nor 2
  D   Both 1 and 2   **(2 marks)**

206   The following statements have been made about performance measurements in not-for-profit organisations.

  (1)   Not-for-profit organisations do not have financial objectives.

  (2)   The outputs produced by not-for-profit organisations are easier to measure than output of commercial companies.

  Which of the above statements is/are true?

  A   1 only
  B   2 only
  C   Neither 1 nor 2
  D   Both 1 and 2   **(2 marks)**

207   Which one of the following figures would be the most suitable for divisional profit for the purpose of performance measurement?

  A   Gross profit
  B   Profit before interest and tax
  C   Profit before tax
  D   Profit after tax   **(2 marks)**

208   A hospital wishes to establish a performance measurement for its 'quality of care', and in particular its adherence to appointment times for patients receiving medical checks. Which one of the following performance measurements would be the most suitable for this purpose?

  A   Average length of appointments
  B   Average number of appointments per day
  C   Average number of days from making an appointment to the appointment date
  D   Average waiting time at the hospital   **(2 marks)**

209　Which one of the following is often used to protect an intranet from unauthorised access by an external hacker?

　　A　Anti-virus software
　　B　Data encryption
　　C　Firewall
　　D　Passwords　　　　　　　　　　　　　　　　　　　　　　　　　　　　　　　　　　**(2 marks)**

210　A company that uses a balanced scorecard approach to performance measurement has recorded the following data for the previous financial year.

	Products made and sold for at least 2 years	Products introduced to market within the previous two years = 'new products'	Total
Number of products	16	4	
Annual sales	$3.0 million	$0.50 million	$3.50 million
Cost of sales	$2.4 million	$0.42 million	$2.82 million
Hours worked	27,500	4,500	
Research and development costs			$150,000

Which one of the following would be the most suitable measure of performance from the innovation and learning perspective in a balanced scorecard?

　　A　Development cost per new product
　　B　Sales revenue per new product
　　C　Sales revenue from new products as a percentage of total revenue
　　D　Sales revenue per hour worked on new products　　　　　　　　　　　　　　**(2 marks)**

211　Which one of the following measures of performance for public sector services is a measure of efficiency?

　　A　Number of patients treated per $1 spent on the state hospital service

　　B　Percentage reduction in the spending budget of a government department compared with the previous year

　　C　Proportion of reported crimes that are solved by the police service

　　D　Proportion of students in a state-owned college achieving good pass grades in their examinations
　　　　　　　　　　　　　　　　　　　　　　　　　　　　　　　　　　　　　　(2 marks)

212　The following statements have been made about data and information.

　　(1)　Automated systems for data capture are generally more reliable than data capture requiring input by individuals.

　　(2)　As a general rule, secondary information is more expensive to collect than primary data.

Which of the above statements is/are true?

　　A　1 only
　　B　2 only
　　C　Neither 1 nor 2
　　D　Both 1 and 2　　　　　　　　　　　　　　　　　　　　　　　　　　　　　　**(2 marks)**

213　When goods are transferred from one division in a company to another division, and there is an intermediate external market for the transferred item in which the goods could be sold, which of the following states the economic transfer pricing rule for what the maximum transfer price should be?

　　A　Marginal cost of the transferring-out division minus any lost contribution of the transferring-out division from having to make the internal transfer

　　B　The higher of the net marginal revenue for the transferring-in division and the external purchase price in the market for the intermediate product

　　C　The lower of the net marginal revenue for the transferring-in division and the external purchase price in the market for the intermediate product

　　D　None of the above　　　　　　　　　　　　　　　　　　　　　　　　　　　**(2 marks)**

214   A company has a call centre to handle queries and complaints from customers. The company is concerned about the average length of calls and the time that it takes to deal with customers. As part of its balanced scorecard, it has set a target for reducing the average time per customer call.

A target for reducing the average time per call would relate to which one of the four balanced scorecard perspectives?

A   Customer perspective
B   Financial perspective
C   Innovation and learning perspective
D   Internal business (operational) perspective   **(2 marks)**

215   The following statements have been made about management information and management information systems.

(1)   Management information is often produced from transaction processing systems.

(2)   The data used in management information systems comes mainly from sources within the organisation and its operations.

Which of the above statements is/are true?

A   1 only
B   2 only
C   Neither 1 nor 2
D   Both 1 and 2   **(2 marks)**

216   The following statements have been made about operational control.

(1)   Budgeting is commonly associated with decision making at the operational planning level within a management hierarchy.

(2)   Operational control decisions in general are more narrowly focused and have a shorter time horizon than management control decisions.

Which of the above statements is/are true?

A   1 only
B   2 only
C   Neither 1 nor 2
D   Both 1 and 2   **(2 marks)**

217   Which one of the following terms is used to describe an information system that provides senior executives with online access to important information obtained from both internal and external sources?

A   Executive information system
B   Enterprise resource planning system
C   Management information system
D   Transaction processing system   **(2 marks)**

218   Data used by the management that has been obtained from an official government source is an example of:

A   External primary data
B   External secondary data
C   Internal primary data
D   Internal secondary data   **(2 marks)**

219 The following statements have been made about data and information.

(1) In-depth analysis of data on a database in order to identify undiscovered trends or patterns in the data is known as data mining.

(2) Large public databases are a major source of feedback for many commercial organisations.

Which of the above statements is/are true?

A 1 only
B 2 only
C Neither 1 nor 2
D Both 1 and 2   **(2 marks)**

220 In a balanced scorecard system of performance measurement, which one of the following is most likely to be used as a measure of performance from the customer perspective?

A Increase in size of product range
B Percentage of customers making repeat orders
C Number of orders won per sales representative
D Speed of processing an order   **(2 marks)**

221 The following statements have been made about performance measurements in not-for-profit organisations.

(1) Providing value for money (VFM) means providing a service that is cheap, efficient and effective.

(2) For the refuse collection department of a local government authority, the efficiency of operations can be measured by the proportion of collected refuse that is recycled.

Which of the above statements is/are true?

A 1 only
B 2 only
C Neither 1 nor 2
D Both 1 and 2   **(2 marks)**

222 The following statements have been made about divisionalisation and performance measurement systems.

(1) Residual income as a measure of performance enables fair comparisons to be made between the performances of different divisions in the company.

(2) When a transfer price is based on cost because there is no external market for the transferred item, at least one of the divisional managers is likely to consider the transfer price as 'unfair'.

Which of the above statements is/are true?

A 1 only
B 2 only
C Neither 1 nor 2
D Both 1 and 2   **(2 marks)**

223 Which one of the following aspects of performance is measured by the average time between receipt of an order from a customer and the time the goods are despatched?

A Quality
B Quantity
C Reliability
D Speed   **(2 marks)**

224 In the Fitzgerald and Moon model of performance measurement in services businesses, which one of the following dimensions of performance reflects past results or achievements rather than provides a guide or determinant for future performance?

A Competitiveness
B Flexibility
C Quality
D Resource utilisation   **(2 marks)**

225 Which of the following is **not** usually a consequence of divisionalisation?

    A   Duplication of some activities and costs
    B   Goal congruence in decision making
    C   Faster decision making at operational level
    D   Reduction in head office control over operations   **(2 marks)**

226 The following statements have been made about the measurement of ROI and residual income.

    (1)   ROI is usually measured as divisional operating profit before deducting depreciation as a percentage of the division's capital employed.

    (2)   Residual income is calculated after deducting both depreciation on non-current assets and notional interest on the division's capital employed.

Which of the above statements is/are true?

    A   1 only
    B   2 only
    C   Neither 1 nor 2
    D   Both 1 and 2   **(2 marks)**

227 For which of the following reasons are controls needed over internally generated information?

    (1)   To prevent information overload
    (2)   To prevent unauthorised dissemination of information

    A   Reason (1) only
    B   Reason (2) only
    C   Neither reason
    D   Reasons (1) and (2)   **(2 marks)**

228 The following statements have been made about information systems.

    (1)   Feedback is information produced from a system that is used by management to take action to control further inputs to the system.

    (2)   Information for benchmarking purposes may be obtained from both internal and external sources.

Which of the above statements is/are true?

    A   1 only
    B   2 only
    C   Neither 1 nor 2
    D   Both 1 and 2   **(2 marks)**

229 The following statements have been made about transfer pricing.

    (1)   Transfer pricing is almost inevitably required when a business is structured as more than one division and some divisions provide goods or services to other divisions.

    (2)   Where a perfect external market price exists and unit variable costs and unit selling prices are constant, the opportunity cost of transfer will be external market price or external market price less savings in selling costs.

Which of the above statements is/are true?

    A   1 only
    B   2 only
    C   Neither 1 nor 2
    D   Both 1 and 2   **(2 marks)**

230 If the performance of a local fire service is judged in terms of its inputs rather than its outputs, which one of the following would be a suitable measure of performance?

    A   Average response times to call-outs

    B   Cost of the local fire service per member of the local population

    C   Number of emergency calls answered per month

    D   Average length of time between call-outs   **(2 marks)**

231 A typical balanced scorecard measures performance from four different perspectives. Which perspective is concerned with measuring 'What must we excel at?'

    A   Customer satisfaction perspective

    B   Financial success perspective

    C   Growth perspective

    D   Process efficiency perspective   **(2 marks)**

232 Which of the following is **not** a correct feature of good performance measurements?

    A   They create an incentive to a manager to make a decision that is in the best interest of the organisation

    B   They measure only factors over which the manager responsible has control or influence

    C   They should be measurable in financial terms

    D   They should include long-term as well as short-term objectives   **(2 marks)**

233 Liquidity is improved by which of the following?

    A   A shorter average receivables payment period and shorter average trade payables period

    B   A longer average receivables payment period and shorter average trade payables period

    C   A shorter average receivables payment period and longer average trade payables period

    D   A longer average receivables payment period and longer average trade payables period   **(2 marks)**

234 A company has a divisionalised structure in which Division A transfers its output to Division B. There is no external market for the transferred item and cost will be used as the basis for setting a transfer price. Which one of the following will be the most appropriate basis for negotiating and agreeing a transfer price?

    A   Actual cost

    B   Actual cost plus a profit margin equal to a percentage of cost

    C   Standard cost

    D   Standard cost plus a profit margin equal to a percentage of cost   **(2 marks)**

(Total = 60 marks)

CBE style OTQ bank – Performance measurement and control

39 mins

235 In a company with a divisionalised structure, Division A transfers its output to Division B. Division A produces just one item, Component X. Division B makes and sells and end product that requires one unit of Component X.

	$ per unit of X
Marginal cost of production in Division A	8
Fixed overhead cost of production	3
Market price in the external market	16
Division B contribution from further processing Component X, before deducting the transfer cost	25

Division A is not working at full capacity, and can meet in full the external market demand and the demand from Division B for internal transfers.

What should be the minimum transfer price per unit and the maximum transfer price per unit for Component X in this situation?

| minimum transfer price | $ | | maximum transfer price | $ | |
| maximum transfer price | $ | | maximum transfer price | $ | | **(2 marks)** |

236 Which of the following is a dimension of performance in a service business, as identified by Fitzgerald and Moon?

☐ Controllability

☐ Innovation

☐ Rewards

☐ Standards   **(2 marks)**

237 In a company with a divisionalised structure, Division A transfers its output to Division B. Division A produces just one item, Component X. Division B makes and sells and end product that requires one unit of Component X.

	$ per unit of X
Marginal cost of production in Division A	8
Fixed overhead cost of production	3
Cost of selling in the external market	1
Market price in the external market	16
Division B contribution from further processing	25
Component X, before deducting the transfer cost	

Division A is working at full capacity.

What should be the minimum transfer price per unit of Component X in this situation?

| $ | |

(2 marks)

238 On which **two** of the following matters would the manager of an investment centre make decisions?

☐ Granting credit to customers.

☐ Administration of centralised departments

☐ Settling inter-departmental disputes

☐ Inventory carrying decisions   **(2 marks)**

239 At the beginning of 20X2, a division has capital employed, consisting of non-current assets of $2 million (at net book value) and working capital of $0.2 million. These are expected to earn a profit in 20X2 of $0.5 million, after depreciation of $0.4 million. A new machine will be installed at the beginning of 20X2. It will cost $0.8 million and will require an additional $0.1 million in working capital. It will add $0.35 million to divisional profits before deducting depreciation. This machine will have a four-year life and no residual value: depreciation is by the straight-line method. When calculating ROI, capital employed is taken at its mid-year value.

What is the expected ROI of the division in 20X2?

☐ 21.7%

☐ 23.2%

☐ 24.1%

☐ 26.0%   **(2 marks)**

240 A company has two Divisions, A and B. Division A manufactures a component which is transferred to Division B. Division B uses two units of the component from Division A in every item of finished product that it makes and sells. The transfer price is $43 per unit of the component.

	$ per unit
Selling price of finished product made in Division B	154
Variable production costs in Division B, excluding the cost of transfers from Division A	32
Variable selling costs, chargeable to the division	1
	33

Fixed costs	$160,000
External sales in units	7,000
Investment in the division	$500,000

The company uses 16% as its cost of capital.

What is the residual income of Division B for the period?

$ [   ]

(2 marks)

241 An investment centre has prepared the following forecasts for the next financial year.

	$
Operating profit before depreciation	85,000
Depreciation	20,000
Net current assets at beginning of year	30,000
Carrying value of non-current assets at beginning of year	180,000

The centre manager is now considering whether to sell a machine that is included in these forecasts. The machine would add $2,500 to divisional profit next year after depreciation of $500. It has a carrying value of $6,000 and could be sold for this amount. He would use the proceeds from the sale plus additional cash from Head Office to purchase a new machine for $15,000. This new machine would add $5,200 to divisional profit next year after depreciation of $2,000.

What will be the expected return on investment (ROI) for the division next year, assuming that the manager acquires the new machine and that non-current assets are valued at the start-of-year carrying amount for the purpose of the ROI calculation.

$ [   ] %

(2 marks)

242 Classify the following into qualitative and quantitative aspects of non-financial performance?

Volume of customer complaints	☐ Quantitative	☐ Qualitative
Employee revenue	☐ Quantitative	☐ Qualitative
Defective products per batch	☐ Quantitative	☐ Qualitative
Customer needs	☐ Quantitative	☐ Qualitative
Employee morale	☐ Quantitative	☐ Qualitative
Brand recognition	☐ Quantitative	☐ Qualitative
Customer satisfaction	☐ Quantitative	☐ Qualitative
Repeat business	☐ Quantitative	☐ Qualitative

(2 marks)

243 The 3Es are often used to assess performance in non-profit making organisations, especially in relation to value for money

Which THREE of the following Es are used?

- [ ] Efficiency
- [ ] Effectiveness
- [ ] Economy
- [ ] Enterprise
- [ ] Efficacy
- [ ] Expediency
- [ ] Endurance   (2 marks)

244 Organisations may need to develop performance measures to ensure that the needs of stakeholders are met.

Which **two** of the following measures are geared towards customer needs?

- [ ] Morale index
- [ ] Percentage of repeat customers
- [ ] Number of warranty claims
- [ ] Dividend yield   (2 marks)

                                                         (Total = 20 marks)

Section B questions

MCQ case questions

Cherry Co   20 mins

The following scenario relates to questions 245 – 249.

Cherry Co has two independent divisions, A and B. Division A produces product X. B is a new division which produces product Y. It requires units of product X to produce product Y. Last year, A sold X exclusively to the external market. Management at Cherry Co did not wish to disrupt the operations of A as B was an experimental division. However, due to the success of product Y, B is now a permanent division of Cherry Co. Management wants A to provide at least some units of product X to B.

The table below shows the contribution margin for each division when B purchases X from an outside supplier.

	B	A
	$	$
Selling price per unit	150	37
Variable cost per unit		
(Div B does not include the cost of X)	65	30
Cost of X purchased from outside suppliers	35	
Contribution margin per unit	50	7

245 What would the minimum transfer price per unit of product X be if A sold 12,000 units of X, assuming that A has capacity for 15,000 units?

    A $36
    B $30
    C $37
    D $35   **(2 marks)**

246 What would the minimum transfer price per unit of product X be if A sold 12,000 units of X, assuming that A has no spare capacity?

    A $36
    B $30
    C $37
    D $35   **(2 marks)**

247 If there was no external market for product X, which of the following approaches could be used to negotiate a transfer price?

    A   Full cost
    B   Management estimated of market cost
    C   Scrap value of product X
    D   All of the above   **(2 marks)**

248 The following two statements have been made about Cherry Co.

profit

    (1)   Cherry Co's transfer pricing system should seek to establish a transfer price for X that will provide an incentive for the managers of A and B to make and sell quantities of products that will maximise sales of Product Y.

                                                     autonomy

    (2)   The manager of division B is likely to be more motivated if she is given freedom in which to operate and is able to purchase from outside suppliers if prices are cheaper.

Which of the above statements is/are correct?

    A   1 only
    (B)   2 only
    C   Both 1 and 2
    D   Neither 1 nor 2   **(2 marks)**

249 The following two statements have been made about Cherry Co.

    (1)   The performance of the managers of A and B will be easier to assess in an environment in which managers are able to control greater elements of the business. ✓

    (2)   In a competitive market, it is likely that suppliers will offer Product X to Division B significantly cheaper than Division A can for a sustained period of time.

Which of the above statements is/are correct?

    A   1 only
    B   2 only
    C   Both 1 and 2
    D   Neither 1 nor 2   **(2 marks)**

                                                     (Total = 10 marks)

Jamair (12/14 adapted)

20 mins

The following scenario relates to questions 250 – 254.

Jamair is one of a growing number of low-cost airlines in the country of Shania.

Jamair's strategy is to operate as a low-cost, high efficiency airline.

The airline was given an 'on time arrival' ranking of seventh best by the country's aviation authority, who rank all 50 of the country's airlines based on the number of flights which arrive on time at their destinations.

The average 'ground turnaround time' for airlines in Shania is 50 minutes, meaning that, on average, planes are on the ground for cleaning, refuelling, etc for 50 minutes before departing again.

The number of passengers carried by the airline has grown from 300,000 passengers on a total of 3,428 flights in 2007 to 920,000 passengers on 7,650 flights in 2013.

The overall growth of the airline has been helped by the limited route licensing policy of the Shanian government, which has given Jamair almost monopoly status on some of its routes. However, the government is now set to change this policy with almost immediate effect, and it has become more important than ever to monitor performance effectively.

Required

250 The _____ perspective considers whether the management in Jamair meets the expectations of its shareholders and how it creates value for them.

Which of the following words is missing from the above statement?

A   Customer
B   Internal business
C   Innovation and learning
D   Financial   (2 marks)

251 The following performance measure has been suggested for Jamair:

Improve on the 'on time arrival' ranking of seventh best in the country's aviation authority ratings.

To which perspective of the balanced scorecard does this measure belong?

A   Customer perspective
B   Internal business perspective
C   Innovation and learning perspective
D   Financial perspective   (2 marks)

252 The following performance objective has been suggested for Jamair:

Improve the turnaround time on the ground

To which perspective of the balanced scorecard does this objective belong?

A   Customer perspective
B   Internal business perspective
C   Innovation and learning perspective
D   Financial perspective   (2 marks)

253 The following performance objective has been suggested for Jamair:

Increase seat revenue per plane

To which perspective of the balanced scorecard does this objective belong?

A   Customer perspective
B   Internal business perspective
C   Innovation and learning perspective
D   Financial perspective   (2 marks)

254   The following statements have been made about Jamair's performance measurement system.

(1)   When performance is not quantified, it is difficult to target and monitor.

(2)   Jamair is more likely to have a reliable and comprehensive system for collecting data about qualitative aspects of performance than a well established system for measuring quantitative data.

Which of the above statements is/are correct?

A   1 only
B   2 only
C   Both 1 and 2
D   Neither 1 nor 2.   **(2 marks)**

(Total = 10 marks)

Stickleback Co   20 mins

The following scenario relates to questions 255 – 259.

Kingfisher is an investment centre within Stickleback Co. Kingfisher has an operating profit of $30,000, and operating assets of $150,000. The cost of capital is 15%. There is a proposed investment of $15,000 which will increase the operating income by $1,900.

255   What is the return on investment (ROI) for Kingfisher with and without the proposed investment?

A   Before investment: 20%, After investment 17%
B   Before investment: 17%, After investment 19.3%
C   Before investment: 19.3%, After investment 20%
D   Before investment: 20%, After investment 19.3%   **(2 marks)**

256   What is the residual income (RI) for Kingfisher with and without the proposed investment?

A   Before investment: $3,350, After investment $7,150
B   Before investment: $7,500, After investment $3,350
C   Before investment: $7,500, After investment $7,150
D   Before investment: $7,150, After investment $7,500   **(2 marks)**

257   The following statements have been made about the use of ROI as a performance measure in Stickleback Co.

(1)   If a manager's performance is being evaluated, a portion of head office assets should be included in the calculation of ROI in Stickleback Co's investment centres.

(2)   It may lead to short termism.

Which of the above statements is/are correct?

A   1 only
B   2 only
C   Both 1 and 2
D   Neither 1 nor 2   **(2 marks)**

258   The divisional manager for Kingfisher wants to increase the ROI for the next period.

The following options are available.

1   Increase payables
2   Reduce interest payments
3   Accept all projects with a positive NPV
4   Keep Kingfisher's old machinery

Which of the above would increase the ROI?

A   1 only
B   1, 2, and 4
C   1 and 4
D   3 and 4

(2 marks)

259   The following statements have been made about Stickleback Co's divisionalised structure.

(1)   There is a danger that managers in the divisions may use their decision-making freedom to make decisions that are not in the best interests of the overall company.

(2)   Stickleback Co's top management must have involvement in the day-to-day operations of the divisions.

Which of the above statements is/are correct?

A   1 only
B   2 only
C   Both 1 and 2
D   Neither 1 nor 2

(2 marks)

(Total = 10 marks)

Squarize (6/13 amended)   20 mins

The following scenario relates to questions 260 – 264.

Squarize is a large company which started as a pay-TV broadcaster and then started offering broadband and telephone services to its pay-TV customers. Customers could take advantage of discounts for 'bundle' packages of all three services.

All contracts to customers of Squarize are for a minimum three-month period. The pay-TV box is sold to the customer at the beginning of the contract; however, the broadband and telephone equipment is only rented to them.

In the first few years after product bundling was introduced, the company saw a steady increase in profits. Then, Squarize saw its revenues and operating profits fall. Several reasons were identified for the deterioration of results:

(1)   In a bid to save cash, many pay-TV customers were cancelling their contracts after the minimum three-month period as they were then able to still keep the pay-TV box. The box comes with a number of free channels, which the customer can still continue to receive free of charge, even after the cancellation of their contract.

(2)   Some bundle customers found that the broadband service that they had subscribed to did not work. As a result, they were immediately cancelling their contracts for all services within the 14 day cancellation period permitted under the contracts.

In a response to the above problems and in an attempt to increase revenues and profits, Squarize made the following changes to the business:

(i)   It made a strategic decision to withdraw the bundle package from the market and, instead, offer each service as a standalone product.

(ii)   It investigated and resolved the problem with customers' broadband service.

It is now one year since the changes were made and the finance director wants to use a balanced scorecard to assess the extent to which the changes have been successful in improving the performance of the business.

260 The following performance objective has been suggested for Squarize:

Reduce the number of contracts cancelled due to the broadband service not working

To which perspective of the balanced scorecard does this objective belong?

A Customer perspective
B Internal business perspective
C Innovation and learning perspective
D Financial perspective (2 marks)

261 The following performance measure has been suggested for Squarize:

Volume of sales to new customers for each product/service

To which perspective of the balanced scorecard does this measure belong?

A Customer perspective
B Internal business perspective
C Innovation and learning perspective
D Financial perspective (2 marks)

262 Which of the following would be the most suitable measure of performance from the innovation and learning perspective in Squarize balanced scorecard?

A Development cost per new standalone service
B Sales revenue per new standalone service
C Sales revenue from new standalone service as a percentage of total revenue
D Sales revenue per hour worked on new standalone service (2 marks)

263 Which of the following is most likely to be used as a measure of performance from the customer perspective in Squarize balanced scorecard?

A Increase in size of the product range
B Percentage of customers renewing their subscription or making repeat orders
C Number of orders won per sales representative
D Speed of processing an order (2 marks)

264 Squarize has been advised that they could also use the Fitzgerald and Moon building block model to attempt to overcome the problems associated with performance measurement of service businesses. Which of the following is not a building block included in this performance management system?

A Rewards
B Innovation
C Standards
D Dimensions of performance (2 marks)

(Total = 10 marks)

CBE OT case questions

Alder Co

The following scenario relates to questions 265 – 269.

An investment centre with capital employed of $750,000 is budgeted to earn a profit of $200,000 next year. A proposed non-current asset investment of $125,000, not included in the budget at present, will earn a profit next year of $20,000. The company's cost of capital is 15%.

265 What is the budgeted ROI for next year, both before and after the investment is made (to the nearest %)?

Before investment: [   ] %

After investment: [   ] %   (2 marks)

266 What is the residual income for next year, both before and after the investment is made?

Before investment: $ [   ]

After investment: $ [   ]   (2 marks)

267 The following statements have been made about the divisionalised structure in Alder Co.

(1) The authority to act to improve performance motivates the divisional managers in Alder Co, more so than if the company was centralised.

(2) Alder Co's top management must have involvement in the day-to-day operations of Alder Co.

Which of the above statements is/are correct?

☐ 1 only
☐ 2 only
☐ Both 1 and 2
☐ Neither 1 nor 2   (2 marks)

268 The following statements have been made about the use of ROI in Alder Co.

(1) If a manager's performance is being evaluated, a portion of head office assets should be included in the calculation of ROI in Alder Co's investment centres.

(2) If the performance of the investment centre is being appraised, head office assets, or investment centre assets controlled by head office should not be included in the calculation of ROI.

Which of the above statements is/are correct?

☐ 1 only
☐ 2 only
☐ Both 1 and 2
☐ Neither 1 nor 2   (2 marks)

269 The following statements have been made about the use of ROI in Alder Co.

(1) The profit figure for ROI should always be the amount before any interest is charged

(2) The asset base of the ratio can be altered by increasing/decreasing payables and receivables (by speeding up or delaying payments and receipts).

Which of the above statements is/are correct?

☐ 1 only

☐ 2 only

☐ Both 1 and 2

☐ Neither 1 nor 2 (2 marks)

(Total = 10 marks)

Apple Co 20 mins

The following scenario relates to questions 270 – 274.

An investment centre in Apple Co generates a profit of $24,000. You have been given the following additional information about the investment centre.

Working capital		20,000
Non-current assets at cost	230,000	
Accumulated depreciation	170,000	
Net book value		60,000

270 What is the ROI for the investment centre? (to the nearest %) ☐ % (2 marks)

271 An investment in a non-current asset could be made which would result in a capital employed figure of $100,000. The investment would result in a new profit figure of $35,000 for the division. If the investment is made, what would the residual income be for the investment centre if the cost of capital is 12%?

$ ☐ (2 marks)

272 The following statements have been made about the use of different performance measures in Apple Co.

(1) Residual income is more flexible, since a different cost of capital can be applied to investments with different risk characteristics.

(2) Residual income does not facilitate comparisons between investment centres.

Which of the above statements is/are correct?

☐ 1 only

☐ 2 only

☐ Both 1 and 2

☐ Neither 1 nor 2 (2 marks)

273 Apple Co operates a transfer pricing system between two divisions based on market price. The following statements have been made about this.

(1) The market price acts as an incentive to use up any spare capacity in the selling division of Apple Co.

(2) Using the market price as the transfer price encourages selling and buying decisions which appear to be in the best interests of the division's performance. This leads to the company as a whole achieving optimal results as each division optimises its performance.

Which of the above statements is/are correct?

☐ 1 only
☐ 2 only
☐ Both 1 and 2
☐ Neither 1 nor 2.   **(2 marks)**

274 Apple Co has two divisions which are set to begin buying and selling a product between themselves. It has been suggested that a cost-based approach to transfer pricing be used.

The following statements have been made about this suggestion.

(1) A cost based approach is suitable for Apple Co in this scenario if there is no external market for the product that is being transferred.

(2) A cost based approach is suitable for Apple Co in this scenario if an imperfect market exists

Which of the above statements is/are correct?

☐ 1 only
☐ 2 only
☐ Both 1 and 2
☐ Neither 1 nor 2   **(2 marks)**

                                                        (Total = 10 marks)

Box Co   **20 mins**

The following scenario relates to questions 275 – 279.

Box Co has an operating profit of $20,000, and operating assets of $95,000. The cost of capital is 12%. There is a proposed investment of $10,000 which will increase the operating profit by $1,400

275 What is the ROI with and without the proposed investment? (to one dp)

Without investment: [   ] %

With investment: [   ] %   **(2 marks)**

276 What is the RI with and without the proposed investment?

Without investment: $ [   ]

With investment: $ [   ]   **(2 marks)**

277   One of the managers in Box Co is critical of the performance measures used. She has said that they are too focused on financial performance and do not take into account any non-financial performance measures.

She has made the following comments:

(1)   Financial performance measures do not necessarily provide sufficient information about ongoing problems with product quality. As a result, there is little attention paid to the generation of information on quality in Box Co.

(2)   Non-financial performance indicators can give a better indication of future prospects.

Which of the above statements is/are true?

☐   1 only
☐   2 only
☐   Both 1 and 2
☐   Neither 1 nor 2   **(2 marks)**

278   Which of the following methods would encourage the managers of Box Co to take a short-term view?

☐   Link managers' rewards to share price
☐   Set quality-based targets as well as financial targets
☐   Keep managers informed about the short term budget targets
☐   Make long-term targets realistic   **(2 marks)**

279   The following statements have been made about Box Co's divisionalised structure.

(1)   There is a danger that managers in Box Co may use their decision-making freedom to make decisions that are not in the best interests of the overall company.

(2)   A good performance measure for the divisional managers in Box Co should include a portion of head office costs in the calculations.

Which of the above statements is/are correct?

☐   1 only
☐   2 only
☐   Both 1 and 2
☐   Neither 1 nor 2   **(2 marks)**

(Total = 10 marks)

Section C questions

280 Biscuits and Cakes (6/12 amended)   39 mins

The Biscuits division (Division B) and the Cakes division (Division C) are two divisions of a large, manufacturing company. Whilst both divisions operate in almost identical markets, each division operates separately as an investment centre. Each month, operating statements must be prepared by each division and these are used as a basis for performance measurement for the divisions.

Last month, senior management decided to recharge head office costs to the divisions. Consequently, each division is now going to be required to deduct a share of head office costs in its operating statement before arriving at 'net profit', which is then used to calculate return on investment (ROI). Prior to this, ROI has been calculated using controllable profit only. The company's target ROI, however, remains unchanged at 20% per annum. For each of the last three months, Divisions B and C have maintained ROIs of 22% per annum and 23% per annum respectively, resulting in healthy bonuses being awarded to staff. The company has a cost of capital of 10%.

The budgeted operating statement for the month of July is shown below:

	B	C
	$'000	$'000
Sales revenue	1,300	1,500
Less variable costs	(700)	(800)
Contribution	600	700
Less controllable fixed costs	(134)	(228)
Controllable profit	466	472
Less apportionment of head office costs	(155)	(180)
Net profit	311	292
Divisional net assets	$23.2m	$22.6m

Required

(a) Calculate the expected annualised Return on Investment (ROI) using the new method as preferred by senior management, based on the above budgeted operating statements, for each of the divisions. **(2 marks)**

The divisional managing directors are unhappy about the results produced by your calculations in (a) and have heard that a performance measure called 'residual income' may provide more information.

(b) Calculate the annualised residual income (RI) for each of the divisions, based on the net profit figures for the month of July. **(3 marks)**

(c) Discuss the expected performance of each of the two divisions, using both ROI and RI, and making any additional calculations deemed necessary. Conclude as to whether, in your opinion, the two divisions have performed well. **(6 marks)**

Division B has now been offered an immediate opportunity to invest in new machinery at a cost of $2·12 million. The machinery is expected to have a useful economic life of four years, after which it could be sold for $200,000. Division B's policy is to depreciate all of its machinery on a straight-line basis over the life of the asset. The machinery would be expected to expand Division B's production capacity, resulting in an 8·5% increase in contribution per month.

Required

(d) Recalculate Division B's expected annualised ROI and annualised RI, based on July's budgeted operating statement after adjusting for the investment. State whether the managing director will be making a decision that is in the best interests of the company as a whole if ROI is used as the basis of the decision. **(5 marks)**

(e) Explain any behavioural problems that will result if the company's senior management insist on using solely ROI, based on net profit rather than controllable profit, to assess divisional performance and reward staff.

(4 marks)

(Total = 20 marks)

281 Story

39 mins

Story is a well-established, global publishing conglomerate. The corporation is structured to allow each country of operation to function as an autonomous business unit, that reports back to head office. The data from each business unit is entered onto the mainframe computer at head office. Each business unit can make use of any service offered by other business units and can also offer services to the other units. The services include translation into different languages, typesetting, printing, storage and so forth. In each country of operation there is at least one, and usually several, retail outlets.

The core business was traditionally based upon the provision of fictional stories for the mass market. For the past decade Story has diversified into publishing textbooks and technical literature. The organisation currently enjoys a good reputation in both areas of the business and global sales are increasing annually at a rate of 5% for fictional books and 2% for textbooks. Last year seven hundred million fictional works and twenty-five million textbooks were sold.

The corporate management team wish to increase the growth in sales of textbooks but realise that they cannot afford to allocate significant resources to this task as the market, and profit margin, for textbooks is very much smaller than for fiction. They also wish to improve the sales performance of the fictional books.

Story is currently having trouble in maintaining a corporate image in some countries of operation. For example, several business units may be unaware of additions to the product range. Another example is that a price change in a book is not simultaneously altered by all the business units leading to pricing discrepancies.

Some members of the corporate management team see possible advantages to upgrading the existing computer system to one that is fully networked. Other members are more sceptical and are reluctant to consider enhancing the system.

Required

(a)   Discuss the issues involved in upgrading the existing information system and the proposed changes, with reference to both the wider business environment and the decision making process.   **(8 marks)**

(b)   Explain what is meant by the terms *open systems* and *closed systems* as applied to systems theory. Identify, with justification and where possible, any examples of these from the information given in, or inferred from, the case study.   **(7 marks)**

(c)   Management Information Systems (MIS) allow managers to make timely and effective decisions using data in an appropriate form. List three types of MIS and how they would be used in an organisation.   **(5 marks)**

(Total = 20 marks)

282 Hammer (6/10 amended)   39 mins

Hammer is a large garden equipment supplier with retail stores throughout Toolland. Many of the products it sells are bought in from outside suppliers but some are currently manufactured by Hammer's own manufacturing division 'Nail'.

The prices (a transfer price) that Nail charges to the retail stores are set by head office and have been the subject of some discussion. The current policy is for Nail to calculate the total variable cost of production and delivery and add 30% for profit. Nail argues that all costs should be taken into consideration, offering to reduce the mark-up on costs to 10% in this case. The retail stores are unhappy with the current pricing policy arguing that it results in prices that are often higher than comparable products available on the market.

Nail has provided the following information to enable a price comparison to be made of the two possible pricing policies for one of its products.

Garden shears

Steel: the shears have 0.4 kg of high quality steel in the final product. The manufacturing process loses 5% of all steel put in. Steel costs $4,000 per tonne (1 tonne = 1,000 kg)

Other materials: Other materials are bought in and have a list price of $3 per kg although Hammer secures a 10% volume discount on all purchases. The shears require 0.1kg of these materials.

The labour time to produce shears is 0.25 hours per unit and labour costs $10 per hour.

Variable overheads are absorbed at the rate of 150% of labour rates and fixed overheads are 80% of the variable overheads.

Delivery is made by an outsourced distributor that charges Nail $0.5 per garden shear for delivery.

Required

(a)   Calculate the price that Nail would charge for the garden shears under the existing policy of variable cost plus 30%.   **(6 marks)**

(b)   Calculate the increase or decrease in price if the pricing policy switched to total cost plus 10%.   **(4 marks)**

(c)   Discuss whether or not including fixed costs in a transfer price is a sensible policy.   **(4 marks)**

(d)   Discuss whether the retail stores should be allowed to buy in from outside suppliers if the prices are cheaper than those charged by Nail.   **(6 marks)**

                                                                                                        (Total = 20 marks)

283 Woodside (6/07 amended)   **39 mins**

Woodside is a local charity dedicated to helping homeless people in a large city. The charity owns and manages a shelter that provides free overnight accommodation for up to 30 people, offers free meals each and every night of the year to homeless people who are unable to buy food, and runs a free advice centre to help homeless people find suitable housing and gain financial aid. Woodside depends entirely on public donations to finance its activities and had a fundraising target for the last year of $700,000. The budget for the last year was based on the following forecast activity levels and expected costs:

Free meals provision: 18,250 meals at $5 per meal
Overnight shelter: 10,000 bed-nights at $30 per night
Advice centre: 3,000 sessions at $20 per session
Campaigning and advertising: $150,000

The budgeted surplus (budgeted fundraising target less budgeted costs) was expected to be used to meet any unexpected costs. Included in the above figures are fixed costs of $5 per night for providing shelter and $5 per advice session representing fixed costs expected to be incurred by administration and maintaining the shelter. The number of free meals provided and the number of beds occupied each night depends on both the weather and the season of the year. The Woodside charity has three full-time staff and a large number of voluntary helpers.

The actual costs for the last year were as follows:

Free meals provision: 20,000 meals at a variable cost of $104,000
Overnight shelter: 8,760 bed-nights at a variable cost of $223,380
Advice centre: 3,500 sessions at a variable cost of $61,600
Campaigning and advertising: $165,000

The actual costs of the overnight shelter and the advice centre exclude the fixed costs of administration and maintenance, which were $83,000.

The actual amount of funds raised in the last year was $620,000.

Required

(a)   Prepare an operating statement, reconciling budgeted surplus and actual shortfall and discuss the charity's performance over the last year.   **(12 marks)**

(b)   Discuss problems that may arise in the financial management and control of a not-for-profit organisation such as the Woodside charity.   **(8 marks)**

                                                                                                        (Total = 20 marks)

284 Ties Only Co (12/07 amended)

Ties Only Co is a new business, selling high quality imported men's ties via the internet. The managers, who also own the company, are young and inexperienced but they are prepared to take risks. They are confident that importing quality ties and selling via a website will be successful and that the business will grow quickly. This is despite the well-recognised fact that selling clothing is a very competitive business.

They were prepared for a loss-making start and decided to pay themselves modest salaries (included in administration expenses in Table 1 below) and pay no dividends for the foreseeable future.

The owners are so convinced that growth will quickly follow that they have invested enough money in website server development to ensure that the server can handle the very high levels of predicted growth. All website development costs were written off as incurred in the internal management accounts that are shown below in Table 1.

Significant expenditure on marketing was incurred in the first two quarters to launch both the website and new products. It is not expected that marketing expenditure will continue to be as high in the future.

Customers can buy a variety of styles, patterns and colours of ties at different prices.

The business's trading results for the first two quarters of trade are shown below in Table 1.

Table 1

	Quarter 1		Quarter 2	
	$	$	$	$
Sales		420,000		680,000
Less cost of sales		(201,600)		(340,680)
Gross profit		218,400		339,320
Less expenses				
Website development	120,000		90,000	
Administration	100,500		150,640	
Distribution	20,763		33,320	
Launch marketing	60,000		40,800	
Other variable expenses	50,000		80,000	
Total expenses		(351,263)		(394,760)
Loss for quarter		(132,863)		(55,440)

Required

(a) Assess the financial performance of the business during its first two quarters using only the data in Table 1 above. **(10 marks)**

(b) Briefly consider whether the losses made by the business in the first two quarters are a true reflection of the current and likely future performance of the business. **(3 marks)**

The owners are well aware of the importance of non-financial indicators of success and therefore have identified a small number of measures to focus on. These are measured monthly and then combined to produce a quarterly management report.

The data for the first two quarters management reports is shown below:

Table 2

	Quarter 1	Quarter 2
Number of ties sold	27,631	38,857
On time delivery	95%	89%
Sales returns	12%	18%
System downtime	2%	4%

The industry average for sales returns was 13%.

Required

(c) Comment on each of the non-financial data in Table 2 above taking into account, where appropriate, the industry averages provided, providing your assessment of the performance of the business. **(7 marks)**

(Total = 20 marks)

285 The Accountancy Teaching Co (12/10)   39 mins

The Accountancy Teaching Co (AT Co) is a company specialising in the provision of accountancy tuition courses in the private sector. It makes up its accounts to 30 November each year. In the year ending 30 November 20X9, it held 60% of market share. However, over the last twelve months, the accountancy tuition market in general has faced a 20% decline in demand for accountancy training leading to smaller class sizes on courses. In 20X9 and before, AT Co suffered from an ongoing problem with staff retention, which had a knock-on effect on the quality of service provided to students. Following the completion of developments that have been ongoing for some time, in 20Y0 the company was able to offer a far-improved service to students. The developments included:

- A new dedicated 24 hour student helpline

- An interactive website providing instant support to students

- A new training programme for staff

- An electronic student enrolment system

- An electronic marking system for the marking of students' progress tests. The costs of marking electronically were expected to be $4 million less in 20Y0 than marking on paper. Marking expenditure is always included in cost of sales

Extracts from the management accounts for 20X9 and 20Y0 are shown below:

	20X9		20Y0	
	$'000	$'000	$'000	$'000
Turnover		72,025		66,028
Cost of sales		(52,078)		(42,056)
Gross profit		19,947		23,972
Indirect expenses:				
Marketing	3,291		4,678	
Property	6,702		6,690	
Staff training	1,287		3,396	
Interactive website running costs	–		3,270	
Student helpline running costs	–		2,872	
Enrolment costs	5,032		960	
Total indirect expenses		(16,312)		(21,866)
Net operating profit		3,635		2,106

On 1 December 20X9, management asked all 'freelance lecturers' to reduce their fees by at least 10% with immediate effect ('freelance lecturers' are not employees of the company but are used to teach students when there are not enough of AT Co's own lecturers to meet tuition needs). All employees were also told that they would not receive a pay rise for at least one year. Total lecture staff costs (including freelance lecturers) were $41.663 million in 20X9 and were included in cost of sales, as is always the case. Freelance lecturer costs represented 35% of these total lecture staff costs. In 20Y0 freelance lecture costs were $12.394 million. No reduction was made to course prices in the year and the mix of trainees studying for the different qualifications remained the same. The same type and number of courses were run in both 20X9 and 20Y0 and the percentage of these courses that was run by freelance lecturers as opposed to employed staff also remained the same.

Due to the nature of the business, non-financial performance indicators are also used to assess performance, as detailed below.

	20X9	20Y0
Percentage of students transferring to AT Co from another training provider	8%	20%
Number of late enrolments due to staff error	297	106
Percentage of students passing exams first time	48%	66%
Labour turnover	32%	10%
Number of student complaints	315	84
Average no. of employees	1,080	1,081

Required

Assess the performance of the business in 20Y0 using both financial performance indicators calculated from the above information AND the non-financial performance indicators provided.

Note: Clearly state any assumptions and show all workings clearly. Your answer should be structured around the following main headings: turnover; cost of sales; gross profit; indirect expenses; net operating profit. However, in discussing each of these areas you should also refer to the non-financial performance indicators, where relevant.

(Total = 20 marks)

286 Jump (6/10 amended) 39 mins

Jump has a network of sports clubs which is managed by local managers reporting to the main board. The local managers have a lot of autonomy and are able to vary employment contracts with staff and offer discounts for membership fees and personal training sessions. They also control their own maintenance budget but do not have control over large amounts of capital expenditure.

A local manager's performance and bonus is assessed relative to three targets. For every one of these three targets that is reached in an individual quarter, $400 is added to the manager's bonus, which is paid at the end of the year. The maximum bonus per year is therefore based on 12 targets (three targets in each of the four quarters of the year). Accordingly the maximum bonus that could be earned is 12 × $400 = $4,800, which represents 40% of the basic salary of a local manager. Jump has a 31 March year end.

The performance data for one of the sports clubs for the last four quarters is as follows.

	Qtr to 30 June 20X1	Qtr to 30 September 20X1	Qtr to 31 December 20X1	Qtr to 31 March 20X2
Number of members	3,000	3,200	3,300	3,400
Member visits	20,000	24,000	26,000	24,000
Personal training sessions booked	310	325	310	339
Staff days	450	480	470	480
Staff lateness days	20	28	28	20
Days in quarter	90	90	90	90

Agreed targets are:

(1) Staff must be on time over 95% of the time (no penalty is made when staff are absent from work).
(2) On average 60% of members must use the clubs' facilities regularly by visiting at least 12 times per quarter.
(3) On average 10% of members must book a personal training session each quarter.

Required

(a) Calculate the amount of bonus that the manager should expect to be paid for the latest financial year.

(6 marks)

(b) Discuss to what extent the targets set are controllable by the local manager (you are required to make a case for both sides of the argument).

(9 marks)

(c) Describe two methods as to how a manager with access to the accounting and other records could unethically manipulate the situation so as to gain a greater bonus.

(5 marks)

(Total = 20 marks)

287 Bridgewater Co (6/08 amended)

Bridgewater Co provides training courses for many of the mainstream software packages on the market.

The business has many divisions within Waterland, the one country in which it operates. The senior managers of Bridgewater Co have very clear objectives for the divisions and these are communicated to divisional managers on appointment and subsequently in quarterly and annual reviews. These are:

- Each quarter, sales should grow and annual sales should exceed budget
- Trainer (lecture staff) costs should not exceed $180 per teaching day
- Room hire costs should not exceed $90 per teaching day
- Each division should meet its budget for profit per quarter and annually

It is known that managers will be promoted based on their ability to meet these targets. A member of the senior management is to retire after quarter 2 of the current financial year, which has just begun. The divisional managers anticipate that one of them may be promoted at the beginning of quarter 3 if their performance is good enough.

The manager of the Northwest division is concerned that his chances of promotion could be damaged by the expected performance of his division. He is a firm believer in quality and he thinks that if a business gets this right, growth and success will eventually follow.

The current quarterly forecasts, along with the original budgeted profit for the Northwest division, are as follows:

	Q1	Q2	Q3	Q4	Total
	$'000	$'000	$'000	$'000	$'000
Sales	40.0	36.0	50.0	60.0	186.0
Less:					
Trainers	8.0	7.2	10.0	12.0	37.2
Room hire	4.0	3.6	5.0	6.0	18.6
Staff training	1.0	1.0	1.0	1.0	4.0
Other costs	3.0	1.7	6.0	7.0	17.7
Forecast net profit	24.0	22.5	28.0	34.0	108.5
Original budgeted profit	25.0	26.0	27.0	28.0	106.0
Annual sales budget					180.0
Teaching days	40	36	50	60	

Required

(a)   Assess the financial performance of the Northwest division against its targets and reach a conclusion as to the promotion prospects of the divisional manager.   **(8 marks)**

The manager of the Northwest division has been considering a few steps to improve the performance of his division.

Voucher scheme

As a sales promotion, vouchers will be sold for $125 each, a substantial discount on normal prices. These vouchers will entitle the holder to attend four training sessions on software of their choice. They can attend when they want to but are advised that one training session per quarter is sensible. The manager is confident that if the promotion took place immediately, he could sell 80 vouchers and that customers would follow the advice given to attend one session per quarter. All voucher holders would attend planned existing courses and all will be new customers.

Software upgrade

A new important software programme has recently been launched for which there could be a market for training courses. Demonstration programs can be bought for $1,800 in quarter 1. Staff training would be needed, costing $500 in each of quarters 1 and 2 but in quarters 3 and 4 extra courses could be offered selling this training. Assuming similar class sizes and the usual sales prices, extra sales revenue amounting to 20% of normal sales are expected (measured before the voucher promotion above). The manager is keen to run these courses at the same tutorial and room standards as he normally provides. Software expenditure is written off in the income statement as incurred.

Delaying payments to trainers

The manager is considering delaying payment to the trainers. He thinks that, since his commitment to quality could cause him to miss out on a well deserved promotion, the trainers owe him a favour. He intends to delay payment on 50% of all invoices received from the trainers in the first two quarters, paying them one month later than is usual.

Required

(b)   Revise the forecasts to take account of all three of the proposed changes.   **(6 marks)**

(c)   Comment on each of the proposed steps and reach a conclusion as to whether, if all the proposals were taken together, the manager will improve his chances of promotion.   **(6 marks)**

(Total = 20 marks)

288 Oliver's Salon (6/09 amended)   39 mins

Oliver is the owner and manager of Oliver's Salon which is a quality hairdresser that experiences high levels of competition. The salon traditionally provided a range of hair services to female clients only, including cuts, colouring and straightening.

A year ago, at the start of his 20X9 financial year, Oliver decided to expand his operations to include the hairdressing needs of male clients. Male hairdressing prices are lower, the work simpler (mainly hair cuts only) and so the time taken per male client is much less.

The prices for the female clients were not increased during the whole of 20X8 and 20X9 and the mix of services provided for female clients in the two years was the same.

The latest financial results are as follows:

	20X8		20X9	
	$	$	$	$
Sales		200,000		238,500
Less cost of sales:				
Hairdressing staff costs	65,000		91,000	
Hair products – female	29,000		27,000	
Hair products – male			8,000	
		94,000		126,000
Gross profit		106,000		112,500
Less expenses:				
Rent	10,000		10,000	
Administration salaries	9,000		9,500	
Electricity	7,000		8,000	
Advertising	2,000		5,000	
Total expenses		28,000		32,500
Profit		78,000		80,000

Oliver is disappointed with his financial results. He thinks the salon is much busier than a year ago and was expecting more profit. He has noted the following extra information:

Some female clients complained about the change in atmosphere following the introduction of male services, which created tension in the salon.

Two new staff were recruited at the start of 20X9. The first was a junior hairdresser to support the specialist hairdressers for the female clients. She was appointed on a salary of $9,000 per annum. The second new staff member was a specialist hairdresser for the male clients. There were no increases in pay for existing staff at the start of 20X9 after a big rise at the start of 20X8 which was designed to cover two years' worth of increases.

Oliver introduced some non-financial measures of success two years ago.

	20X8	20X9
Number of complaints	12	46
Number of male client visits	0	3,425
Number of female client visits	8,000	6,800
Number of specialist hairdressers for female clients	4	5
Number of specialist hairdressers for male clients	0	1

Required

(a) Calculate the average price for hair services per male and female client for each of the years 20X8 and 20X9.

(3 marks)

(b) Assess the financial performance of the Salon using the data above.   **(11 marks)**

(c) Analyse and comment on the non-financial performance of Oliver's business, under the headings of quality and resource utilisation.   **(6 marks)**

(Total = 20 marks)

Answers

Part A answers

MCQ bank – Specialist cost and management accounting techniques

1   D   (Syllabus area A3(a))

A product's life cycle costs are incurred from its design stage through development to market launch, production and sales, and finally to its eventual decline and withdrawal from the market.

2   C   (Syllabus area A3(c))

Financial returns can be improved over the life cycle of a product by minimising the breakeven time, minimising the time to get a new product to market and maximising the length of the product life cycle.

3   A   (Syllabus area A4(b))

Throughput per unit of Product X = $(40 − 10) = $30
Throughput per bottleneck hour = $30/0.01 hours = $3,000
Factory costs per year = $2,920,000 + (50,000 × $12) = $3,520,000
Factory cost per bottleneck hour = $3,520,000/4,000 hours = $880
Throughput accounting ratio = $3,000/$880 = 3.41

4   D   (Syllabus area A5(b))

In MFCA, a distinction is made between good finished output (positive output) and waste and emissions (negative output). Both types of output are given a cost. Performance can be improved by finding ways to reduce the amount of negative output – and so achieve the same amount of output with less input materials.

5   B   (Syllabus area A1 (a))

A is incorrect. The cost driver for quality inspection costs is likely to be either the number of units produced or the number of batches produced, depending on whether quality inspection is linked to batches produced or total production output. The batch size is not a factor that drives total inspection costs.

C is incorrect. Some costs of activities may vary with the volume of the activity, but other costs of the activity will be fixed costs. D is incorrect. A cost driver is not the cost itself; it is a measure of the volume or quantity of an activity.

6   D   (Syllabus area A3 (b))

Variable costs	$
Year 1: $(30 + 6 + 4) × 25,000	1,000,000
Year 2: $(25 + 5 + 3) × 100,000	3,300,000
Year 3: $(20 + 4 + 2) × 75,000	1,950,000
R&D costs	940,000
Other fixed costs	3,000,000
Total life cycle costs	10,190,000
Total units made and sold	200,000
Average life cycle cost per unit	$50.95

7   C   (Syllabus area A4 (a))

In throughput accounting, all inventory, including work in progress and finished goods, should be valued at the cost of their materials. They should not include any other costs (labour or overhead costs). The aim should not be to maximise the use of all available resources, because this will simply create unwanted inventory. The aim should be to maximise the use of the bottleneck resource and efficiency is achieved by meeting production schedules and delivery dates to customers.

| 8 | B | (Syllabus area A5 (a)) |

The US Environment Protection Agency in 1998 suggested classifying environmental costs into four types: conventional costs, hidden costs (costs hidden because they are included in general overheads and not identified separately), contingent costs and image and relationship costs.

| 9 | D | (Syllabus area A4 (a)) |

Factory labour costs are always treated as a part of the factory cost/conversion cost of a product. Throughput accounting does not make a distinction between direct and indirect costs. It is also assumed that labour costs are a fixed cost, so if machine time is the bottleneck resource, nothing is gained by improving labour efficiency, because this will not increase throughput.

| 10 | C | (Syllabus area A1 (c)) |

ABC can be used for cost-plus pricing. Traditional absorption costing tends to allocate insufficient overhead costs to low-volume products that use up a disproportionate amount of time for order handling, production runs and set-ups. ABC is expensive and time consuming to implement. It is therefore important to assess whether the benefits will outweigh the costs before implementing ABC.

| 11 | C | (Syllabus area A1 (c)) |

The correct answer is: Capping.

Operation	Wash Units	Fill Units	Cap Units	Label Units
(a) Capacity in mins	$(1,200 \times 60)$	(700×60)	(250×60)	(450×60)
(b) Time per 12 units	6	3	1.5	2
Capacity in groups of 12 units ((a)/(b))	12,000	14,000	10,000	13,500

| 12 | D | (Syllabus area A1 (c)) |

Environmental management accounting measures physical quantities as well as monetary amounts.

| 13 | D | (Syllabus area A1 (c)) |

'Input' costs consist of material costs, waste management costs, energy costs and system costs (labour and overhead costs).

Output costs are allocated between positive products (good finished output) and negative product costs (cost of waste and emissions).

| 14 | C | (Syllabus area A1 (c)) |

The aim should be to improve the output capacity of the binding constraint. This can be done by achieving more output per unit of binding resource (improving efficiency) or obtaining more of the resource that is the binding constraint.

By increasing output through the binding constraint, a point will eventually be reached where it ceases to be the binding constraint, and another resource becomes the binding constraint.

| 15 | D | (Syllabus area A1 (c)) |

Reducing material costs or increasing the sales price will increase throughput per machine hour. Reducing factory costs will reduce the factory cost per machine hour. These will increase the TA ratio. Reducing the machine time per unit will increase throughput per hour and factory cost per hour by the same proportion, leaving the TA ratio unchanged.

CBE style OTQ bank – Specialist cost and management accounting techniques

16   Both are true (Syllabus area A5(a))

A system of environmental management accounting provides environmental information for internal use by management, but not for external reporting. It is distinct from environmental accounting, which is concerned with external reporting (as well as internal reporting). Environmental management accounting systems typically make use of life cycle costing, given that there may be substantial clean-up and disposal costs at the end of the life of an activity or operation.

17   'Unless output capacity is greater than sales demand, there will always be a binding constraint' and 'The production capacity of a bottleneck resource should determine the production schedule for the organisation as a whole'.

(Syllabus area A4(a))

Output from a binding constraint should be used immediately, not built up as inventory, because it is the factor that constrains output and sales. Some inventory may build up before the binding constraint, but the general principle in throughput accounting is that any inventory is undesirable.

The production capacity of a bottleneck resource should determine the production schedule for the organisation as a whole. This means inevitably that there will be idle time in other parts of production where capacity is greater.

18   Products should be discontinued if there is a target cost gap

(Syllabus area A2(a/b))

For services that have a large fixed cost based, other methods of cost control may be more appropriate, such as activity based management, and a key to reducing costs is often increasing sales volumes rather than reducing expenditures. To achieve a target cost, one approach is to remove design features from a product specification that do not add value for customers (so do not affect the price that customers are willing to pay).

If there is a target cost gap that cannot be eliminated, management may consider whether or not to continue with the product, since it will not be achieving the required profit margin. However, a decision to discontinue a product on whether to continue making it should not be based on target costs or profit margins alone.

19   'In a system of ABC, for costs that vary with production levels, the most suitable cost driver is likely to be direct labour hours or machine hours' and 'Activity based costing is a form of absorption costing'

(Syllabus area A1 (a/c))

Implementation of ABC is likely to be cost effective when variable production costs are a low proportion of total production costs and overhead costs, traditionally assumed to be fixed costs, are a large proportion of total production costs.

At a unit level, the cost driver for production-related overheads is likely to be direct labour hours or machine hours.

It is a mistake to associate activity based costs with the variable costs of an activity. Some of the costs may be variable in the short run, but others are not. So ABC costs should **not** be treated as relevant costs for the purpose of short-term decision making. It is more appropriate to think of ABC as a form of absorption costing, where overheads are allocated to activities and products on a more meaningful basis than with traditional absorption costing.

20 'Target costing may be applied to services that are provided free of charge to customers' is false and the others are true.

(Syllabus area A2 (b/c))

Cost reduction measures may reduce the perceived value of a product to customers, so that the target selling price becomes unachievable for the sales volume required. The projected cost of a new product may be reduced by simplifying the design (such as using more standard components, fewer components in total and removing design features that do not add value), but simplification of the design should not reduce the value of the product for customers.

Overhead costs are usually a large proportion of total costs; therefore it is important to have reliable estimates of sales demand at a given target sales price in order to establish a target cost. Target costing is dependent on identifying a target selling price for an item, so it is not appropriate for costing services provided free of charge. Call centre costs, for example, should be managed using other methods of cost control.

21 'An important use of life cycle costing is to decide whether to go ahead with the development of a new product ' and 'Life cycle costing encourages management to find a suitable balance between investment costs and operating expenses'.

(Syllabus area A3 (c)/A4(a))

A product is usually most profitable during the maturity phase of its life cycle. Life cycle costing is not particularly useful for deciding the selling price for a product, because the appropriate selling price changes over the life of a product.

By looking at the costs over the entire life cycle of a product, and comparing these with expected sales revenues, a decision can be taken at an early stage, before too much cost has been committed, about whether to go ahead with developing a new product. Life cycle costing also helps management to consider the merits of investing more money at the design stage for a new product if this will reduce operating costs over the product life cycle.

22 The correct answer is: $362.50

(Syllabus area A2(a))

Required return: $500,000 × 30% = $150,000
Total sales revenue: $550 × 800 units = $440,000
Therefore total cost = $440,000 − $150,000 = $290,000
Unit cost = $290,000/800 = $362.50

23 'The majority of environmental costs are already captured within a typical organisation's accounting system. The difficulty lies in identifying them' is true. ' Input/output analysis divides material flows within an organisation into three categories: material flows; system flows; and delivery and disposal flows' is false.

(Syllabus area A5(a))

Statement 2 refers to flow cost accounting rather than input/output analysis. Under the flow cost accounting technique, material flows within an organisation are divided into three categories: material flows; system flows; and delivery and disposal flows.

24 The correct answer is: 500 units.

(Syllabus area A4(d))

	A	B	C	D
Maximum sales demand	1,000	500	2,000	1,000
Selling price per unit	$15	$21	$18	$25
Material cost per unit	$6	$10	$9	$16
Throughput per unit	$9	$11	$9	$9
Machine hours per unit	0.1	0.2	0.3	0.2
Throughput per machine hour	$90	$55	$30	$45
Priority for manufacture	1st	2nd	4th	3rd

In the 750 hours available, the company should make 1,000 units of A (100 hours), then 500 units of B (100 hours), then 1,000 units of D (200 hours) leaving 350 hours available to make 1,166 units of Product C.

25   The correct answer is $92.00

(Syllabus area A3 (b))

	Year 1 $'000	Year 2 $'000	Year 3 $'000	Year 4 $'000	Total $'000
R&D costs	900	300			1,200
Marketing	300	300	100	100	800
Production	400	400	750	300	1,850
Customer services	100	150	250	50	550
Disposal				200	200
Total					4,600
Units					50,000
Life cycle cost per unit					$92.00

26      $80

(Syllabus area A1 (c))

The return per factory hour is measured using the bottleneck resource as a measure of factory hours. Return = Throughput

Return per machine hour = $(30 − 10)/0.25 hours = $80.

27   2.4

(Syllabus area A1 (c))

Throughput per unit of Product X = $(50 − 14) = $36.

Throughput per bottleneck hour = $36/0.05 hours = $720

Factory costs per year = $1,620,000 + (18,000 × $10) = $1,800,000 Factory cost per bottleneck hour = $1,800,000/6,000 hours = $300 Throughput accounting ratio = $720/$300 = 2.40.

28   (Syllabus area A1 (a))

The correct answers are:

- ABC recognises the complexity of modern manufacturing by the use of multiple cost drivers
- ABC establishes separate cost pools for support activities

29   (Syllabus area A1 (a))

The correct answers are:

- Labour costs are a relatively minor proportion of total costs
- Overheads vary with many different measures of activity

That overheads are difficult to predict and cost drivers difficult to identify are not reasons to prefer ABC.

30   (Syllabus area A1 (a))

The correct answers are:

- Set up costs.
- Raw material handling costs.

These two costs are likely to increase, as batch sizes get smaller.

Remember, the whole aim of JIT is to hold no inventory. Thus raw material storage costs should fall, not rise. Customer order costs will not be changed by the introduction of JIT.

Triple

31   The correct answer is:

Product D: $65

Traditional cost per unit

	Product D $
Material	20
Labour @$6 per hour	3
Direct costs	23
Production overhead @ $28 per machine hour	42
Total production cost per unit	65

32   The correct answer is: **$7,000**.

Product C uses 1,250 machine hours (W1) × $5.60 per hour (W2) = $7,000

Workings

(1)   Total machine hours (needed as the driver for machining overhead)

Product	Hours/unit	Production units	Total hours
D	1½	750	1,125
C	1	1,250	1,250
P	3	7,000	21,000
Total machine hours			23,375

(2)

Type of overhead	Driver	%	Total overhead	Level of driver activity	Cost/driver
Machining	Machine hours	20	$130,900	23,375 (W1)	$5.60

33   The correct answer is: **$9,818**.

Type of overhead	Driver	%	Total overhead	Level of driver activity	Cost/driver
Materials handling	Material movements	15	98,175	120	818.13

Product D:

Activity	Level of activity	Cost
Material handling	12	818.13 × 12 = 9,818

34   Number of inspections

The number of inspections per product is likely to be the main driver of quality control costs. The number of set ups is unlikely to have an effect on the quality control costs. Some product lines may require more inspections than others, therefore, number of units produced is not sufficient to use as the cost driver. Labour hours will not reflect the quality control aspect of individual products.

35   The benefits obtained from ABC might not justify the costs.

Some companies find the costs of implementing ABC to be prohibitive. If Triple Co believe that the difference in cost per unit of each product under ABC and traditional based costing systems is not material, they should not adopt ABC.

Distractors:

- ABC can be applied to all overheads, not just production overheads.
- The cost per unit provided under ABC principles will be more accurate.
- ABC costing will provide much better insight into what drives overhead costs.

Brick by Brick

36 **The correct answer is $3,000**

Overhead absorption rate is calculated as $400,000/40,000hrs = $10/hr

A GC takes 300 labour hours to complete.

$300 \times \$10/hr = \$3,000$

37 **The correct answer is:**

GC: $180

Supervisor costs of the **GC using ABC**.

1   Cost drivers

	Costs $	Number of drivers	Cost per driver $
Supervisor	90,000	500	180

2   Cost per product

	Supervisor
Cost per driver (W1)	$180
GC	$180 \times 1 = 180$

38 **The correct answer is:**

EX: 1,400

Planning costs of the **EX using ABC**.

1   Cost drivers

	Costs $	Number of drivers	Cost per driver $
Planning	70,000	250	280

2   Cost per product

	Planning
Cost per driver (W1)	$280
EX	$280 \times 5 = 1,400$

39   1 only

Statement 1 is true. ABC leads to more competitive pricing of the GC because it is allocated a fairer proportion of the total overheads. This will reflect the reality of the overheads that the GC is actually generating. Traditional absorption costing is more arbitrary which can lead to uncompetitive pricing.

Statement 2 is false. Total overhead costs will be the same no matter which method of allocation is used.

40   The correct answer is: ABC improves pricing decisions

It is ABC which gives a better indication of where cost savings can be made. BBB uses cost plus pricing and so more accurate costs will lead to better pricing decisions.

ABC is expensive to implement and BBB currently has an absorption costing system set up.

ABC does not eliminate the need for cost apportionment. It may still be required at the cost pool stage for shred items such as rent.

Jola Publishing Co

41 **The correct answer is: $2.57 per unit**

Number of units produced per year = 1,000,000 + (12 × 10,000) = 1,120,000 units

Overhead absorption rate is calculated as $2,880,000/1,120,000 units = $2.57/unit

42 **4, 5, 3, 2, 1**

Identify major activities within each department which create cost	4
Create a cost centre/cost pool for each activity – 'the activity cost pool'	5
Determine what causes the cost of each activity – the 'cost driver'	3
Calculate the absorption rate for each 'cost driver'	2
Calculate the overhead cost per unit of CB and TJ	1

43 **The correct answer is $1,800,000**

Production of CB takes a total of 100,000 hours at **$18 per machine hour**

Cost per driver

Cost pool	Cost $'000	Quantity of cost drivers	Rate per cost driver $	
Production costs	2,160	120,000*	18	per machine hour

* Number of machine hours

CB
1,000,000 units × 6 mins/60 = 100,000 hours

TJ
(10,000 × 12) units × 10 mins/60 = 20,000 hours

44 **The correct answer is $66,800**

Quality control of the TJ : $3,340 per inspection × 20 inspections

Cost per driver

Cost pool	Cost $'000	Quantity of cost drivers	Rate per cost driver $	
Quality control	668	180 + 20 = 200	3,340	per inspection

45 The correct answer is: More accurate costs per unit.

Distractors:

There will not be a reduction in overhead costs as a result of the adoption of ABC. However, management of Jola Publishing Co may benefit from improved decision making regarding cost control, if they understand the cost drivers better.

ABC tends to be a more expensive approach to absorption costing

ABC is a more complex form of costing

Corrie

46 **The correct answer is $360,000.**

Profit per day = throughput contribution – conversion cost

= [($80 × 6,000) + ($80 × 4,500) + ($200 × 1,200)] – $720,000 = $360,000

47 **The correct answer is 125%.**

Product	Minutes in alpha per unit	Minutes in alpha per day
X	60/1,200 = 0.05	6,000 × 0.05 = 300
Y	60/1,500 = 0.04	4,500 × 0.04 = 180
Z	60/600 = 0.10	1,200 × 0.10 = 120
		600

Total hours = 600 minutes ÷ 60 = 10 hours

Hours available = 8, hours produced = 10, ∴ **Efficiency** = 10/8 × 100% = 125%

48 **The correct answer is: $90,000**

Conversion cost per factory hour = $720,000/8 = $90,000

49 **The correct answer is:**

X 1.2

Y 1.5

Z 1.5

TA ratio = throughput contribution per factory hour/conversion cost per factory hour

Product	Throughput contribution per factory hour	Cost per factory hour	TA ratio
X	$80 × (60 ÷ 0.05 mins) = $96,000	$80,000	1.2
Y	$80 × (60 ÷ 0.04 mins) = $120,000	$80,000	1.5
Z	$200 × (60 ÷ 0.10 mins) = $120,000	$80,000	1.5

50 The correct answers are:

TA assumes that labour costs are largely fixed and TA assumes that material costs can be controlled in the short term. There is a technical article on ACCA's website called 'Throughput accounting and the theory of constraints' which explains this.

'The TA ratio for each product should be less than 1' in incorrect. The TA ratio should be greater than 1.

'Corrie Co's priority, using TA, should be given to products with the highest throughput contribution per unit' is incorrect. Priority should be given to products with the highest throughput contribution per unit of bottleneck resource.

A Co

51 The correct answer is:

B1 Department 1   **40 units**

B1 Department 2   **42 units**

B2 Department 1   **30 units**

B2 Department 2   **56 units**

	Maximum number of B1 units	Maximum number of B2 units
Department 1	480/12 = 40	480/16 = 30
Department 2	840/20 = 42	840/15 = 56

52   The correct answer is $1.93.

The question requires us to use **traditional contribution analysis**:

We need to calculate the contribution (sales less direct materials, labour and variable overheads) per unit of the bottleneck resource, which is time in Department 1. The contribution maximising output is found by dividing contribution per unit by the time in minutes required in department 1.

	$	B1 $
Sales price		50.00
Less variable costs		
Direct materials	10.00	
Direct labour	10.40	
Variable overheads	6.40	
		(26.80)
Contribution		23.20

Contribution per unit of limiting factor $\dfrac{\$23.20}{12} = \$1.933$

53   The correct answer is $3.13

The **throughput approach** is based on throughput maximisation. Throughput is defined as **sales less direct materials**.

	B2 $
Sales price	65
Less direct materials	(15)
	50

Throughput per minute of bottleneck resource is:

	B2 $
	50/16 = 3.125

54   The throughput accounting approach is more suitable for short term decision making than limiting factor analysis

The fundamental belief in throughput accounting is that all costs except direct material costs are largely fixed, therefore, to work on the basis of maximising contribution is flawed because to do so is to take into account costs that cannot be controlled in the short term anyway. In most businesses, it is simply not possible to hire workers on a daily basis and lay workers off if they are not busy.

Distractors:

- In throughput accounting idle time must be accepted. To do otherwise can lead to non-bottleneck activities being falsely identified as bottleneck activities, and possibly obsolescence if products need to be stored for a period of time

- Bottlenecks cannot be eliminated, only the activity identified as the bottleneck can change

- A certain amount of buffer material may need to be held in order to maximise throughput through the bottleneck activity

55   Step 1 Identify A Co's bottlenecks

Before any other work can be carried out, the bottleneck must first be identified.

Step 2   Decide how to exploit the system's bottlenecks

This involves making sure that the bottleneck resource is actively being used as much as possible and is producing as many units as possible.

Step 3   Subordinate everything else to the decisions made about exploiting the bottlenecks

The production capacity of the bottleneck resource should determine the production schedule for the organisation as a whole

Step 4   Elevate the system's bottlenecks

It is important that an organisation does not ignore Step 2 and jump straight to Step 4, which often happens. This ensures that no unnecessary capital investment occurs.

Cam Co

56   **The correct answer is $130**

Target selling price per unit $200
Profit margin 35%

Target cost $200 − ($200 × 35%) = $130

57   **The correct answer is $21.60**

Direct material cost

Parts to be replaced by standard parts = $40 × 80% = $32
New cost of standard parts at 45% (100% − 55%) = $14.40
Unique irreplaceable parts (original cost) = $40 × 20% = $8
New cost = $8 × 90% = $7.20
Revised direct material cost = $14.40 + $7.20 = $21.60

58   **The correct answer is $10.98.**

Direct labour

$Y = ax^b$

b = − 0.152 (given in question)

The question states that a learning curve of 90% is expected to occur until the 100th unit has been completed.

Total labour time for first 100 units

 x = 100

The question states that the first unit is expected to take 45 minutes (a = 45)

$Y = 45 × 100^{-0.152}$
   = 45 × (1/2.0137)
   = 22.3469 minutes

Therefore, labour time for 100 units = 22.3469 × 100 = 2,234.69 minutes

Labour time for the 100th unit

Time for 99 units

$Y = 45 × 99^{-0.152}$
   = 45 × (1/2.01065)
   = 22.38082 minutes

Therefore, labour time for 99 units = 22.38082 × 99 = 2,215.70 minutes

Therefore, time for 100th unit = 2,234.69 − 2,215.70 = 18.99 minutes, say 19 minutes

Labour time for remaining 49,900 units × 19 = 948,100 minutes
Total labour time for 50,000 units = 2,234.69 + 948,100 = 950,334.69 minutes

Therefore, total labour cost = (950,334.69/60) × $34.67 per hour = $549,135
Average labour cost per unit = $549,135/50,000 = $10.98

59   Neither 1 nor 2

Cam Co's target costing system may take product development costs into consideration, but recovery of product design and development costs is associated more with life cycle costing. Even with life cycle costing, recovery of design and development costs is not ensured: much depends on whether customers will buy enough webcams at the target price.

In target costing, a cost gap is the difference between the current estimate of the cost per webcam and the target cost that the Cam Co wants to achieve.

60   Redesign the webcam

Changes to selling price will have no effect upon target cost. The remaining options (employ more specialist staff; increase the number of bespoke components) would serve to increase the target cost gap rather than decrease it. If a product cannot be made within the target cost, so that a cost gap exists, the targets must be reduced, or the product redesigned.

Part B answers

MCQ bank – Decision-making techniques

61   B   (Syllabus area B6(e))

The decision options are given expected values, not the various different possible outcomes from each decision option. Each possible outcome is given a value, but not an expected value (EV).

62   A   (Syllabus area B4(b))

In circumstances of inelastic demand, prices should be increased because revenues will increase and total costs will reduce (because quantities sold will reduce).

Price elasticity of demand is measured as the amount of change in quantity demanded (measured as a percentage of the current sales volume) divided by the amount of change in sales price (measured as a percentage of the current sales price)

$$\frac{\text{The change in quantity demanded, as a \% of demand}}{\text{The change in price, as a \% of the price}}$$

63   B   (Syllabus area B4(g))

A price in excess of full cost per unit will not necessarily ensure that a company will cover all its costs and make a profit. Making a profit with cost plus pricing also depends on working at a sufficient capacity level, so that all fixed costs are covered by sales revenue.

Cost plus pricing is an appropriate pricing strategy when there is no comparable market price for the product or service.

64   D   (Syllabus area B3(c))

Statement (1) is a simple definition of slack for a production resource. When there is a minimum sales constraint for a product, surplus will occur when the quantity of production and sales for the product in the optimal solution exceeds the minimum sales requirement in the constraint.

65   A   (Syllabus area B6(b))

Expected value is a more reliable guide to the outcome from a situation that will occur many times over than for an outcome that will happen only once. A risk-averse decision maker makes decisions on the basis that the worst outcome will occur, but no one can avoid risk entirely in decision making.

66   A   (Syllabus area B4(g))

Price discrimination involves charging different prices in two or more different markets. This is only effective when the markets can be kept entirely separate – such as charging different prices for different age groups (children and old age pensioners), or charging a different price for a product or service at different times of the day or week.

67   D   (Syllabus area B2(b))

The correct answer is: $2,802,000

When sales revenue is $1.5 million, total contribution is 45% × $1.5 million = $675,000.

This leaves a further $625,000 of fixed costs to cover. To achieve breakeven, sales in excess of $1.5 million need to be $625,000/0.48 = $1.302 million.

Total sales to achieve breakeven = $1.5 million + $1.302 million = $2.802 million.

68   D   (Syllabus area B6(f))

The correct answer is: $7,500

EV of Project 1 = (0.1 × 70,000) + (0.4 × 10,000) − (0.5 × 7,000) = $7,500
EV of Project 2 = (0.1 × 25,000) + (0.4 × 12,000) + (0.5 × 5,000) = $9,800

EV of Project 3 = (0.1 × 50,000) + (0.4 × 20,000) − (0.5 × 6,000) = $10,000

Project 3 would be chosen on the basis of EV without perfect information. With perfect information, this decision would be changed to Project 1 if market research indicates strong demand and Project 2 if market research indicates weak demand.

EV with perfect information: (0.1 × 70,000) + (0.4 × 20,000) + (0.5 × 5,000) = $17,500

Value of perfect information = $(17,500 − 10,000) = $7,500 − ignoring the cost of obtaining the information.

69   A   (Syllabus area B4(b))

If demand is price-inelastic, a reduction in price will result in a fall in total sales revenue. At the lower price, there will be some increase in sales demand, so total costs will increase. With falling revenue and increasing costs, profits will fall.

70   A   (Syllabus area B5(d))

The correct answer is: $2,750

	FP1	FP2	Total
Input to further processing (kg)	5,500	4,000	
Finished output (kg)	4,950	3,800	
	$	$	$
Revenue from sales of FP1/FP2	44,550	34,200	
Relevant further processing costs	(11,000)	(12,000)	
Revenue from sales of CP1/CP2	(33,000)	(20,000)	
	550	2,200	2,750

71   A   (Syllabus area B5(b))

Product	W	X	Y	Z
Extra cost of external purchase	$1	$2.1	$2	$1
Direct labour hours per unit	0.1	0.3	0.25	0.2
Extra cost per hour saved by purchasing	$10	$7	$8	$5
Priority for external purchasing	4th	2nd	3rd	1st
Priority for making in-house	1st	3rd	2nd	4th

72   D   (Syllabus area B4(d))

The correct answer is: $110

For every $1 increase in price, demand will fall by 10,000 × (1/5) = 2,000 units
Demand will be 0 when the price is $120 + $(200,000/2,000) = $220
The demand curve $P = 220 − (1/2,000) × Q = 220 − 0.0005Q$
Total revenue = $(220 − 0.0005Q) × Q = 220Q − 0.0005Q^2$
Marginal revenue MR = $220 − 0.001Q$
Revenue is maximised when marginal revenue = 0
$220 − 0.001Q = 0$; therefore Q = 220/0.001 = 220,000 units, and P = 220 − (220,000 × 0.0005) = 110

73   B   (Syllabus area B2(b))

	$
Total cost at sales of $6.8 million	6,560,000
Deduct step increase in fixed costs	(400,000)
Total cost excluding step cost increase	6,160,000
Total cost at sales of $5.2 million	5,440,000
Therefore variable cost of sales of $1.6 million	720,000

Variable cost = 720,000/1,600,000 = 45% of sales. Contribution/sales ratio is 55%.

	$
Total cost at sales of $6.8 million	6,560,000
Variable cost (45%)	(3,060,000)

Fixed cost   <u>3,500,000</u>

If fixed costs are $3.5 million at the higher sales level and so $3.1 million at the lower sales level.

When fixed costs are $3.1 million, breakeven sales = $3.1 million/0.55 = $5.636 million

When fixed costs are $3.5 million, breakeven sales = $3.5 million/0.55 = $6.363 million

74   **C**   (Syllabus area B6(a))

A unique feature of simulation modelling using the Monte Carlo method is the use of random numbers to determine the value of input variables to the model.

75   **B**   (Syllabus area B6(b))

The 'What if' refers to the type of question used in sensitivity analysis. For example, what if the volume of sales is 10% less than expected? What if variable unit costs are 5% more than expected?

76   **C**   (Syllabus area B2(c))

The correct answer is: $1.968 million

Breakeven sales = $(2.4 million − 400,000) = $2,000,000

Contribution at this level of sales = $360,000. Therefore contribution/sales ratio = 360,000/2,000,000 = 18%

Variable costs = 82% of sales. At a sales level of $2.4 million, variable costs = 82% × $2.4 million = $1.968 million

77   **C**   (Syllabus area B3(d))

The shadow price of a limiting resource is the amount above the normal variable cost that will be added to the objective function (total contribution) if one extra unit of the resource is made available. This means that the company would increase contribution by paying up to $(8 + 4.50) = $12.50 per hour for additional labour time. However, it would not pay exactly $12.50, as this would leave it no better and no worse off than if it did not have the extra labour hour.

78   **A**   (Syllabus area B4(b))

When the price elasticity of demand is elastic, a reduction in price by x% will increase the quantity demanded by more than x% and as a result total sales revenue will increase. Without knowing about marginal costs, it is not possible to determine whether profits would increase or fall.

79   **A**   (Syllabus area B3(d))

The correct answer is: $1.50 per hour for the next 38,000 direct labour hours

If one extra direct labour hour is available, the optimal solution will change to the point where:

(1): sales demand for X	x	=	10,000
(2): direct labour	5x + 4y	=	60,001
Multiply (1) by 5			
(3)	5x	=	50,000
Subtract (3) from (2)	4y	=	10,001
	y	=	2,500.25

Total contribution = $(10,000 × $8) + $(2,500.25 × $6) = $80,000 + $15,001.15 = $95,001.5

Total contribution in original solution = $(10,000 × $8) + $(2,500 × $6) = $95,000

The shadow price per direct labour hour is therefore $1.50

The solution is changing because each additional labour hour allows the company to produce an additional 0.25 units of Product Y, to increase total contribution by $1.50.

This shadow price will cease to apply when the direct labour hours constraint is replaced in the optimal solution by the sales demand for Product Y constraint. At this level of output, total labour hours would be (10,000 units of X at 5 hours) + (12,000 units of Y at 4 hours) = 98,000 hours.

The shadow price of $1.50 per hour therefore applies for an additional 38,000 hours above the current limit.

80   C   (Syllabus area B3(d))

The correct answer is: $4.00

If one extra direct labour hour is available, the optimal solution will change to the point where:

(1): direct labour hours	$2x + 4y$	=	10,001
(2): materials	$4x + 2y$	=	14,000
Multiply (1) by 2			
(3)	$4x + 8y$	=	20,002
Subtract (2) from (3)	$6y$	=	6,002
	y	=	1,000.333
Substitute in (2)	$4x + 2,000.667$	=	14,000
	x	=	2,999.8333

Total contribution = $(2,999.833 \times $12) + $(1,000.333 \times $18) = $35,998 + $18,006 = $54,004

Total contribution in original solution = $(3,000 \times $12) + $(1,000 \times $18) = $54,000

The shadow price per direct labour hour is therefore $54,004 - $54,000 = $4

CBE style OTQ bank – Decision-making techniques

81   (Syllabus area B6(b))

The correct answers are:

- Identify all possible outcomes and their probabilities
- Assume the investor is risk neutral

Using EV for decision-making is more appropriate when the decision will often be repeated, because an EV is an estimate of the long-run average outcome. However EV can be used as the basis for making a one-off decision, even though this has severe limitations.

82   (Syllabus area B1(c))

The correct answer is: An opportunity cost

The question provides a definition of opportunity cost. An opportunity cost is a relevant cost for the purpose of decision making, but the definition in the question is too narrow to fit the term 'relevant cost'.

83   (Syllabus area B1(b))

The correct answer is: $376

	$
Additional purchases (5 tonnes × $50)	250
Relevant cost of material M already held: higher of	
$126 and (3 × $35)	126
Relevant cost total	376

84   (Syllabus area B6(d))

The correct answer is: P1

	Weekly contribution			
	Price P1	Price P2	Price P3	Price P4
	$	$	$	$
Best possible	30,000	31,500	32,000	31,500
Most likely	24,000	26,250	28,000	27,000
Worst possible	18,000	17,500	16,000	13,500

The maximin decision rule is to select the price offering the maximum possible benefit under the worst of circumstances. (It is similar to the minimax rule for decisions on minimising cost.) Price P1 will provide the biggest weekly contribution under the worst of circumstances, which is a contribution of $18,000 if the worst possible demand occurs. Only the bottom line of the above table needs to be calculated for your answer. The full table is shown here for the sake of completeness.

85   (Syllabus area B6(e))

The correct answer is: Choice 4

EV of Choice 1 = $9,500
EV of Choice 2 = (0.3 × 14,000) + (0.3 × 10,000) + (0.4 × 5,000) = $9,200
EV of Choice 3 = (0.4 × 10,000) + (0.6 × 9,000) = $9,400
EV of Choice 4 = (0.7 × 8,000) + (0.3 × 14,000) = $9,800

86   (Syllabus area B5(b))

The correct answer is: 4,000 units of W and 4,000 units of Z

Material	W	X	Y	Z
	$	$	$	$
Extra cost per unit of external purchase	1	6	3	2
Total extra cost of external purchase	4,000	12,000	9,000	8,000
Fixed costs saved by not making in-house	(5,000)	(8,000)	(6,000)	(7,000)
Difference	(1,000)	4,000	3,000	1,000

It would save $1,000 in cash to buy Material W externally. If full production can be achieved for the other materials, only W would be purchased externally. However, there is insufficient capacity to produce all three materials in-house.

Only 8,000 units can be produced in-house. If all the requirement for W is purchased externally (4,000 units), at least 1,000 units of X, Y or Z must be purchased externally too. The additional cost of buying Z externally is the least of these three.

If in-house production of Material Z is reduced to 3,000 units, the additional cost of external purchase would be only $6,000, so that $1,000 would be saved by purchasing all of Z externally.

87   (Syllabus area B4(d))

The correct answers are:

- Demand is 'perfectly inelastic'
- There is no change in the quantity demanded, regardless of any change in price

Demand is perfectly inelastic (that is, price elasticity is zero) when price changes have no impact upon demand.

The formula for the price elasticity of demand is percentage change in demand divided by percentage change in price; it will equal zero only if demand remains unchanged. A perfectly inelastic demand curve is a vertical straight line.

88   (Syllabus area B6(d))

The correct answer is: P2

	Weekly contribution			
	Price P1	Price P2	Price P3	Price P4
	$	$	$	$
Best possible	30,000	31,500	32,000	31,500
Most likely	24,000	26,250	28,000	27,000
Worst possible	18,000	17,500	16,000	13,500

	Regret			
	Price P1	Price P2	Price P3	Price P4
	$	$	$	$
Best possible	2,000	500	0	500
Most likely	4,000	1,750	0	1,000
Worst possible	0	500	2,000	4,500
Maximum regret	4,000	1,750	2,000	4,500

The maximum regret is minimised by selecting Price P2

89   (Syllabus area B6(f))

The correct answer is: $1,500

EV of Project 1 = (0.2 × 80,000) + (0.4 × 50,000) – (0.4 × 5,000) = $34,000
EV of Project 2 = (0.2 × 60,000) + (0.4 × 25,000) + (0.4 × 10,000) = $26,000

Project 1 would be chosen on the basis if EV without perfect information. With perfect information, this decision would be changed to Project 2 if market research indicates weak demand.

EV with perfect information: (0.2 × 80,000) + (0.4 × 50,000) + (0.4 × 10,000) = $40,000

Value of perfect information = $(40,000 – 34,000) – $4,500 cost = $1,500

90   (Syllabus area B2(d))

The correct answer is: $5.188 million

Weighted average sales price per unit = [(20 × 2) + (18 × 3) + (24 × 5)]/((2 + 3 + 5) = $21.40
Weighted average variable cost per unit = [(11 × 2) + (12 × 3) + (18 × 5)]/((2 + 3 + 5) = $14.80
Therefore weighted average contribution per unit = $(21.40 – 14.80) = $6.60
Weighted average C/S ratio = 6.60/21.40 = 0.3084112

Sales required to achieve target contribution of $1.6 million = $1.6 million/0.3084112 = $5.188 million.

91   (Syllabus area B6(a))

The correct answer is:

•   To gain insight into which assumptions or variables in a situation are critical

Sensitivity analysis can be used to identify how much the outcome from a situation or decision would be different if the value of an input variable changes. In this way, the input variables that are most critical to the situation or decision can be identified. Sensitivity analysis can also be described as assessing how projected performance or outcome will be affected by changes in the assumptions that have been used.

92   (Syllabus area B4(f))

The correct answer is: $96

An increase in price of $25 will result in a fall in demand quantity by 6,250 units. Each $1 change in price therefore results in a change in demand by 6,250/25 = 250 units.

Demand Q will be 0 when the price P is $145 + $(5,000/250) $165
Demand function = 165 – Q/250 = 165 – 0.004Q
Marginal revenue = 165 – 0.008Q

Profit is maximised when marginal revenue equals marginal cost:

When 27 = 165 – 0.008Q, so Q = 138/0.008 = 17,250

Price = 165 – (17,250/250) = $96

93   (Syllabus area B2(b))

The correct answer is: $914,000

Product	A	B	C	Total
	$'000	$'000	$'000	$'000
Sales revenue	360	720	200	1,280
Variable costs	90	240	110	440
Contribution	270	480	90	840
Fixed costs	180	360	60	600

Contribution/sales ratio = 840/1,280 = 0.65625

Breakeven point in sales revenue = $600,000/0.65625 = $914,286

With CVP analysis for a company that sells several products, a fixed sales mix has to be assumed.

94   (Syllabus area B5(d))

The correct answers are:

- The final sales value of the joint product
- he further processing cost of the joint product

When deciding whether or not to process further a joint product, the final sales value of the joint product is deducted from the sum of the further processing cost of the joint product and the opportunity cost of further processing (ie the sales value of the joint product at the separation point).

95   (Syllabus area B3(c))

The correct answers are:

- If the aim is to minimise costs, the solution is where the total cost line touching the feasible area at a tangent, is as close to the origin as possible.

- If the aim is to maximise profit, the solution is where the total contribution line touching the feasible area at a tangent, is as far away from the origin as possible.

If the aim is to minimise costs, the solution is where the total cost line touching the feasible area at a tangent, is as close to the origin as possible as this will allow the company to make as little as possible given constraints. If the aim is to maximise profit, the solution is where the total contribution line touching the feasible area at a tangent, is as far away from the origin as possible as this will allow the company to make as much as possible given contraints.

All other statements are false.

BDU Co

96   A   **The correct answer is: $425**

Maximax $425

The **maximax criterion** looks at the **best possible results**. Maximax means 'maximise the maximum profit'. In this case, we need to **maximise the maximum contribution**.

Demand/price	Maximum contribution
1,000/$425	$255,000
730/$500	$240,900
420/$600	$180,600

BDU would therefore set a price of **$425**.

97   B   **The correct answer is: $500**

Maximin $500

The **maximin** decision rule involves choosing the outcome that offers the **least unattractive worst outcome**, in this instance choosing the outcome which **maximises the minimum contribution**.

Demand/price	Minimum contribution
1,000/$425	$165,000
730/$500	$175,200
420/$600	$142,800

BDU would therefore set a price of **$500**.

98   A   **The correct answer is: $425**

Minimax regret $425

The **minimax regret** decision rule involves choosing the **outcome that minimises the maximum regret** from making the wrong decision, in this instance choosing the outcome which **minimises the opportunity loss** from making the wrong decision.

We can draw up an **opportunity loss table.**

Variable cost	Price		
	$425	$500	$600
$170	–	$14,100	$74,400 (W1)
$210	–	$3,300	$51,200 (W2)
$260	$10,200	–	$32,400 (W3)
Minimax regret	$10,200	$14,100	$74,400

Minimax regret strategy (price of $425) is that which minimises the maximum regret ($10,200).

Workings

(1) At a variable cost of $170 per day, the best strategy would be a price of $425. The opportunity loss from setting a price of $600 would be $(255,000 − 180,600) = $74,400.

(2) At a variable cost of $210 per day, the best strategy would be a price of $425. The opportunity loss from setting a price of $600 would be $(215,000 − 163,800) = $51,200.

(3) At a variable cost of $260 per day, the best strategy would be a price of $500. The opportunity loss from setting a price of $600 would be $(175,200 − 142,800) = $32,400.

99   **A** $425

Expected values calculations:

$425: (255,000 × 0.4) + (215,000 × 0.25) + (165,000 × 0.35) = $213,500

$500: (240,900 × 0.4) + (211,700 × 0.25) + (175,200 × 0.35) = $210,605

$600: (180,600 × 0.4) + (163,800 × 0.25) + (142,800 × 0.35) = $163,170

100   **B**   Market research

Market research is used to obtain data about customer/consumer attitudes and preferences to products or markets, and the quantitative or qualitative information obtained from market research can help to reduce uncertainty for some elements of decision making, such as pricing and product design decisions.

Cement Co

101   C   **The correct answer is: 200,000 bags**

Maximin

Select the least unattractive worst outcome (the option that maximises the minimum profits).

	SUPPLY (number of bags)		
	350,000	280,000	200,000
	$'000	$'000	$'000
Worst	325	640	1,000

The highest of these is $1,000,000 therefore choose to supply only 200,000 bags to meet poor conditions.

102   A   **The correct answer is: 350,000 bags**

Maximax

Select the best possible outcome (the option that maximises the maximum profit).

	SUPPLY (number of bags)		
	350,000	280,000	200,000
	$'000	$'000	$'000
Best	1,750	1,400	1,000

The highest of these is $1,750,000 therefore choose to supply 350,000 bags to meet good conditions.

BPP
LEARNING MEDIA

103 B **The correct answer is: 280,000 bags**

Minimax regret **280,000**

The **minimax regret** decision rule involves choosing the **outcome that minimises the maximum regret** from making the wrong decision, in this instance choosing the outcome which **minimises the opportunity loss from making the wrong decision.**

We can draw up an **opportunity loss table.**

Demand	Supply		
	350,000	280,000	200,000
	$'000	$'000	$'000
Good	–	350	750 (W1)
Average	315	–	400 (W2)
Poor	675	360	– (W3)
Minimax regret	990	710	1,150

Minimax regret strategy (supply of 280,000 bags) is that which minimises the maximum regret ($710,000).

Workings

(1)   If demand is good, the best strategy would be a supply of 350,000. The opportunity loss from supplying 200,000 bags would be $(1,750,000 − 1,000,000) = $750,000.

(2)   If demand is average, the best strategy would be a supply of 280,000. The opportunity loss from supplying 200,000 bags would be $(1,400,000 − 1,000,000) = $400,000.

(3)   If demand is poor, the best strategy would be a supply of 200,000. There is no opportunity loss from supplying 200,000 bags.

104 B **The correct answer is: 280,000 bags**

Expected values

Use the probabilities shown to calculate the expected value of each of the supply levels.

Good   (0.25 × $1,750,000) + (0.45 × $1,085,000) + (0.30 × $325,000) = $1,023,250
Average   (0.7 × $1,400,000) + (0.3 × $640,000) = $1,172,000
Poor   1 × $1,000,000 = $1,000,000

The expected value of producing 280,000 bags when conditions are average is the highest at $1,172,000, therefore this supply level should be chosen.

105 C **Neither 1 nor 2**

Statement 1 is false. Expected values are used to support the risk-neutral decision-maker, who will ignore any variability or extremities in the range of possible outcomes and be interested only in the overall average expected value. By contrast, a risk averse decision maker is likely to be more interested in those extreme outcomes, and so an overall average will not give enough information. Statement 2 is false. The average profit calculated may not correspond to any of the possible outcomes, and this is a limitation of expected value analysis.

Ennerdale

106 **C** **The correct answer is $30,870**

Relevant cost – Material K

Since the material is regularly used by the company, the relevant cost of material K is the current price of the material.

Cost last month $= \dfrac{\$19,600}{2,000\,\text{kg}}$

$= \$9.80$

Revised cost (+5%) $= \$9.80 \times 1.05$

$= \$10.29$

∴ Relevant cost of material K $= 3,000\,\text{kg} \times \$10.29 \text{ per kg}$

$= \$30,870$

107 **A** **The correct answer is $2,200**

Relevant cost – Material L

Since the material is not required for normal production, the relevant cost of this material is its net realisable value if it were sold.

∴ Relevant cost of material L $= 200\,\text{kg} \times \$11 \text{ per kg}$

$= \$2,200$

108 **B** **The correct answer is $15,600**

Relevant cost – skilled labour

Skilled labour is in short supply and therefore the relevant cost of this labour will include both the actual cost and the opportunity cost of the labour employed.

	$
Cost of skilled labour (800 hours × $9.50)	7,600
Opportunity cost of skilled labour (see working)	8,000
Relevant cost – skilled labour	15,600

Working

Skilled labour cost per unit of Product P = $38

Cost per skilled labour hour = $9.50

∴ Number of hours required per unit of Product P $= \dfrac{\$38}{\$9.50}$

$= 4 \text{ hours}$

Contribution per unit of Product P $= \$40$

∴ Contribution per skilled labour hour $= \dfrac{\$40}{4\,\text{hours}}$

$= \$10 \text{ per hour}$

∴ Opportunity cost of skilled labour $= 800 \text{ hours} \times \$10 \text{ per hour}$

$= \$8,000$

109 **B** $15 × 8 hours = $120

The cost of hiring an accountant is $25 × 75% × 8 hours = $150. As this cost is greater than if the work were done by the finance team, the finance team overtime cost of $120 is the relevant cost.

110 **D** These are fundamental statements about relevant costing.

Metallica Co

111 C   **The correct answer is:**

Product P4   70

Product P6   100

	Product P4	*Product P6*
	$	$
Selling price	125	175
Opportunity cost		
Direct materials:		
M1	15	10
M2	10	20
Direct labour	20	30
Variable overhead	10	15
Total variable costs	55	75
Contribution/unit	70	100

112 B   **The correct answer is:**

The contribution per limiting factor of P4 and P6 is \$113.33 and \$190 respectively, therefore P6 should be produced first.

The most profitable course of action can be determined by ranking the products and components according to **contribution per unit of the limiting factor**. Direct material M1 is the limiting factor in this case, therefore the highest rank will be given to the product/component with the greatest contribution per m^2 of this material.

Contribution/unit	85	95
m^2 of M1/unit	0.75	0.5
Contribution/m^2	$113.33	$190
Ranking	2	1

113 C   In throughput accounting, a very similar calculation to limiting factor analysis is performed. However, in throughput accounting, it is not contribution per unit of scarce resource which is calculated, but throughput return per unit of bottleneck resource. Throughput is calculated as 'selling price less direct material cost'. This is different from the calculation of 'contribution', in which both labour costs and variable overheads are also deducted from selling price.

114 D   Firms face many constraints on their activities and have to plan accordingly.

115 D

    Step 1: Calculate the contribution per unit for each product

    Step 2: Calculate the contribution per unit of the scarce resource for each product

    Step 3: Rank the products in order of the contribution per unit of the scarce resource

    Step 4: Allocate resources using the ranking

Pixie Pharmaceuticals

116 C **The correct answer is: $48,000**

	Fairyoxide $'000	Spriteolite $'000	Goblinex $'000	Total $'000
Sales value	80	200	160	440
Variable costs	56	136	112	304
Contribution	24	64	48	136
Fixed costs	16	40	32	88
Profit	8	24	16	48

If we produce our three drugs in-house our total profits are $48,000.

117 B **$0.05 per unit**

	Fairyoxide $
Unit variable costs:	
direct material	0.80
direct labour	1.60
direct expense	0.40
Total variable cost	2.80
Imported price	2.75
Saving/(increased cost) of purchasing	0.05

118 A **$(0.80) per unit**

	Spriteolite $
Unit variable costs:	
direct material	1.00
direct labour	1.80
direct expense	0.60
Total variable cost	3.40
Imported price	4.20
Saving/(increased cost) of purchasing	(0.80)

119 D **$(0.60) per unit**

	Goblinex $
Unit variable costs:	
direct material	0.40
direct labour	0.80
direct expense	0.20
Total variable cost	1.40
Imported price	2.00
Saving/(increased cost) of purchasing	(0.60)

120 A Pixie Pharmaceutical should consider a number of other factors before making a final decision on whether to produce all of its products in house, or to purchase from the overseas supplier. Those factors include the reliability of the overseas supplier, customer reaction, and any legal implications.

T Co

121   D   **$500**

One of the three engineers has spare capacity to complete the installation and his/her salary will be paid regardless of whether they work on the contract for Push Co. The relevant cost is therefore $Nil.

The other two engineers are currently fully utilised and earn a contribution of $200 per week each on Contract X. The engineers could be temporarily taken off of Contract X to work on the contract for Push Co. Work on Contract X would recommence in one week's time when there is no other scheduled work for the engineers.

Delaying the work on Contract X would result in T Co missing the contractual completion deadline and having to pay a one-off penalty of $500.

Relevant cost = $500

122   B   **$2,184**

120 handsets would need to be supplied to Push Co. Though 80 handsets are already in inventory, the handsets are frequently requested by T Co's customers and so would need to be replaced if supplied to Push Co. The current cost of a handset is $18.20.

Relevant cost = $18.20 × 120 handsets = $2,184

123   A   **$7,600**

The current market price of Swipe 2 is $10,800.

The original cost of Swipe 1 ($5,400) is a sunk cost and not relevant to the decision.

The current market price of Swipe 1 ($5,450) is also not relevant to the decision as T Co has no intention of replacing Swipe 1.

The company could sell Swipe 1 for $3,000 if it does not use it for this contract. This represents an opportunity cost.

In addition to the $3,000, Swipe 1 could be modified at a cost of $4,600, bringing the total cost of converting Swipe 1 to $7,600.

124   C   An opportunity cost is the benefit forgone taking one course of action instead of the next most profitable course of action.

The effect that the decision to accept the Push Co contract has on profit or cost is an important factor in decision making, but non-financial factors should also be taken into consideration.

125   A   The cost of the demonstration has already been incurred and cannot be recovered. It is therefore, a sunk cost and is not relevant to the decision about whether or not to accept the Push Co contract.

Rotanola Co

126   **The correct answer is: P = 210 – 0.005Q**

Find the price at which demand would be nil: Each price increase of $10 results in a fall in demand of 2,000 phones. For demand to be nil, the price needs to rise by as many times as there are 2,000 units in 20,000 units (20,000/2,000 = 10) ie to $110 + (10 × $10) = $210. So a = 210

b = change in price/change in quantity = 10/2,000 = 0.005

The demand equation is therefore P = 210 – 0.005Q

Alternatively
P = a - bQ
110 = a – (0.005 × 20,000)
a = 110 + 100 = 210
P = 210 – 0.005Q

127 The correct answer is: TC = 460,000 +62Q

Cost behaviour can be modelled using equations. These equations can be highly complex but in this case are quite simple.

b = variable cost = 30 + 18 + 14 = $62
a = fixed cost = $23 × 20,000 = 460,000
TC = 460,000 + 62Q where Q = number of units

128 The correct answer is: TC = 460,000 +59Q

With the **volume based discount**:

b = 27 + 18 + 14 = 59
TC = 460,000 + 59Q

129 The correct answer is $969,000.

Materials

Probability	Forecast material cost	Expected value
	$	$
0.6	50	30
0.3	60	18
0.1	40	4
		52

Sales units

Probability	Forecast sales units	Expected value
	$	$
0.5	25,000	12,500
0.4	22,500	9,000
0.1	26,250	2,625
		24,125

Expected profit

		$	$
Sales	(24,125 × $150)		3,618,750
Materials	(24,125 × $52)	1,254,500	
Labour	(24,125 × $18)	434,250	
Variable overheads	(24,125 × $16)	386,000	
			2,074,750
Attributable fixed overheads			575,000
Expected profit			969,000

130 1 only

Statement 1 is true. Decision makers need data to reduce uncertainty and risk when planning for the future and to monitor business performance. Market researchers provide the data that helps them to do this.

Statement 2 is false. Sensitivity analysis could be used by Rotanola to estimate by how much costs and revenues would need to differ from their estimated values before the decision would change.

131 RB Co

(a) **Managing director's pricing strategy**

The managing director has adopted what is known as a **full cost plus** pricing strategy, which means that a profit margin (in this case, of 50%) is added to the budgeted full cost of the product.

Given the information in the question, the **selling price used by RB Co** is calculated as follows.

	$
Full cost	400
50% mark up	200
Selling price	600

Disadvantages of this pricing strategy

Its **focus** is **internal** – internal costs and internal targets. It therefore takes **no account of the market conditions** faced by RB Co, which is why the company's selling price bears little resemblance to those of competitors. By adopting a fixed mark-up, **it does not allow the company to react to competitors'** pricing decisions.

Absorption bases used when calculating the full cost are **decided arbitrarily**. The current basis of absorption is based on the budgeted level of production, which is lower than the current capacity. **Depending on the absorption basis** used in the calculation of total cost, the strategy can **produce different selling prices.**

Advantages of this pricing strategy

It is **quick**, **cheap** and relatively **easy** to apply. Pricing can therefore be delegated to more junior management if necessary.

It ensures that **all costs are covered** and that the organisation **makes a profit**, provided budget figures used in the pricing calculation are reasonably accurate. This was the case in the first two years for RB Co.

The **costs of collecting market information** on demand and competitor activity are **avoided.**

(b) **Alternative pricing strategies**

    (1) **Market penetration pricing**

        Market penetration pricing is a policy of **low prices** when a product is first launched in order to achieve **high sales volumes** and hence gain a **significant market share**. If RB Co had adopted this strategy it might have discouraged competitors from entering the market.

    (2) **Market skimming**

        This pricing strategy involves charging **high prices** when a product is first launched and **spending heavily on advertising and promotion** to obtain sales so as to exploit any price insensitivity in the market. Such an approach would have been particularly suitable for RB's circumstances: demand for the software would have been relatively inelastic, customers being prepared to pay high prices for the software given its novelty appeal. As the product moves into later stages of its life cycle, prices can be reduced in order to remain competitive.

(c) When demand is linear the equation for the demand curve is:

$P = a - bQ$

where   P   = the price

        Q   = the quantity demanded

        a   = the price at which demand would be nil

        $b = \dfrac{\text{change in price}}{\text{change in quantity}}$

a = $750

$b = \dfrac{\$10}{1,000}$

  = 0.01

∴ P = 750 − 0.01Q

(d) **Cost behaviour** can be modelled using a **simple linear equation** of the form $y = a + bx$ where 'a' represents the fixed costs, which for RB are $1,200,000 (15,000 × $80), and 'b' represents the variable costs per unit ie $320 (400 − 80) per unit for RB. This cost model assumes fixed costs remain unchanged over all ranges of output and a constant unit variable cost.

(e) **Price elasticity of demand**

Price elasticity of demand is a measure of the extent of change in market demand for a good in response to a change in its price. It is measured as:

$$\frac{\text{The change in quantity demanded, as a \% of demand}}{\text{The change in price, as a \% of the price}}$$

Since the demand goes up when the price falls, and goes down when the price rises, the elasticity has a negative value, but it is usual to ignore the minus sign.

The value of demand elasticity may be anything from zero to infinity.

Elastic and inelastic demand

Demand is referred to as **inelastic** if the absolute value is less than 1. Where demand is **inelastic**, the **quantity demanded falls by a smaller percentage than the percentage increase in price.**

Where demand is **elastic, demand falls** by a **larger percentage than the percentage rise in price** the absolute value is greater than 1.

Pricing decisions

An awareness of the concept of elasticity can assist management with **pricing decisions**.

In circumstances of **inelastic demand, prices should be increased** because revenues will increase and total costs will reduce (because quantities sold will reduce).

In circumstances of **elastic demand**, increases in prices will bring decreases in revenue and decreases in price will bring increases in revenue. Management therefore have to **decide** whether the **increase/decrease in costs will be less than/greater than the increases/decreases in revenue**.

In situations of **very elastic demand**, overpricing can lead to a massive drop in quantity sold and hence a massive drop in profits whereas underpricing can lead to costly stock outs and, again, a significant drop in profits. **Elasticity must therefore be reduced by creating a customer preference which is unrelated to price** (through advertising and promotional activities).

In situations of **very inelastic demand**, customers are **not sensitive to price. Quality, service, product mix and location** are therefore **more important** to a firm's pricing strategy.

Cost-plus pricing

Cost-plus pricing is based on the **assumption** that demand for the company's software is **inelastic** and prices should be increased in order to increase total revenue and hence profit. The market research information for RB Co does not support this view, however. It suggests that increasing prices will lead to a drop in demand and hence a reduction in profit.

132 The Cosmetic Co

Text reference. Graphical linear programming is covered in Chapter 4.

Top tips. Perhaps the biggest challenge in this question is time management. There is a lot to do in the time allowed.

Use the step by step approach in part (a), clearly labelling your workings to make it easy for the marker to follow. Make sure your read the question scenario very carefully as it is easy to miss an element.

Easy marks. There are plenty of easy marks available throughout for establishing the constraints and clearly drawing and labelling each line on the graph.

Examiner's comments. Much of this question could have been examined at F2. Why then, was it in the F5 paper? It is becoming more and more apparent that the assumed F2 knowledge for F5 simply isn't there and it is therefore necessary to make candidates realise that it is examinable under F5 and that, if they don't know the subject matter, they need to go away and study it!

Candidates who had revised this area made a decent attempt at this question, with many of them scoring full marks in part (a) at least. It is important, when answering a linear programming question like this, to set out your workings clearly, with a logical progression in steps from defining the variables and constraints, through to drawing the graph and finding the solution. This makes it easier to mark. The recommended approach is to use the iso-contribution line to find the optimum solution; it is the quickest way to do it. Candidates weren't penalised if they used the simultaneous equations method, because they were not told which method to use, but they penalised themselves because it took them longer to do it.

It is essential to show all of your workings. So, for example, the iso-contribution line needs to be worked out and then drawn onto the graph. If you didn't show how you worked it out, you stood to lose some marks.

Where you are asked to work to 2 decimal places, you should do it. In this question, it was necessary in order to keep a level of accuracy required to answer part (b) as well. Whilst we gave follow on marks for part (b) wherever possible, if fundamental mistakes had been made in part (a) so that, for example, there was no slack for amino acids, it was hard to award marks.

Marks

(a) Optimum production plan:

Assigning letters for variables	½
Defining constraint for silk powder	½
Defining constraint for amino acids	½
Defining constraint for labour	½
Non-negativity constraint	½
Sales constraint: x	½
Sales constraint: y	½
Iso-contribution line worked out	1
The graph:	
Labels	½
Silk powder	½
Amino acids	½
Labour line	½
Demand for x line	½
Demand for y line	½
Iso-contribution line	½
Vertices a–e identified	½
Feasible region shaded	½
Optimum point identified	1
Equations solved at optimum point	3
Total contribution	1
	14

(b) Shadow prices and slack:

Shadow price	4
Slack	2
	6
	20

(a) **Define variables**

Let x = number of jars of face cream to be produced
Let y = number of bottles of body lotion to be produced
Let C = contribution

Establish objective function

The objective is to maximise contribution (C).

Face cream contribution (x) = $9.00 per unit

Body lotion contribution (y) = $8.00 per unit

Maximise C = 9x + 8y, subject to the constraints below.

Establish constraints

Silk powder:	$3x + 2y \leq 5{,}000$
Silk amino acids:	$1x + 0.5y \leq 1{,}600$
Skilled labour:	$4x + 5y \leq 9{,}600$
Non-negativity constraints:	$x, y \geq 0$
Maximum demand for body lotion:	$y \leq 2{,}000$

Establish coordinates to plot lines representing the inequalities

Silk powder: $3x + 2y \leq 5,000$

If $x = 0$, $y = 2,500$
If $y = 0$, $x = 1,666.7$

Silk amino acids: $1x + 0.5y \leq 1,600$
If $x = 0$, $y = 3,200$
If $y = 0$, $x = 1,600$

Skilled labour: $4x + 5y \leq 9,600$
If $x = 0$, $y = 1,920$
If $y = 0$, $x = 2,400$

Also plot the line $y = 2,000$ (maximum weekly demand for body lotion).

Draw the graph

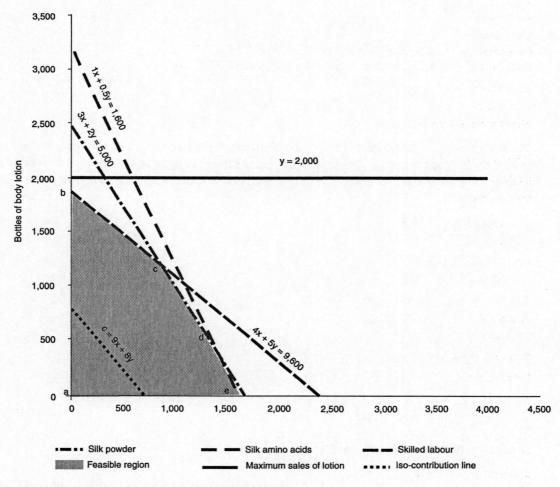

Find the optimal solution using an iso-contribution line

$C = 9x + 8y$

If $C = (8 \times 800) = 6,400$, then:

If $y = 0$, $9x = 6,400$

Therefore $x = 711.11$

By moving the iso-contribution line out across the graph, it is clear that the optimal solution lies as point C, the intersection of the constraints for skilled labour and silk powder.

Solving the simultaneous equations for these constraints:

$4x + 5y = 9,600 \qquad \times 3$

$3x + 2y = 5,000 \qquad \times 4$

$12x + 15y = 28,800 \quad (1)$

$12x + 8y = 20,000 \quad (2)$

Subtract (2) from (1):

$7y = 8,800$

$y = 1,257.14$

If y = 1,257.14 and;

$4x + 5y = 9,600$

The $5 \times 1,257.14 + 4x = 9,600$

Therefore x = 828.58

The **optimal solution** is therefore to make 828.58 jars of face cream and 1,257.14 bottles of body lotion.

Maximum profit

$

Contribution

		$
Face cream:	828.58 units × unit contribution of $9.00	7,457.22
Body lotion:	1,257.14 units × unit contribution of $8.00	10,057.12
		17,514.34

(b)   **Shadow price for silk powder**

The shadow price for silk powder can be found by solving the two simultaneous equations that intersect at point C on the graph in part (a). The **shadow price** is the **increase in value which would be created by having one additional unit** of limiting factor. For this reason, we must add one more hour to the equation for silk powder.

$4x + 5y = 9,600 \qquad \times 3$

$3x + 2y = 5,001 \qquad \times 4$

$12x + 15y = 28,800 \quad (1)$

$12x + 8y = 20,004 \quad (2)$

Subtract (2) from (1):

$7y = 8,796$

$y = 1,256.57$

$3x + (2 \times 1,256.57) = 5,001$

$x = 829.29$

$C = (9 \times 829.29) + (8 \times 1,256.57) = \$17,516.17$

Original contribution = $17,514.34

The **shadow price for silk powder** is therefore $1.83 per gram.

Slack for amino acids

Each unit of face cream requires 1 gram of silk amino acids and each unit of body lotion requires 0.5 grams of amino acids.

$(828.58 \times 1) + (0.5 \times 1,257.14) = 1,457.15$ grams used.

Grams available = 1,600 grams.

Therefore slack = 142.85 grams.

133 Bits and Pieces

> **Text references.** Incremental costs and revenues are covered in Chapters 5 and 6.
>
> **Top tips.** In part (a), use a clear layout, read the information carefully and make sure you state which costs should be excluded rather than not mentioning them at all.
>
> In part (b) use your common sense to make sensible suggestions and don't be afraid to state the obvious.
>
> **Easy marks.** There are plenty of easy marks available for the calculations in part (a).
>
> **Examiner's comments.** Marks gained for part (a) were reasonable but the incremental heating cost was often incorrectly calculated for the whole year, rather than just the winter months as stated in the question.
>
> This question required some common business sense which was lacking in many candidates with a lack of understanding or experience demonstrated in parts (b) and (c).

Marking scheme

		Marks	
(a)	Existing total sales	1	
	Existing total gross profit	1	
	New sales	1	
	New gross profit	1	
	Incremental gross profit	1	
	Existing purchasing	1	
	Discount allowed for	1	
	Incremental Sunday purchasing costs	1	
	Staff cost	1	
	Lighting cost	1	
	Heating cost	1	
	Manager's bonus	1	
			12
(b)	Time off at normal rate not time and a half	1	
	Lack of flexibility	1	
	Bonus per day worked calculation and comment	1	
	Risk	1	
			4
(c)	Changing customer buying pattern	2	
	Complaints risk	2	
	Quality link	2	
	Maximum		4
			20

(a) Incremental revenue

	Sales	Gross profit	Gross profit
	$	%	$
Average	10,000	70	
Sunday (60% more than average)	16,000	50	8,000
Annual Sunday sales (50 weeks)	800,000	50	400,000

Purchasing costs

Current annual spending = 50 weeks × 6 days × 10,000 × 30%
= $900,000

New annual spending with discount $= (900{,}000 + 400{,}000) \times 95\%$

$= \$1{,}235{,}000$

Incremental purchasing cost $= \$(1{,}235{,}000 - 900{,}000)$

$= \$335{,}000$

Staff costs

Additional staff costs on a Sunday $= 5$ sales assistants $\times 6$ hours $\times 50$ weeks $\times 1.5 \times \$20$

$= \$45{,}000$

Manager's costs

The salary of the manager is a sunk cost and there will be no additional costs for his time.
He will be entitled to an extra bonus of $1\% \times \$800{,}000 = \$8{,}000$

Lighting costs

50 weeks $\times$ 6 hours $\times$ \$30 = \$9,000

Heating costs

25 weeks $\times$ 8 hours $\times$ \$45 = \$9,000

Rent

The rent of the store is a sunk cost so is not relevant to this decision.

Net incremental revenue

Net incremental revenue $= 800{,}000 - (335{,}000 + 45{,}000 + 9{,}000 + 9{,}000 + 8{,}000)$

$= \mathbf{\$394{,}000}$

Conclusion

Incremental revenue exceeds incremental costs by \$394,000 so Sunday opening is **financially justifiable**.

(b) **Manager's pay deal**

Time off

If the manager works on a Sunday he will take the equivalent **time off** during the week. He is not entitled to extra pay in the same way as the sales assistants and this does not seem fair. Weekend working is disruptive to most people's family and social life and it is reasonable to expect **extra reward** for giving up time at weekends. It is unlikely that time off in lieu during the week will motivate the manager.

Bonus

The bonus has been calculated as \$8,000 which equates to an extra \$160 per day of extra work. The sales assistants will be paid \$180 per day (6 × \$20 × 1.5) so again the manager is **not getting a fair offer**.

The bonus is based on **estimated sales** so could be higher if sales are higher than predicted. However, there is a **risk** that sales and therefore the bonus could be lower. It is therefore again unlikely that this bonus will motivate the manager.

(c) **Price discounts and promotions**

B & P plans to offer substantial discounts and promotions on a Sunday to attract customers. This may indeed be a good **marketing strategy** to attract people to shop on a Sunday, but it is not necessarily good for the business.

Customer buying pattern

B & P wants to attract **new** customers on a Sunday but customers may simply **change the day** they do their shopping in order to take advantage of the discounts and promotions. The effect of this would be to **reduce the margin** earned from customer purchases and not increase revenue.

Customer dissatisfaction

Customers who buy goods at full price and then see their purchases for sale at lower prices on a Sunday may be disgruntled. They could then complain or switch their custom to another shop.

The **reputation** of B & P could be damaged by this marketing policy, especially if customers associate lower prices with **lower quality**.

Part C answers

MCQ bank – Budgeting and control

134   **C**   (Syllabus area C6(b))

With road haulage and distribution, drivers' times on the road are measured automatically. Variable costs can be high (labour and fuel, for example). Standard costing is more common in manufacturing but in principle can be applied to service industries. The problem is to identify a standard item for which a cost can be measured and variances subsequently calculated. In road haulage for example a standard measure may be cost per tonne/kilometre delivered: this does not lend itself easily to variance analysis.

135   **D**   (Syllabus area C6(c))

Material usage is within the control of a production manager, whereas material price variances are usually the responsibility of the purchasing manager. Line managers are responsible for operational variances, but planning variances are commonly assumed to be the responsibility of someone in senior management.

136   **B**   (Syllabus area C4(b))

Mix variances should only be calculated when a product contains two or more materials that can be mixed together in different proportions. For example, calculating a mix variance for the production of a bicycle out of its component parts would be meaningless. It is important to be aware of the interdependence between variances: a favourable mix variance – meaning a cheaper mix of materials in a product – may result in adverse total output of the product (adverse yield).

137   **D**   (Syllabus area C3(c))

Flexible budgets enable actual results to be compared with expected results for the same volume of activity, such as production and sales. To reconcile an original budgeted profit to actual profit with variances there must be a sales volume variance (measured in terms of either budgeted/standard contribution or profit, depending on the type of costing system used).

138   **A**   (Syllabus area C5(a))

The loss of the advertising campaign means that sales of Product Y will be less than budgeted, which should lead us to expect adverse sales volume variance for Y and an adverse sales quantity variance for both products together. The price discounting for Product Y should lead us to expect an adverse sales price variance. The increase in the proportion of Product X units sold in the total sales mix should lead us to expect a favourable sales mix variance, because Product X has a bigger standard contribution, both per unit and per $1 of standard sales price, than Product Y.

139   **B**   (Syllabus area C3(d))

This should be a fundamental principle of management control, but it is not always applied in practice.

140   **C**   (Syllabus area C5(a))

Mix and yield variances measure costs and output quantities, not quality. A potential problem is that persistent **favourable** mix variances may have an adverse effect on sales volume variances and direct labour efficiency variances, because the cheaper materials mix may affect the quality of the product sold to customers and also make the product more difficult to handle. These consequences could lead to adverse sales volume and labour efficiency variances.

141   **B**   (Syllabus area C7(e))

Standard costing systems are not compatible with a Total Quality Management approach to operations. With standard costing, the aim is to achieve standard cost or perhaps obtain some favourable variances. With TQM, guiding principles are 'continuous improvement' and 'zero defects'.

Existing standards and methods of operating are always unsatisfactory and improvements should always be sought. This is not compatible with a standard costing 'philosophy'.

Standard costing tends to be of little value in a rapidly changing environment because products are not standardised for a sufficient length of time to make the preparation of standard costs worthwhile.

142   D   (Syllabus area C1(d))

The cumulative average time falls to r% of what it was previously every time that output doubles. Between the first unit and the 16th unit, output has doubled four times.

Therefore $3.3/6 = r^4$

$r^4 = 0.55$

$r = 0.861$ or 86.1%

143   A   (Syllabus area C2(d))

If an EV is used as a value in a budget, it represents a weighted average value that may not be expected to occur. If so, comparing actual results against the budget for control purposes would have limited value. The use of expected values and probabilities in budgeting is most useful when there is some, but a limited, amount of uncertainty about the future. When uncertainty is very high, the use of probabilities becomes little more than guesswork.

144   B   (Syllabus area C4(a))

In the Fitzgerald and Moon model, there are three building blocks. Dimensions are the bases for measuring performance, such as financial performance and quality. For each dimension of performance there must be standards or targets for achievement. And there should be a reward system to provide incentives to managers and other employees to achieve the targets or standards.

145   D   (Syllabus area C1(d))

In an article in *Student Accountant* on incremental budgeting and zero based budgeting, ACCA examination team described two reasons why ZBB is often considered more suitable for public sector service organisations than for private sector companies. One is that ZBB is more suited to costs where there is a lot of discretionary spending, as in the public sector services. The second reason is that activities of public sector organisations are more easily definable and so can usually be put into decision packages. (For example the activities of a local authority can be grouped into packages for local housing local education, local refuse collection and waste disposal, and so on.)

146   D   (Syllabus area C2(e))

The advantages of spreadsheets in budgeting include time-saving in preparing figures and the ability to carry out sensitivity analysis by analysing the effect of alterations to the value of key variables. It is also relatively easy to prepare alternative draft budgets or new draft budgets, simply by altering the value of variables in the spreadsheet budget model.

147   C   (Syllabus area C1(d))

If it is difficult to forecast or plan costs and revenues accurately for more than three months ahead, it would be appropriate to prepare new annual budgets every three months, giving most emphasis to the budget for the next three-month period. The disadvantage is that this would require four annual budgets in every 12-month period.

148   B   (Syllabus area C1(d))

$Y = ax^b$

$b = \log 0.75/\log 2 = -0.1249/0.3010 = -0.415$

When $x = 6$, $x^{-0.415} = 1/6^{-0.415} = 0.4754$

Average time for six jobs:

$Y = 5 \times 0.4754 = 2.377$ hours

Total time required for six jobs $= 6 \times 2.377$ hours $= 14.262$ hours

Average time for five jobs: $5 \times 5^{-0.415} = 2.564$ hours

Total time required for five jobs = 5×2.564 hours = 12.820 hours

Time required to perform the 6th job = Total time required for six jobs − Total time required for five jobs.

Therefore, time required to perform the 6th job = 14.262 hours − 12.820 hours = 1.442 hours

CBE style OTQ bank– Budgeting and control

149 (Syllabus area C3(a))

The correct answer is: $1,248 (F)

Standard yield from actual input of materials at standard cost: $19,552

Actual yield at standard materials cost: $20,800

Mix variance (19,552 − 20,800): $1,248 (F)

150 (Syllabus area C4(a))

The correct answers are:

- This standard makes allowances for expected wastage and inefficiencies.
- This standard should give employees a realistic, but challenging target of efficiency.

The least useful and most rarely used type of standard is the basic standard, which is kept unaltered over a long period of time and may be out of date. The standard that is based on perfect operating conditions is the ideal standard which makes no allowances for wastage or inefficiencies.

151 (Syllabus area C2(b))

The correct answer is: $645 (A)

When $Y = ax^b$, $b = \log 0.90 / \log 2 = -0.0457575 / 0.30103 = -0.1520031$

Average labour time for first 49 batches = $2,000 \times 49^{-0.1520031} = 2,000 \times 0.5534584 = 1,106.916731$ hours

Average labour time for first 50 batches = $2,000 \times 50^{-0.1520031} = 2,000 \times 0.5517614 = 1,103.522743$

	Hours
Total labour time for first 50 units ($\times$ 1,103.522743)	55,176.14
Total labour time for first 49 units ($\times$ 1,106.916731)	54,238.92
Labour cost for the 50th batch	937.22

Standard time = 937 hours. Actual time = 980 hours. Labour efficiency variance for this unit = 43 hours (A) $\times$ $15 = $645 (A).

152 (Syllabus area C4(a))

The correct answer is: $880 (F)

	Actual mix kg	Standard mix kg	Mix variance kg	Std price $	Mix variance $
P	820	750	70 (A)	3.0	210 (A)
Q	1,740	1,500	240 (A)	2.5	600 (A)
R	2,300	2,250	50 (A)	4.0	200 (A)
S	2,640	3,000	360 (F)	5.25	1,890 (F)
	7,500	7,500	0		880 (F)

153 (Syllabus area C4(a))

The correct answer is: $1,475 (A)

	Actual sales in	Sales mix		Sales mix

Product	Actual sales	std mix	variance	Std profit	variance
	Units	Units	Units	$	$
X	700	750.0	50.0 (A)	10	500 (A)
Y	1,200	937.5	262.5 (F)	6	1,575 (F)
Z	350	562.5	212.5 (A)	12	2,550 (A)
	2,250	2,250.0	0		1,475 (A)

154   (Syllabus area C3(a))

The correct answers are:

- For standard costing to be useful for control purposes, it requires a reasonably stable environment

- The ethos behind a system of standard costing is that performance is satisfactory if it meets predetermined standards

In a standard costing environment, products or processes must be standardised and repetitive, so that standards can be established for budgeting and control. In a TQM environment, the objective is continuous improvement, which may involve continuous changes in procedures, input quantities and prices. A stable standard is never achieved.

Standard costing assumes that there is a target level of performance and achieving that target represents success. With TQM the view is that performance can be improved continually. There is no 'target'.

155   (Syllabus area C6(c))

The correct answer is: $40 (F)

	Kg
120 units of product should use (× 3.50)	420
They did use	410
Operational usage variance in kg	10 (F)

Operational usage variance in $ (× Standard price per kg $4) = $40 (F)

156   (Syllabus area C5(a))

The correct answer is: $1,325 (A)

	Budgeted sales	Std profit	Budgeted profit
	Units	$ per unit	$
X	800	10	8,000
Y	1,000	6	6,000
Z	600	12	7,200
	2,400		21,200

Weighted average standard profit per unit = $21,200/2,400 = $8.8333

Quantity variance in units = 2,400 − 2,250 = 150 units (A)

Quantity variance in $ (standard profit) = 150 (A) × $8.8333 = $1,325 (A)

157   (Syllabus area C2(b))

The correct answers are:

- Control reports are provided too late
- Targets are not communicated
- Budgets are imposed by senior management

If targets are too easy, they cannot provide an incentive, but they cannot be a disincentive either.

If targets are set at high levels that cannot realistically be achieved, this can be demotivating. Demotivation can also occur if targets are imposed by senior management; or if control reports are provided late so that the manager responsible is unable to take prompt action to deal with problems that may arise.

158 (Syllabus area C8(g))

The correct answers are:

- It is dependent upon a close and mutually beneficial working relationship with suppliers.
- It can result in much reduced inventory holding costs
- It requires suppliers to operate sound quality control procedures

The aim of JIT is to increase efficiency of inventory control systems in order to reduce company costs, principally by minimising inventory levels and thus stockholding costs. This is achieved by using local, reliable suppliers who can deliver goods of the right quality in the right quantity at the right time. The burden of quality control is generally passed back to the supplier to cut costs of the company.

JIT works best when a tied supplier relationship is formed, where the orders form a large part, if not the entirety, of the supplier's business. This precludes the use of many different suppliers. In a JIT system, steps will also be taken to improve customer relations and communications, so that demand can be more accurately determined. This means that reorder levels, and thus safety inventories, can be minimised without necessarily increasing the risks (and thus costs) of stock outs.

159 (Syllabus area C4(a))

The correct answers are:

- There is often no measurable output from service functions.
- The activities of many service functions are of a non-standard nature.

The output of services functions is not as easily measurable as it is with goods which are physically manufactured. This makes it difficult to establish standard unit rates, because there are no easily available standard times or usages.

160 (Syllabus area C4(a))

The correct answer is:

- The quantity of work achievable at standard performance in an hour

161 (Syllabus area C4(a))

The correct answer is: Rolling budget.

If it is difficult to forecast or plan costs and revenues accurately for more than two or three months ahead, it would be appropriate to prepare new annual budgets every two or three months, giving most emphasis to the budget for the next three-month period. The disadvantage is that this would require four or six annual budgets in every 12-month period.

162 (Syllabus area C4(a))

The correct answer is: A standard which can be attained if production is carried out efficiently, machines are operated properly and/or materials are used properly. Some allowance is made for waste and inefficiencies.

Attainable standards may provide an incentive to work harder as they represent a realistic but challenging target of efficiency

163 (Syllabus area C4(a))

The correct answer is: Current standard.

Budgeted capacity is associated with current standards. Budgeted capacity is not associated with basic standards. Practical capacity is associated with attainable standards.

Full capacity is associated with ideal standards.

Crush Co

164 B **The correct answer is: 565.6 hours**

Cumulative average time per batch for the first 64 batches

$Y = ax^b$

Where Y = the cumulative average time per unit to produce x units
       x = the cumulative number of units
       a = the time taken for the first unit of output
       b = the index of learning (logLR/log2)

The cumulative average time per batch, with a learning curve of 85% is therefore

$Y = aX^{-0.2345}$

where a = the time for the first batch (1,500 hours) and X is the number of the batch. For the 64th batch, X = 64.

$Y = 1,500 \times 64^{-0.2345}$

$= 1,500 \times 0.37709 = 565.6$

The cumulative average time per batch for the first 64 batches is 565.6 hours.

165 C

Batches	Total time	Average time/unit
1	1,500	1,500
2		1,500 × r
4		1,500 × r2
8		1,500 × r3
16	9,000	1,500 × r4

$9,000 = 16 \times 1,500\ r^4$

$9,000/(16 \times 1,500) = r^4$

$r = 0.78$ or 78%

166 A Decisions about allocating resources and costing of the new product should be based on the time taken to produce the 64th batch because this is when the learning effect stops. After this point, the product will reach a point of steady state production. Using information regarding labour costs from a point prior to steady state level will result in too high a price being assigned to labour costs. The learning process starts when the first batch comes off the production line.

167 D Statement 1 is one of the main assumptions of the learning effect. Employees must have some motivation to improve and learn, otherwise the learning effect will not appear. The second statement is also true.

168 D A, B, and C are all conditions which allow the learning curve to flourish.

BBB Co

169 B **The correct answer is: 330.75 hours**

Cumulative average time per batch for the first 71 batches

$Y = ax^b$

Where Y = the cumulative average time per unit to produce x units
       x = the cumulative number of units
       a = the time taken for the first unit of output
       b = the index of learning (logLR/log2)

The cumulative average time per batch, with a learning curve of 90% is therefore

$Y = aX^{-0.152}$

where a = the time for the first batch (750 hours) and X is the number of the batch. For the 71st batch, X = 71.

$Y = 750 \times 71^{-0.152}$

$= 750 \times 0.5231 = 392.35$

The cumulative average time per batch for the first 71 batches is 392.35 hours.

Time taken for the 71st batch

The cumulative average time per batch for the first 70 batches is $Y = 750 \times 70^{-0.152}$

$= 750 \times 0.5243 = 393.23$

	Hours
Total time for 1st 71 batches (71 × 392.35)	27,856.85
Total time for 1st 70 batches (70 × 393.23)	27,526.10
Time for the 71st batch	330.75

170   **A**

Batches	Total time	Average time/unit
1	750	750
2		750 × r
4		750 × r2
8		750 × r3
16	8,500	750 × r4

$8,500 = 16 \times 750\ r^4$

$8,500/(16 \times 750) = r^4$

r = 0.92 or 92%

171   **C**   The learning curve will eventually come to an end in all cases.

The use of learning curve is not restricted to the manufacturing industries that it is traditionally associated with. It is also used in other less traditional sectors such as professional practice, financial services, publishing and travel.

172   **B**   The learning effect leads to a reduction in labour hours per batch, which therefore lowers the labour costs. The other factors are not affected by the learning rate.

173   **B**   Increasing staff training could lead to an extension of the learning curve as the higher skilled employees should demonstrate an even greater improvement than if they were not trained.

Ash Co

174   **A**   **$28.75 (F)**

Usage variance

	Std usage for actual output of 50 units 'Should have used' Kg	Actual usage 'Did use' Kg	Variance Kg	Standard cost per kg $	Variance $
A	100	110	10 (A)	1.50	15.00 (A)
B	250	225	25 (F)	1.75	43.75 (F)
	350	335			28.75 (F)

175 **C** **$3.57 (F)**

Mix variance

		Actual usage	Act total usage in standard mix	Mix Variance	Standard price per kg	Mix variance
		Kg	kg	kg	$	$
A		110	95.71	14.29 (A)	1.50	21.44 (A)
B		225	239.29	14.29 (F)	1.75	25.01 (F)
		335	335.00			3.57 (F)

176 **B** **$25.15 (F)**

Yield variance

	Units
335 kg of material should produce (÷ 7)	47.86
They did produce	50
Yield variance in units of output	2.14 (F)
Standard material cost per unit	$11.75
Yield variance in $	$25.15 (F)

177 **D** **1, 2 and 3**

Each of the factors outlined above may lead to an adverse material usage for Ash Co.

178 **B** The production manager in Ash Co deviates from the standard mix

Distractors:

A   This may lead to the production manager deviating from the standard mix, however, it will not lead directly to a mix variance.

C   This may influence the behaviour of the production manager, eg if the price has to be lowered, and cost savings made, so the mix may be reviewed. However, it will not lead directly to a mix variance.

D   This may lead to a yield variance, however, it will not lead to a mix variance, unless the use of the inferior material forces the manager to alter the mix, perhaps due to how the inferior material reacts in production.

Birch Co

179 **C** **$3,750 (A)**

The sales volume planning variance compares the revised budget with the original budget. It may be called a market size variance.

Revised sales volume	17,500 units
Original budgeted sales volume	20,000 units
Sales volume planning variance in units of sales	2,500 units (A)
× standard contribution per unit	$1.5
Sales volume planning variance in $	3,750 (A)

180 **B** **$2,250 (A)**

The operational variance is calculated in a similar way to the planning variance, except that actual results are compared with the revised standard or budget.

Actual sales volume	16,000 units
Revised sales volume	17,500 units
Operational sales volume variance in units	1,500 units (A)
× standard contribution per unit	$1.5
Operational sales volume variance in $ contribution	2,250 (A)

181 **A** **$440 (A)**

Fixed production overhead total variance:

Units produced × standard fixed costs per unit – actual cost

[18,000 × ($3,000/17,500 units)] – $3,500
[18,000 × ($3,000/17,500 units)] – $3,500
[18,000 × 0.17] – $3,500
$3,060 – $3,500
=$440 (A)

182 **C** An improvement in technology led to an international reduction in sales price of Product X.

The improvement in technology is outside the control of the managers in Birch Co, and would therefore give rise to a planning variance. All of the other distractors are examples of operational issues.

183 **B** The sales volume operational variance

A sales volume operational variance, or market share variance is caused by the difference between actual sales volume and the sales volume in the revised budget.

Elm Co

184 The correct answer is $44,000 F

Planning (selling price) variance

	$ per unit
Original budgeted sales price	8
Revised budgeted sales price	10
Sales price planning variance	2 (F)
× actual units sold	22,000
Planning variance for sales price	44,000 (F)

185 The correct answer is $22,000 (A)

Operational (selling price) variance

	$
Actual sales revenue	198,000
Should have sold for (× $10)	220,000
Operational (selling price) variance	**22,000 (A)**

186 The correct answer is $13,000 (A)

Labour rate variance

	$
4,000 hours should have cost (× $15)	60,000
But did cost	73,000
Labour rate variance	**13,000 (A)**

187 The correct answer is 2 only.

The first statement is false because operational variances are the only variances within the control of the managers, so performance must be assessed with only operational variances in mind.

The second statement is true. One might question the validity of the revised price. The person responsible for the revised price should have sufficient evidence to support setting the revised price at that level to ensure that there is no manipulation of figures.

188 The correct answer is: Neither 1 nor 2

An operational manager cannot appraise variances in isolation from each other. A favourable material price variance from using lower quality material may result in a much larger adverse usage variance, reaching the overall conclusion that the performance is poor.

Statement 2 is false because a change in the economic circumstances in Sealand is clearly outside of the control of the managers of Elm Co and will therefore not result in operational variances.

Maple Co

The original standard cost was 2.5 kg × $4 = $10. The revised standard cost is 4 kg × $5.50 = $22.

189 **The correct answer is: $22,000 (A)**

Material price planning variance

This is the difference between the original standard price for Material X and the revised standard price.

	$ per kg
Original standard price	4
Revised standard price	5
Material price planning variance	1 (A)
× Actual quantity of material used (22,000 kg)	$22,000 (A)

190 **The correct answer is: $13,000 (A)**

Material price operational variance

This compares the actual price per kg of material with the revised standard price. It is calculated using the actual quantity of materials used.

	$
22,000 kg of Material X should cost (revised standard $5)	110,000
They did cost	123,000
Material price operational variance	13,000 (A)

191 **The correct answer is: $8,000 (A)**

Material usage operational variance

This variance is calculated by comparing the actual material usage with the standard usage in the revised standard, but is then converted into a monetary value by applying the original standard price for the materials, not the revised standard price.

	kg of X
8,000 units of Bark should use (× 2.5kg)	20,000
They did use	22,000
Material usage (operational) variance in kg of X	2,000 (A)
Original standard price per kg of Material X	$4
Material usage (operational) variance in $	$8,000 (A)

192 2 only

Statement 1 is an example of a controllable variance, and would therefore give rise to an operational variance. The second statement is outside the control of management and is therefore a planning variance.

193 1 only

Operational variances compare actual performance with a realistic standard cost or budget, and so should provide a realistic reflection of what the causes of the variances have cost Maple Co.

Planning variances are not the responsibility of operational managers, therefore there is no need for operational managers to immediately investigate their causes. However, their causes could be investigated by someone in Maple Co, since lessons may be learned for the future.

Pine Co

194   The correct answer is $24,300 (F)

Labour rate planning variance

This is the difference between the original standard rate per hour and the revised standard rate per hour.

	$ per hour
Original standard rate	15
Revised standard rate	14
Labour rate planning variance	1 (F)
× actual no of hours worked	24,300
	24,300 (F)

195   The correct answer is $180,000 (A)

Labour efficiency planning variance

This is the difference between the original standard time per unit and the revised standard time for the quantity of units produced.

	Hours
8,000 units of product should take: original standard (× 3)	24,000
8,000 units of product should take: revised standard (× 4.5)	36,000
Labour efficiency planning variance in hours	12,000 (A)
Original standard rate per hour	$15
Labour efficiency planning variance in $	$180,000 (A)

196   The correct answer is: $12,150 (A)

Labour rate operational variance

This is calculated using the actual number of hours worked and paid for.

	$
24,300 hours should cost (revised standard $14)	340,200
They did cost	352,350
Labour rate operational variance	12,150 (A)

197   The correct answer is: $175,500 (F)

Labour efficiency operational variance

	Hours
8,000 units of product should take (× 4.5 hours)	36,000
They did take	24,300
Labour efficiency (operational variance in hours)	11,700 (F)
Original standard rate per hour	$15
Labour efficiency (operational variance in $)	$175,500 (F)

198   1 only

The second statement is false. It is operational variances which provide a more realistic and fair reflection of actual performance since these are within the control of management.

199 Mic Co

Marking scheme

			Marks
(a)	Cost each month: July and August (1.5 mark per month)	3	
	Cost each month: September and October (1.5 marks per month)	3	
	Cost in November	3	
			9
(b)	**End of learning period**		
	Each point discussed -maximum	2	
	Maximum		4
(c)	**Advantages and disadvantages**		
	Each advantage	1	
	Each disadvantage	1	
	Maximum		7
	Total marks		20

(a) Every time output doubles, the average time per batch is 88% of what it was previously. The learning curve effect ends in October and does not apply in November, when the average time per unit is the same as the time required to make the eighth batch in October.

Month	Cumulative batches	Average time per batch Hours	Total time Hours	Incremental time in the month Hours	Labour cost per month at $12 per hour $
July	1	200.00	200.00	200.00	2,400
August	2	176.00	352.00	152.00	1,824
September	4	154.88	619.52	267.52	3,210
October	8	136.294	1,090.35	470.83	5,650

Average time to produce first 7 batches = $200 \times 7 -0.1844245 = 200 \times 1/1.4317157 = 139.6925$ hours

Total time for first 7 batches = $7 \times 139.6925 = 977.85$ hours

Average time to produce first 8 batches = $200 \times 8 -0.1844245 = 200 \times 1/1.4674115 = 136.2944$ hours

Total time for first 8 batches = $8 \times 136.2944 = 1,090.35$ hours

Time to make the 8th batch = $1,090.35 - 977.85 = 112.50$ hours

Total labour cost in November = 8 batches × 112.50 per batch × $12 per hour = $10,800.

(b)   The company sets selling prices on a cost plus basis, but in the first few months the cost per unit falls due to the 88% learning curve effect. The average time per batch was 200 hours for the first batch in July, but falls to 112.5 hours per batch from November onwards.

If cost plus pricing is used, and if the company wants to charge a stable price for its product, it should consider a cost plus price based on the longer-term unit cost from November onwards.

The company appears to have used actual cost plus to set the selling price on its initial batches, with the result that the price was high. This probably explains the disappointing initial sales.

Budgeting for labour time and labour costs should also take the learning curve into effect, because of the reduction in incremental labour time per batch in the months July – October.

(c)   Involving senior staff at Mic Co in the budget setting process

Advantages

- Since they are based on information from staff who are most familiar with the department, they are more likely to improve the accuracy of the budget. In Mic Co's case, the selling price could have been set more accurately and sales may have been higher if the production manager had been consulted.

- Staff are more likely to be motivated to achieve any targets as it is 'their' budget and they therefore have a sense of ownership and commitment. The production manager at Mic Co seems resigned to the fact that he is not consulted on budgetary matters.

- Morale amongst staff is likely to improve as they feel that their experience and opinions are valued.

- Knowledge from a spread of several levels of management is pooled.

- Co-ordination is improved due to the number of departments involved in the budget setting process.

Disadvantages

- The whole budgeting process is more time consuming and therefore costly.

- The budgeting process may have to be started earlier than a non-participative budget would need to start because of the length of time it takes to complete the process

200 ZBB

Marks

(a) Explanation:

Difficulty setting objectives quantifiably	2
Difficulty in saying how to achieve them	1
Outputs difficult to measure	2
No relationship between inputs and outputs	2
Value for money issue	2

max 5

(b) Incremental and zero-based budgeting:

Explaining 'incremental budgeting'	2
Explaining 'zero-based budgeting'	2

4

(c) Stages involved in zero-based budgeting:

1 mark per stage	3

(d)

Any disadvantage of incremental budgeting that supports the statement	1
Incremental budgeting is quick and easy	1
Any disadvantage of ZBB that refutes the statement	1
Easier to define decision packages in public sector	2
More appropriate for discretionary costs	2
Conclusion	1

8

20

(a) **Difficulties when budgeting in the public sector**

The main objective for most companies is to **maximise profit**. Effective budgeting can assist in meeting this objective by focussing efforts on reducing certain costs and increasing revenues by a certain amount or percentage. The **objectives of public sector organisations** are more **difficult to define in a quantifiable way**.

The **objectives of public sector organisations** such as hospitals are likely to **be largely qualitative**. For example, ensuring that ambulances reach patients within 20 minutes from an emergency call being received. Such objectives are difficult to define in a quantifiable way, whilst identifying how the objective is actually achieved can also be problematic.

Another problem why budgeting is so difficult in public sector organisations is that outputs in the public sector can seldom be measured in a way that is generally agreed to be meaningful. Whilst outputs for private companies can be measured in terms of sales revenue, outputs in the public sector are harder to pin down. For example in the education sector, are good exam results alone an adequate measure of the quality of teaching? In the public sector, **comparisons are often made between the funds available and the funds actually required**. Therefore, public sector budgeting naturally focuses on inputs, rather than the relationship between inputs and outputs.

Public sector organisations are under constant pressure to prove that they are economical, efficient and effective (offering value for money). **Resources are always kept to a minimum and each item of expenditure must be justified**. This makes the budgeting process more difficult.

(b) **Incremental budgeting**

Incremental budgeting **bases the budget on the current year's results plus an extra amount for estimated growth or inflation next year**. This form of budgeting is a reasonable procedure if current operations are as effective, efficient and economical as they can be. **Zero-based budgeting (ZBB)**

ZBB rejects the assumption that underpins the concept of incremental budgeting; that next year's budget can be based on this year's costs plus an extra amount for estimated growth or inflation. ZBB involves **preparing a budget for each cost centre from a zero base**. Every item of **expenditure must be justified** in its entirety in order to be included in next year's budget.

(c) **Stages in zero-based budgeting**

ZBB involves three main stages.

Define activities (decision packages)

At the first stage, management identify the **key activities** within the organisation. These activities are described within a decision package. The decision package is originally **prepared at a base level** which shows the minimum level of resource required to meet the organisations objectives. **Incremental packages** may be prepared to show any **additional work** that could be done, at what cost and for what benefit.

Evaluate and rank each activity

Management will then rank each activity (decision package) on the basis of its benefit to the organisation. Minimum work requirements (those that are essential to get the job done) will be given high priority and so too will work which meets legal obligations. This process will **help management to decide what to spend and where to spend it**.

Allocate resources

At the final stage, management allocate resources in the budget **according to the funds available and the evaluation and ranking of the competing packages**.

(d) **No longer a place for incremental budgeting and the drawbacks of ZBB**

Incremental budgeting can encourage **slack** and **wasteful spending** as past inefficiencies are perpetuated because cost levels are rarely subjected to close scrutiny. However, the view that there is no longer a place for it in any organisation is rather misleading. Whilst inappropriate for public sector organisations where all expenditure must be justified, to say that it is of no use in any organisation effectively ignores the limitations of zero-based budgeting (ZBB). These limitations are analysed below.

The limitations of ZBB

The major limitation of ZBB is the volume of **extra paperwork** created. Assumptions about costs and benefits in each package must be continually updated and new packages must be developed as new activities occur within the organisation.

ZBB is likely to require **management skills both in constructing decision packages and in the ranking process**. If management do not possess such skills they will require training in ZBB techniques which takes time and money.

The ranking process can also prove problematic. It can be difficult **to rank packages which appear to be equally vital**, for legal or operational reasons. Furthermore, it is difficult to rank activities which have **qualitative rather than quantitative benefits**.

ZBB can **give the impression that all decisions have to be made in the budget**. As a result, management may feel unable to carry out new ideas because they were not approved by a decision package and did not pass through the ranking process.

ZBB in practice

As all costs need to justified under a ZBB system, it would seem inappropriate to use it as the sole system within a private sector organisation where **certain costs will always be incurred in order to meet basic production requirements**. In such a scenario, incremental budgeting is likely to prove more efficient as it is quick and easily understood.

ZBB could be considered more **appropriate for public sector organisations**. The majority of costs in such organisations are **discretionary** and emphasis is placed on obtaining **value for money**. This objective is directly linked to the decision package ranking process within a ZBB system. Furthermore, it is easier to put activities into decision packages in organisations which undertake a number of set definable activities. Hospitals for example have set activities including outpatient wards, children's wards and A&E departments.

Conclusion

Whilst ZBB is more suitable for public sector organisations particularly in the current economic climate, its limitations should not be overlooked. Incremental budgeting can still be of use to organisations.

201 Designit

Text reference. Budgetary systems are covered in Chapter 9. The use of spreadsheets in budgeting is covered in Chapter 10.

Top tips. There are easy marks available throughout this question so ensure you allocate enough time to each requirement. Refer to the scenario throughout your answer and, as a guide, aim for 1 mark per well explained point.

Easy marks. You should be able to score well in part (a) by briefly explaining what a rolling budget is and how it would operate in Designit.

			Marks
(a)	Explanation:		
	Updated after one month elapsed	1	
	Always 12 months	1	
	Example given	1	
	First month in detail	1	
	Later month less detail	1	
	Need to revisit earlier months	1	
			max 4
(b)	Problems:		
	More time	1	
	Lack of experience	1	
	Too regular	2	
	Managers' resistance	2	
	Work harder	1	
	Holding back work	2	
			max 6
(c)	Simpler incentive scheme:		
	Current target too easy	1	
	Second target too hard	1	
	Other valid point re current scheme	1	
	New scheme outlined	3	
			6
(d)	Using spreadsheets:		
	Errors entering data	1	
	Rolling budgets more complex	1	
	Formulae may be wrong	1	
	Corruption of model	1	
	No audit trail	1	
			max 4
			20

(a)   **Rolling budget**

A **monthly rolling** budget is a budget which is **continuously updated** by adding a further month when the earliest month has passed.

For example, Designit would begin by preparing a 12-month budget covering the period 1 December 20X2 to 30 November 20X3. At the end of December 20X2, a budget for December 20X3 would be prepared, so that the **unexpired period covered by the budget is always 12 months**.

When the budget is initially prepared for the year ending 30 November 20X3, the budget for December 20X2 (the first month in the budget) should be prepared in detail. The later months will contain a lot **less detail** as there will be greater uncertainty regarding **internal resources** and **market conditions**.

When the budget for December 20X2 has elapsed and the budget for December 20X3 is prepared, the budget for January 20X3 should be **revised in greater detail**.

(b)   **Problems**

Monthly rolling budgets **take time to prepare** and can be **complex**. The company's accounts department consists of a single part-qualified accountant who already has a **heavy workload**. As such it is unlikely that he has the **time or experience** required to successfully implement a system of monthly rolling budgets.

Rolling budgets are best suited to organisations that operate in **rapidly-changing environments**. Designit is a **mature business and trading is fairly stable** year on year. A rolling budget updated on a **quarterly basis** (as opposed to a monthly basis) would probably be sufficient.

A monthly rolling budget will require **input from many staff**, reducing the time they have to dedicate to other tasks.

Sales managers are unlikely to embrace the new budgeting and incentive system. They will have become accustomed to **knowing their target for the whole year in advance** and will **be used to working to targets that are easily achievable**.

Under the proposed system sales managers may hold back work once they have achieved their monthly target and let it run into the following month to increase their chances of meeting next month's target. This is **not in the best interests of the business**.

(c)   **Problems with the current bonus scheme**

The current bonus scheme consists of **two targets**. The first target ($1.5m of fee income) is **too easily reached** whilst the second target (a further $1.5m of fee income) appears **unrealistic** and has not been achieved by any of the sales managers.

Due to the above, sales managers are **not motivated to earn additional fees** once they have reached the first target of $1.5m.

Alternative bonus scheme

The company is currently paying each sales manager a bonus of $30,000 each year (20% of $150,000). This is 2% of $1.5m. Changing the bonus to **2% commission on all sales** as opposed to a percentage of salary would motivate the sales managers to bring in fees throughout the year.

Alternatively, the company may consider **revising the current bonus scheme** to include smaller bonuses paid out at more regular intervals. For example, a bonus equivalent to 5% of salary for every $500,000 of fee income.

(d)   **Using the company accountant's own spreadsheets for budgeting**

The company should ensure that the accountant has the **necessary skills** to operate the budget spreadsheet. Even a minor error in the design of a budgeting model can **affect the validity of data throughout the spreadsheet**.

Even if the accountant does have the necessary skills, he is likely to have **to input large amounts of data** from the company's systems into the spreadsheet. The **opportunity for error is high**, especially if nobody is available to check his work.

It is **very easy to corrupt a model** by accidentally changing a cell or inputting data in the wrong place. The accountant is unlikely to spot this due to his **lack of experience** and the **time pressure** on him.

Finally, when data is input from a company's system into a spreadsheet, the **audit trail is lost**. This can make it difficult to trace/check the numbers.

202 Crumbly Cakes

Text references. Variance analysis is covered in Chapters 12 and 13.

Top tips. You may find part (a) quite tricky. You need to plan a structured answer using the headings suggested by the question. Make some sensible, common sense suggestions and if you run out of ideas, move on to parts (b) and (c) where easier marks are available. Read the information very carefully and layout your workings clearly.

Easy marks. There are some easy variance calculations in parts (b) and (c) as well as some trickier mix and yield variances.

Examiner's comments. Many candidates completely missed the point in part (a). If a business fundamentally changes its business process without altering the standard costs of the process, it renders the variances that are produced meaningless. Some candidates tried to discuss each variance in turn rather than carry out a performance assessment of each manager. This is not as effective a method. Motivation is a complex topic and credit was given for any sensible comments.

Part (b) was well done with many candidates scoring good marks.

Marking scheme

			Marks
(a)	Production manager assessment	2	
	Sales manager assessment	2	
	Bonus scheme comment	3	
			7
(b)	Price variance	3	
	Mix variance	3	
	Yield variance	3	
			9
(c)	Planning variance and comment	2	
	Operational variance and comment	2	
			4
			20

(a)   Production manager

The production manager instigated the new organic cake production approach and this has **fundamentally changed** the nature of the business. Before the new system started, there were **favourable material variances** for price and yield and the production manager would have received a bonus as a result.

Organic ingredients are **more expensive** and this results in **adverse** material price and mix variances in March. The **material yield** variance is favourable but not by enough to compensate for the adverse variances. This means that the production manager would not receive a bonus under the current scheme.

Sales of the cakes have improved significantly so customers presumably appreciate the new flavour and mix of ingredients. The production manager does not receive any credit for the favourable sales variances and that does not seem fair.

Sales manager

In contrast, the **sales variances** that the sales manager is responsible for have moved from adverse in February to favourable in March. The new organic approach has therefore been a **success** with customers. The sales manager will have had to sell the new organic cakes to customers and is therefore **partly responsible** for the improvement, but the original impetus came from the production manager.

Bonus scheme

The bonus scheme does not seem to be fair as it will **not reward** the two managers fairly for their efforts. They are both responsible for the improved sales but it is very difficult to **fairly allocate responsibility** in this situation. Some form of **sharing** of responsibility and reward is required.

The **standards** that the variances are based on need to be changed to reflect the new approach that the business is taking. For example, the standard price of the materials needs to be increased.

(b) **Material price variances**

	$
5,700 kg of flour should have cost (× $0.12)	684
but did cost	741
Material price variance	57 (A)

	$
6,600 kg of eggs should have cost (× $0.70)	4,620
but did cost	5,610
Material price variance	990 (A)

	$
6,600 kg of butter should have cost (× $1.70)	11,220
but did cost	11,880
Material price variance	660 (A)

	$
4,578 kg of sugar should have cost (× $0.50)	2,289
but did cost	2,747
Material price variance	458 (A)

	$
Total material price variance	2,165 (A)

Material mix variances

Total quantity used = 5,700 + 6,600 + 6,600 + 4,578 = 23,478 kg
Standard mix of actual use of each ingredient is in equal proportions = 23,478/4 = 5,869.5 kg

	Actual quantity Actual mix Kg	Actual quantity Standard mix Kg	Variance Kg	Standard cost per kg $	Variance $
Flour	5,700	5869.5	169.5 (F)	0.12	20.34 (F)
Eggs	6,600	5869.5	730.5 (A)	0.70	511.35 (A)
Butter	6,600	5869.5	730.5 (A)	1.70	1,241.85 (A)
Sugar	4,578	5869.5	1,291.5 (F)	0.50	645.75 (F)
	23,478	23,478			1,087.11 (A)

Material yield variance

Standard cost of a cake

		$
Flour	0.1 kg × $0.12	0.012
Eggs	0.1 kg × $0.70	0.070
Butter	0.1 kg × $1.70	0.170
Sugar	0.1 kg × $0.50	0.050
		0.302

	Cakes
The actual quantity of inputs are expected to yield (23,478/0.4)	58,695
Actual output	60,000
Yield variance in cakes	1,305 (F)
× standard cost per cake ($0.302)	$394.11 (F)

Alternative method

	Standard quantity Standard mix Kg	Actual quantity Standard mix Kg	Variance Kg	Standard cost per kg $	Variance $
Flour	6,000	5869.5	130.5	0.12	15.66
Eggs	6,000	5869.5	130.5	0.70	91.35
Butter	6,000	5869.5	130.5	1.70	221.85
Sugar	6,000	5869.5	130.5	0.50	65.25
	24,000	23,478			394.11 (A)

(c) **Total operational variance**

	$
Revised standard cost of actual production (60,000 × $0.40)	24,000
Actual cost	20,978
Total operational variance	3,022 (F)

The variance is **favourable** because the actual cost was lower than the expected cost using the revised basis.

Total planning variance

	$
Revised standard cost (60,000 × $0.40)	24,000
Original standard cost (60,000 × $0.302)	18,120
Total planning variance	5,880 (A)

The planning variance reveals the extent to which the original standard was at fault. It is an **adverse variance** because the original standard was too optimistic, overestimating the expected profits by understating the standard cost. More simply, it is adverse because the revised standard cost is much higher than the original standard cost.

203 Secure Net

Text reference. Planning and operational variances are covered in Chapter 13.

Top tips. Part (a) should not cause any problems. In part (b) ACCA examination team has stated that any methods applied consistently would score full marks. This answer shows the BPP approach and the approach used in the article previously written by ACCA examination team. If you get stuck on the details of which numbers to use where, makeFsy an attempt at something sensible and move on.

Part (c) is a straightforward discussion of the production manager's performance. Even if you struggled with the calculations in part (b), you should be able to pick up on the clues given in the scenario for factors that would have been controllable and uncontrollable.

Easy marks. Part (a) should be an easy 4 marks and there are easy marks available in part (c) just from describing factors in the scenario.

Marking scheme

			Marks
(a)	Behavioural problems with standard costing – 1 mark per point	Max 2	
	Ways to reduce problems – ½ mark per point	Max 2	
			4
(b)	Planning price variance	2	
	Planning usage variance	2	
	Operational price variance	2	
	Operational usage variance	2	
			8
(c)	Explanation of external problems beyond control of manager	4	
	Assessment of factors within the control of the manager	4	
	Conclusion	1	
	Maximum		8
			20

(a) **Behavioural problems that may arise from using standard costs**

Standard costing is principally used to value inventories, to prepare budgets and to act as a **control device**. The focus in using a standard cost system should not be to attribute blame, but to influence behaviour through **positive support** and **appropriate motivation**.

The perception of a standard costing system can affect its success or failure. A **negative perception** is often the consequence of unreasonable standards, lack of transparency in setting standards, poor communication or uneven reward systems. Such situations can make a good standard cost system a failure.

Ways to reduce negative perceptions / motivation

Organisations should set **understandable** and **achievable** standards, otherwise it neither motivates nor rewards employees. Complex financial measures and reports mean nothing to most employees.

Employees should be **involved** in setting standards and developing performance measures. This should result in realistic targets and increase **employee motivation**.

Standards should be **well defined** and **communicated** to all employees so that operational efficiency can be achieved. Management should ensure that any performance-related scheme does not reward behaviour that goes against the best interests of the organisation.

Finally, **performance pay plans** should be **reviewed and updated** on a regular basis to meet the changing needs of employees and the business as a whole.

(b) **Total materials planning variance**

		$
Original flexed budget cost	(100,000 × $4 × 0.04kgs)	16,000
Revised flexed budget cost	(100,000 × $4.80 × 0.042kgs)	20,160
		4,160 (A)

BPP
LEARNING MEDIA

Planning price variance

Actual units × revised standard usage × (original standard price – revised standard price)

= 100,000 units × 0.042 kgs × ($4.00 – $4.80) = $3,360 (A)

Planning usage variance

Actual units × original standard price × (original standard usage – revised standard usage)

= 100,000 units × $4.00 × (0.04 kgs – 0.042 kgs) = $800 (A)

Planning price variance + planning usage variance = total planning variance

$3,360 + $800 = $4,160 (A)

Total materials operational variance

	$
Actual cost (for 100,000 units)	18,375
Revised standard cost (for 100,000 units) (0.042 kgs × $4.80)	20,160
Total operational variance	1,785 (F)

Operational price variance

	$
Actual price of actual materials (3,500 kg)	18,375
Revised standard price of actual materials ($4.80 × 3,500 kg)	16,800
Operational price variance	1,575 (A)

Operational usage variance

Actual quantity should have been	4,200 kgs
but was	3,500 kgs
Operational usage variance in kgs	700 kgs (F)
× revised standard cost per kg	× $4.80
Operational usage variance in $	$3,360 (F)

(c)   **Worldwide standard size**

The size of the security card has to fit the reader of that card and if the **industry specification changes** there is nothing that the production manager can do about it. This is **beyond his control** and therefore a planning error and should not be used to assess his performance.

Oil prices

World-wide oil prices have increased which have **increased plastic prices** and again the production manager **cannot control** that. This is another planning error and should be ignored in an assessment of his performance.

New supplier

The decision to use a new supplier cost an extra $1,575 which is the **operational price variance** and could be regarded as **poor performance** by the production manager. However, the manager seems to have agreed to the higher price on the promise of **better quality** and **reliability**.

The **operational usage variance** is $3,360 favourable and this could be as a result of improved quality.

Increase in production and sales

Production levels increased significantly from 60,000 to 100,000 which could potentially have caused problems for the production manager. However, the ability to increase production suggests that the new supplier's reliability was good.

The total materials operational variance shows a favourable variance of $1,785 which reflects well on the performance of the production manager. The ability to react and be flexible can often form a part of a performance assessment.

In **conclusion** the manager could be said to have performed well.

204 Noble

Marking scheme

		Marks
(a)	Flexed budget:	
	Food sales	1
	Drink sales	1
	Total revenue	1
	Staff wages	1½
	Food costs	1
	Drink costs	1
	Energy costs	1½
	Variable costs total	1
	Contribution	1
	Manager's and chef's pay	½
	Rent & rates	½
	Operating profit	1
		12
(b)	Explanation of variances	2
	Suggestions of reason for variances	2
		4
(c)	Discussion of variance 1	Max 2
	Discussion of variance 2	Max 2
		4
		20

(a) **Flexed budget**

Number of meals	1,560	
	$	$
Revenue:		
Food sales (W1)	62,400	
Drink sales (W1)	15,600	
		78,000
Variable costs:		
Staff wages (W2)	(12,672)	
Food costs (W3)	(7,800)	
Drink costs (W4)	(3,120)	
Energy costs (W5)	(4,234)	
		(27,826)
Contribution		50,174
Fixed costs:		
Manager's and chef's pay	(8,600)	
Rent, rates and depreciations	(4,500)	
		(13,100)
Operating profit		37,074

Workings

1   *Revenue*
Food revenue = 1,560 × (($45 + $35)/2) = $62,400
Drinks revenue = 1,560 × ($2.50 × 4) = $15,600

2   *Staff wages*
Average number of orders per day = 1,560/(6 days × 4 weeks) = 65 orders per day
Therefore extra orders = 15 per day (65 – 50). 15/5 = 3 therefore, 3 × 0.5 hours (1.5 hours) of overtime must be paid.
8 staff × 1.5 hours × 6 days × 4 weeks = 288 extra hours
Extra wages = 288 extra hours × $12 = $3,456 extra wages
Total flexed wages = $9,216 + $3,456 = $12,672

3   *Food costs*
Food costs = 12.5% × $62,400 = $7,800

4   *Drink costs*
Drink costs = 20% × $15,600 = $3,120

5   *Energy costs*
Standard total hours worked = (8 staff × 6 hours) × 6 days × 4 weeks = 1,152 hours
Extra hours worked = 288 (W2)
Total hours = 1,152 + 288 = 1,440
Total energy costs = 1,440 hours × $2.94 per hour = $4,234

(b) **Sales mix contribution variance**

The sales mix contribution variance measures the effect on profit when the proportions of products sold are different from those in the standard mix.

The sales mix variance is adverse. Meal B generates a higher contribution than meal A. This means that more of meal A must have been sold, relative to meal B, than budgeted.

Sales quantity contribution variance

The sales quantity contribution variance shows the difference in contribution/profit because of a change in sales volume from the budgeted number of sales.

The sales quantity variance is favourable. This means that the total number of meals sold (in the standard mix) was higher than expected. Indeed, 1,560 meals were sold (budget was 1,200 meals).

(c)   **Food sales**

The half-price drinks promotion has attracted more customers to the restaurant. Calculating variances such as the sales volume variance for food sales would help to show how the promotion on drinks has impacted upon the number of meals sold.

Drink sales

The sales volume variance could also be calculated for drinks sales. This will compare the standard number of drinks sold (1,560 × 4 drinks) to the actual number of drinks sold as a result of the drinks promotion (1,560 × 6 drinks). The sales volume variance will be favourable as the variance is calculated by applying the increase in volume to the standard margin per unit.

The restaurant manager should only be held accountable for matters within his control. As such, the total sales margin price variance could be split into a planning and an operational variance.

The restaurant manager is only accountable for any operational variance and should not be held accountable for any part of the sales margin price variance that relates to bad planning.

Part D answers

MCQ bank – Performance measurement and control

205 D (Syllabus area D5(b))

Internal transfers should be preferred to external purchases because the company will have better control over output quality from Division A and the scheduling of production and deliveries. Transfer prices determine how total profit will be shared between the divisions.

206 C (Syllabus area D6(a))

Not-for-profit organisations do have financial objectives, which may sometimes be described as financial constraints. For example a charity organisation may want to maximise its funding and a government department may seek to carry out its activities within the spending budget for the department.

The outputs produced by commercial organisations can be measured simply by profit, which is a measure of the value created by the organisation in a period. Outputs of not-for-profit organisations cannot be measured as easily because they often have many different objectives, each measured in different ways.

207 B (Syllabus area D5(d))

Gross profit ignores other expenses other than cost of sales. Profit before tax and profit after tax are after deducting items that do not relate to divisional performance (costs of interest on company debt and tax charges). Profit before interest and tax is the most appropriate measure of the four, and it will often be the same as operating profit.

208 D (Syllabus area D6(b))

Adherence to appointment times means starting an appointment at the scheduled time. One suitable measure might be the percentage of appointments that begin late more than a certain amount of time, say 15 minutes. Of the performance measurements in the question, average waiting time on the appointment date would be the most appropriate.

209 C (Syllabus area D3(b))

Passwords are used to prevent access to files and programs within a system, rather than preventing access to the system at all.

210 C (Syllabus area D4(e))

R&D expenditure on its own is not a measure of performance, and costs in the previous year will not relate to all four products introduced to the market in the past two years.

The most appropriate of these measures as an indication of innovation within the organisation is revenue from new products as a percentage of total revenue. (This is more meaningful for comparison purposes than simply measuring average revenue per new product.)

211 A (Syllabus area D6(b))

Number of patients treated per $1 spent relates outputs to inputs, and is a measure of efficiency. Reducing a departmental budget is a measure of economy. A crime clear-up rate and an examination pass rate are measures of effectiveness for the police force and the state-owned college respectively.

212 A (Syllabus area D2(b))

For example systems for recording attendance times at work are more reliable when recorded automatically by a card reader system than if individuals sign in and sign out in a manual attendance record. However, time recording systems (such as time sheets for recording time spent on different jobs) must sometimes rely on human records. Secondary information is usually much cheaper to collect than primary data.

213 C (Syllabus area D5(a))

For example if the marginal cost of a transferred item is $5 and it has an external intermediate market of $7 but external selling costs of $0.50; and if the transferring-in division can use the transferred item to make an end product that earns a contribution of $10, the maximum transfer price should be the lower of $7 and $10. The minimum transfer price should be $5 + $(7 − 5 − 0.50) = $6.50.

214 D (Syllabus area D4(e))

The target is to improve the efficiency of dealing with customer calls. This may affect customer satisfaction and profitability, but its prime objective is to reduce call times and improve efficiency in the call centre.

215 D (Syllabus area D1(b))

Management information, often of an operational nature, is often produced as summary data output from a transaction processing system. Management information systems are based mainly on internal data sources rather than sources that are external to the organisation.

216 B (Syllabus area D1(a))

Budgeting is commonly associated with decision making at the tactical planning level (management control level) within a management hierarchy.

217 A (Syllabus area D1(b))

EIS systems often present key information in a 'visually friendly' format.

218 B (Syllabus area D2(a))

Data from a government source is external data since it comes from a source outside the organisation. It is secondary data because it was not produced for the specific purpose for which management are using it.

219 A (Syllabus area D2(b))

Feedback is information captured within an organisation by measuring output from the system. Information from an external source cannot be feedback.

220 B (Syllabus area D4(e))

Making repeat orders is possibly a measure of customer satisfaction, and so might be used as a measure of performance from a customer perspective in a balanced scorecard. The growth in the product range is more relevant to innovation, and speed of order processing and orders per sales representative are measures of operational efficiency and effectiveness rather than customer attitudes to the organisation and its products.

221 C (Syllabus area D6(d))

Providing value for money (VFM) means providing a service that is economical, efficient and effective. 'Economical' means getting the best price, but this does not necessarily mean 'cheap'. Measuring the percentage of collected refuse that is recycled is a measure of effectiveness, if recycling refuse is an objective of the service. (Efficiency measures an amount of output or benefit per unit of resource input.)

222 B (Syllabus area D5(c))

When divisional performance is measured by residual income, a fair comparison of divisional performances is not possible, because the divisional residual incomes are not related to the size and asset value of each division. For example residual income of $50,000 when divisional assets are $10 million is not as impressive as residual income of $50,000 when divisional assets are only $100,000.

When a transfer price is based on cost, the size of the profit mark-up is a matter for negotiation, and one of the divisional managers (or even both of them) are likely to consider the agreed transfer price as 'unfair', favouring the other division.

223 D (Syllabus area D4(b))

Time between order and despatch is a measure of speed, which is an aspect of efficiency.

224   **A**   (Syllabus area D4(e))

In the Fitzgerald and Moon model there are six dimensions of performance. Two of these reflect past results and achievements: financial performance and competitiveness. The other four dimensions of performance are determinants of future performance: flexibility, innovation, quality and resource utilisation.

225   **B**   (Syllabus area D4(d))

There is a risk of dysfunctional decision making and a lack of goal congruence with divisionalisation. Divisional managers may base investment decisions on whether they will improve ROI, which is inappropriate. Transfer pricing disputes too may lead to bad decisions by divisional managers. However, the risk can be avoided or minimised if divisional management and head office management are aware of the potential problem.

Authority is delegated to divisional managers; therefore there is some loss of head office control over operations, but decision making at 'local' operational level should be faster since the decision does not have to be referred to head office for a decision. There is likely to be some duplication of costs, since each division will have its own administration activities.

226   **B**   (Syllabus area D5(c))

ROI is measured as divisional operating profit: this is after deducting depreciation charges.

227   **D**   (Syllabus area D3(a))

Controls are needed over internally-produced information to prevent excessive amounts of information being circulated - leading to waste of management time. Controls are also needed to ensure that unauthorised information is not circulated. Controls may extend to the use of e-mails containing 'off the record' comments which could potentially have legal implications for the organisation.

228   **D**   (Syllabus area D2(b))

Feedback is information produced by a system as control information for management. Benchmarking means comparing performance of an organisation, or part of an organisation, with a 'benchmark'. The benchmark may be an external organisation, such as a competitor company, or another department or division within the same organisation.

229   **D**   (Syllabus area D5(a))

When an organisation is structured into divisions, there will almost inevitably be some transfer of goods or services between divisions, for which transfer prices are required.

Statement 2 is one of the guiding rules for identifying the optimal transfer price.

230   **B**   (Syllabus area D6(b))

The cost of resources (inputs) per member of the local community is a measure of the resources spent on the fire service, without providing any measure of outputs obtained from the resources. A measure of the cost of the service provides an indication of the resources committed to it, but does not measure the value or benefits obtained from them.

231   **D**   (Syllabus area D4(e))

The growth perspective is concerned with: 'Can we continue to improve and create value?' The process efficiency perspective, also called the operational perspective, is concerned with operational efficiency and excellence.

232   **C**   (Syllabus area D7(d))

Good performance measurements may be either financial or non-financial measurements.

233   **C**   (Syllabus area D4(a))

Liquidity and cash flow are improved by reducing the average time that customers take to pay and by extending the length of credit taken from suppliers.

234   D   (Syllabus area D5(a))

Transfers should not be at actual cost, because there is no incentive for the transferring division to control the costs of the transferred item. A transfer price based on actual cost plus would be even worse, since the transferring division (Division A) would make a profit on any overspending that it incurs. Standard cost plus is preferable to standard cost because the profit margin provides an incentive for Division A to make and transfer the item.

CBE style OTQ bank – Performance measurement and control

235   (Syllabus area D5(a))

The correct answer is: Minimum transfer price $8, maximum transfer price $16

The minimum transfer price is the marginal cost of production in Division A, because any transfer price in excess of this amount will add to the division's contribution and profit. The maximum transfer price is the external market price of Component X, because any price in excess of this amount will lead to Division B sourcing Product X externally.

236   (Syllabus area D4(e))

The correct answer is:

* Innovation

Fitzgerald and Moon identified six dimensions or aspects of performance in a service business: financial performance, competitiveness, quality, resource utilisation, flexibility and innovation.

237   (Syllabus area D5(a))

The correct answer is: $15

The minimum transfer price is a price that should be sufficient to make the manager of Division A wiling to transfer units of Component X to Division B. This is the marginal cost of manufacture plus the opportunity cost of not being able to sell the component in the external market.

This is $8 + $(16 − 8 − 1) = $15.

238   (Syllabus area D5(c))

The correct answers are:

* Granting credit to customers
* Inventory carrying decisions

The investment centre manager would have power to make decisions over granting credit to customers and the level of inventory carried. This affects the investment centre's level of working capital and hence is the responsibility of the investment centre manager.

239   (Syllabus area D5(c))

The correct answer is: 23.2%

Capital employed at start of 20X2 = $2 million + $0.2 million + $0.8 million + $0.1 million = $3.1 million

Capital employed at the end of 20X2 is the capital employed at the beginning of the year minus depreciation of $0.4m on the 'old' assets and $0.2m on the 'new' asset.

Capital employed at end of 20X2 = $1.6 million + $0.2 million + $0.6 million + $0.1 million = $2.5 million

Mid-year capital employed = $(3.1 m + 2.5m)/2 = $2.8 million

Profit = $0.5 million + $0.35 million − depreciation $0.2 million = $0.65 million

ROI = 0.65/2.8 = 0.232 = 23.2%

240   (Syllabus area D5(c))

The correct answer is: $5,000

	$'000	$'000
Sales (7,000 units × $154)		1,078
Variable costs in Division B; (7,000 × $33)	231	
Costs of transfers (14,000 × $43)	602	
		833
		245
Fixed costs		160
Operating profit		85
Notional interest (16% × $500,000)		80
Residual income		5

241   (Syllabus area D5(c))

The correct answer is: 30.9%

	Profit	Capital employed
	$	$
Original forecast	65,000	210,000
Effect of machine sale	(2,500)	(6,000)
Effect of machine purchase	5,200	15,000
	67,700	219,000

Revised ROI = 67,700/219,000 = 30.9%

242   (Syllabus area D7(d))

The correct answers are:

- Volume of customer complaints - Quantitative
- Employee revenue - Quantitative
- Defective products per batch - Quantitative
- Customer needs - Quantitative
- Employee morale - Qualitative
- Brand recognition - Qualitative
- Customer satisfaction - Qualitative Repeat business - Qualitative

Quantitative performance measures are something that can be actually measured and a value assigned.

Volume of customer complaints, employee revenue, defective products per batch and repeat business are all performance measures which can be regularly monitored, values assigned and benchmarks made.

Qualitative performance measures are more difficult to measure and are based on judgement. It is only possible to gain an opinion as opposed to a concrete value. They are still important as many decisions are swayed by the strength of the qualitative arguments rather than the cold facts presented as part of qualitative analysis.

Customer needs, customer satisfaction, employee morale and brand recognition are all examples of qualitative performance measures. They are very difficult to measure accurately and their rating tends to be based on judgement.

There are still ways to devise quantitative measures for these areas. For example volume of repeat business may give an indication of customer satisfaction. Additionally, surveying a sample of customers may help to devise some measure of satisfaction.

243   (Syllabus area D6(b))

The correct answers are:

- Effectiveness
- Efficiency
- Economy

Effectiveness is the relationship between an organisation's outputs and its objectives (i.e. getting done what was supposed to be done). Efficiency is the relationship between inputs and outputs (i.e. getting out as much as possible for what goes in).

Economy is attaining the appropriate quantity and quality of inputs at lowest cost (i.e. spending money frugally). Enterprise, efficacy, expediency and endurance although perhaps relevant are all red herrings in this context.

244   (Syllabus area D4(e))

The correct answers are:

- Percentage of repeat customers
- Number of warranty claims

Dividend yield is a shareholder measure and morale index is an employee measure.

Cherry Co

245 **B** $30

Division A has available capacity of 15,000 units. Division A does not want to lose its contribution margin of $7 per unit, and therefore the minimum price it would now accept is $30 as shown below.

$30 (variable cost) + $0 (opportunity cost) = $30

In this case Division A and B should negotiate a transfer price within the range of $30 and $35 (cost from outside supplier).

246 **C** $37

Division A charges $37 and derives a contribution margin of $7 per unit of Product X. Division A has no spare capacity.

Therefore, Division A must receive from the Division B a payment that will at least cover its variable cost per unit plus its lost contribution margin per unit (the opportunity cost). If Division A cannot cover that amount (the minimum transfer price), it should not sell units of Product X to Division B.

The minimum transfer price that would be acceptable to Division A is $37, as shown below.

$30 (variable cost) + $7 (opportunity cost) = $37

247 **A** Full cost

Under this approach, the full cost (including fixed overheads absorbed) incurred by the supplying division in making the 'intermediate' product is charged to the receiving division. It can be used when there is no external marker for the product being transferred, or if an imperfect market exists.

248 **B** 2 only

Statement 1 is false. Cherry Co's transfer pricing system should seek to establish a transfer price for X that will provide an incentive for the managers of A and B to make and sell quantities of products that will maximise the company's total profit. Statement 2 is true.

249 **A** 1 only

Statement 1 is true. Statement 2 is false because Division A is likely to save money on selling and distribution expenses if they can sell product X to Division B.

Jamair

250 D Financial

The financial perspective considers whether the management in Jamair meets the expectations of its shareholders and how it creates value for them.

This perspective focuses on traditional measures such as growth, profitability and cost reduction.

251 A Customer perspective

The customer perspective considers how new and existing customers view Jamair. The objective is to ensure that flights land on time.

252 B Internal business perspective

The internal business perspective makes Jamair consider what processes it must excel at in order to achieve financial and customer objectives. The measure may be: Reduction in 'on the ground' time from 50 minutes.

253 D Financial perspective

The measure could be 'Revenue per available passenger mile'. The financial perspective considers whether the management in Jamair meets the expectations of its shareholders and how it creates value for them.

254 A 1 only

Statement 1 is true. By its very nature, qualitative data is not quantified. At best, qualitative measures are converted into quantitative measures using a subjective scoring system.

Statement 2 is false. An organisation is much more likely to have a well-established system for measuring quantitative data, especially in the areas of accounting and sales statistics.

Stickleback Co

255 D Before investment: 20%, After investment 19.3%.

	Before Investment $	After Investment $
Divisional profit	30,000	31,900
Capital employed	150,000	165,000
ROI	20%	19.3%

256 C Before investment: $7,500, After investment $7,150.

	Before Investment $	After Investment $
Divisional profit	30,000	31,900
Imputed interest (15% of $150,000)	(22,500)	
Imputed interest (15% of $165,000)		(24,750)
Residual income	7,500	7,150

257 B 2 only.

Statement 1 is false because if a manager's performance is being evaluated, only those assets which can be traced directly to the division and are controllable by the manager should be included.

The second statement is true. Short-termism is when there is a bias towards short-term rather than long-term performance. It is often due to the fact that managers' performance is measured on short term results such as ROI.

258   C   1 and 4

'Increase payables' and 'Keep Kingfisher's old machinery'

One of the problems with using ROI as a performance measure is that it can be manipulated. Allowing non-current assets to depreciate (giving a lower NBV) and delaying payments to suppliers, both reduce the capital employed and therefore increase the ROI.

Accepting all projects with a positive NPV may not necessarily increase the ROI. Projects may have lower ROIs than Kingfisher's current ROI and this could cause Kingfisher's overall ROI to reduce.

ROI is calculated using profit before interest and so interest makes no difference to the ROI.

259   A   1 only

Statement 1 is a danger of decentralisation. Managers may make dysfunctional decisions.

Statement 2 is false. The divisional organisation frees top management from detailed involvement in day-to-day operations and allows them to devote more time to strategic planning.

Squarize

260   B   Internal business perspective

This is measuring the effectiveness of improving the broadband service (an internal process) and is therefore part of the Internal business perspective,

261   A   Customer perspective

The performance objective associated with this measure would be to 'Increase number of new customers'. It measures whether customers are willing to pay the individual prices for each service.

262   C   Sales revenue from new standalone service as a percentage of total revenue
The most appropriate of these measures as an indication of innovation within the organisation is revenue from new standalone services as a percentage of total revenue. (This is more meaningful for comparison purposes than simply measuring average revenue per new standalone service.)

263   B   Renewing subscription or making repeat orders is possibly a measure of customer satisfaction, and so might be used as a measure of performance from a customer perspective in a balanced scorecard. The growth in the product range is more relevant to innovation, and speed of order processing and orders per sales representative are measures of operational efficiency and effectiveness rather than customer attitudes to the organisation and its products.

264   B   Innovation

Innovation is an element of the 'Dimensions of performance' building block, but it is not included as a standalone building block.

The three building blocks are:

- Dimensions of performance
- Standards
- Rewards

Alder Co

265   The correct answer is: Before investment 27%, after investment 25%.

	Before investment $	After investment $
Controllable divisional profit	200,000	220,000
Capital employed	750,000	875,000
ROI	27%	25%

266   The correct answer is: Before investment: $87,500, After investment $88,750.

	Before investment $	After investment $
Divisional profit	200,000	220,000
Imputed interest		
(750,000 × 0.15)	(112,500)	
(875,000 × 0.15)		(131,250)
Residual income	87,500	88,750

267   1 only

Statement 1 is said to be one of the key advantages of a divisionalised structure.

Statement 2 is false. The divisional organisation frees top management from detailed involvement in day-to-day operations and allows them to devote more time to strategic planning.

268   Neither 1 nor 2.

Statement 1 is false because if a manager's performance is being evaluated, only those assets which can be traced directly to the division and are controllable by the manager should be included.

Statement 2 is false because an investment centre could not operate without the support of head office assets and administrative backup.

269   Both 1 and 2

The first statement is true and is a key exam focus point that should be remembered for your exam.

The second statement is true, and it is a risk associated with the use of ROI. If a manager in Alder Co's bonus depends on ROI being met, the manager may feel pressure to massage the measure.

Apple Co

270   The correct answer is: 30%

	Investment $
Divisional profit	24,000
Capital employed (20,000 + 60,000)	80,000
ROI	30%

271   The correct answer is: $23,000.

	Investment $
Divisional profit	35,000
Imputed interest (100,000 × 12%)	(12,000)
Residual income	23,000

272   Both 1 and 2

Statement 1 is a key advantage of working with RI.
Statement 2 is a key disadvantage of working with RI.

273   2 only

Statement 1 is false. The market price can act as a disincentive to use up any spare capacity in the selling division of Apple Co, particularly if the market price does not provide a significant mark-up. A price based on incremental cost, in contrast, might provide an incentive to use up the spare resources in order to provide a marginal contribution to profit.

Statement 2 is true and is a key advantage of using market price as a basis for transfer pricing.

274 Both 1 and 2

Both statement are examples of the conditions under which market based transfer prices are not suitable, and therefore a cost based approach would be preferable.

Box Co

275 The correct answers are: Before investment: 21%, After investment 20.4%.

	Before Investment	After Investment
	$	$
Divisional profit	20,000	21,400
Capital employed	95,000	105,000
ROI	21.1%	20.4%

276 The correct answers are: Before investment: $8,600, After investment $7,950.

	Before Investment	After Investment
	$	$
Divisional profit	20,000	21,400
Depreciation		(850)
Imputed interest (12% of $95,000)	(11,400)	
Imputed interest (12% of $105,000)		(12,600)
Residual income	8,600	7,950

277 Both 1 and 2

Both statements are reasons for the growing emphasis on NFPIs.

Traditional responsibility accounting systems fail to provide information on the quality of products, and therefore statement 1 is true.

Financial performance indicators tend to focus on the short term. They can give a positive impression of what is happening now but problems may be looming. Therefore statement 2 is true.

278 Keep managers informed about the short term budget targets

Options A, B, and D are all methods to encourage managers to take a long term view, so that the 'ideal' decisions are taken.

Providing sufficient management information to allow managers to see what trade-offs they are making is a method of encouraging managers to take a long-term view. Managers must be kept aware of the long-term aims as well as shorter-term (budget) targets.

279 1 only

Statement 1 is a danger of divisionalised structures. Managers may make dysfunctional decisions.

Statement 2 is false. Only factors for which the manager can be held accountable should be included in calculations, and therefore head office costs would not be included.

280 Biscuits and Cakes

Marking scheme

			Marks
(a)	ROI/RI calculations:		
	ROI for B	1	
	ROI for C	1	
			2
(b)	ROI/RI discussion:		
	RI for B	1½	
	RI for C	1½	
			3
(c)	Discussion:		
	ROI discussion	2	
	RI discussion	2	
	Extra ROI calculation under old method	1	
	Valid conclusion drawn	1	
			6
(d)	ROI/RI after investment:		
	ROI calculation	2	
	RI calculation	1	
	Comments and conclusion	2	
			5
(e)	Behavioural issues:		
	ROI of investment – 1 mark per valid point	Max 4	
			20

(a) **Annualised return on investment (ROI)**

ROI = (Net profit / Net assets) × 100%

Division B

Net profit = $311,000 × 12 months = $3,732,000
ROI = ($3,732,000 / $23,200,000) × 100%
= 16.09%

Division C

Net profit = $292,000 × 12 months = $3,504,000
ROI = ($3,504,000 / $22,600,000) × 100%
= 15.5%

(b) **Annualised residual income (RI)**

	Division B $'000	Division C $'000
Net profit (part (a))	3,732	3,504
Less: imputed interest charge:		
$23.2m × 10%	(2,320)	nil
$22.6m × 10%	nil	(2,260)
	1,412	1,244

(c) **Performance based on ROI**

The ROIs calculated for each division in part (a) are both significantly below the company's **target ROI** (20%). This would suggest that both divisions are performing poorly.

However, both divisions are now required to deduct a share of **head office costs** in their respective operating statements before arriving at 'net profit' which is then used to calculate ROI. The company's target ROI has not been reduced to take account of these **uncontrollable costs**.

Using the old method (prior to head office costs being recharged to divisions), ROI for both divisions would have **exceeded the 20% target**, and increased on ROIs for the last three months (Division B: 22% pa, Division C: 23%pa) showing that both divisions have actually **improved their performance**.

ROI using the old method

Division B net profit = ($311,000 + $155,000) × 12 = $5,592,000

Division B ROI = $5,592,000 / $23,200,000 × 100% = **24.1%**

Division C net profit = ($292,000 + $180,000) × 12 = $5,664,000

Division C ROI = $5,664,000 / $22,600,000 × 100% = **25.06%**

Performance based on RI

Division B and Division C both have healthy RI figures of $1.4m and $1.2m respectively. These figures are impressive when you consider that they are based on **net profits** as opposed to **controllable profits**.

However, the company's cost of capital of 10% is significantly lower than the target return on investment (20%). This makes the residual income figure show a more **positive position**.

(d) **Division B's revised annualised net profit and opening net assets after investment**

Depreciation = ($2,120,000 − $200,000) / 48 months = $40,000 per month

Net profit for July = $311,000 + ($600,000 × 8.5%) − $40,000 = $322,000

Annualised net profit = $322,000 × 12 = $3,864,000

Opening net assets after investment = $23,200,000 + $2,120,000 = $25,320,000

Division B ROI

ROI = (Net profit / Net assets) × 100%
= $3,864,000 / $25,320,000 × 100% = 15.26%

Division B will not proceed with the investment as it will cause a decrease in ROI.

Division B RI

	$'000
Net profit	3,864
Less: imputed interest charge:	
$25.32m × 10%	(2,532)
Residual income	1,332

Based on the above calculation, it is clear that **RI is higher** with the investment. This would suggest that the company should **proceed with the investment** and shows that the use of ROI as a performance measure is likely to result in the manager of Division B making a decision that is **not in the best interests** of the company as a whole.

(e)   **Behavioural problems**

Staff in both divisions are used to exceeding the target ROI of 20% and being rewarded for doing so. As a result of including head office costs in the calculation of net profit, staff will see that their respective divisions are **no longer meeting the target ROI** despite performance actually improving.

The target ROI should be revised to take account of the these **uncontrollable allocated costs**.

Staff are likely to become **demotivated** by the fact that they are no longer meeting the target ROI despite continuing to operate at the same level as before. They may feel that management have deliberately altered how performance is measured in order to **avoid paying staff bonuses** for exceeding targets.

Staff may deliberately work slowly and refuse to work overtime to show their opposition to the new system. The company should resolve the situation as soon as possible to avoid a decrease in **production output** and **product quality.**

281 Story

> **Text reference.** Management information systems are discussed in Chapter 14.
>
> **Top tips.** This is quite a long and complicated scenario. You'll improve your chances of writing a good answer by reading the scenario carefully and then planning your answer.
>
> We suggest that you start by making notes as a rough sketch for your answer. Spend around ten minutes doing this. Then elaborate your notes into your answer, using headings and paragraphs, and picking out the main points from the question. So, for example, head up a paragraph 'open systems' and write a paragraph on open systems. This makes it much clearer to mark and uses the key phrases ACCA examination team is looking for in a good answer.
>
> Part (b) of this question illustrates the importance of being able to apply theory to the scenario. You may not be able to give any examples of closed systems as these rarely occur. Just make sure you put down an explanation so that you get credit for knowing what a closed system is.
>
> We have put our answer to Part (c) in a table though you could also use headings and paragraphs to answer the question.

(a)   **Issues in upgrading the existing information system**

The issues involved in an upgrade of the existing information system include achieving the potential advantages at minimum cost and anticipating and managing necessary changes.

(i)   **Advantages of upgrade**

A networked system would allow the **transmission** of information both to and from the business units and head office at Story. As such it is likely that performance indicators, financial statistics and similar **information** could be **rapidly gathered, processed and disseminated. Improved**

communication between units and head office should improve, leading to **rapid reaction** to changes both within the organisation and outside it. This should result in a responsive, evolving organisation capable of meeting the challenges of the market place. It would also get rid of the problems currently experienced where some countries do not have the most up-to-date information on products and prices.

(ii) **Costs**

The **costs** of providing a fully networked computer system, changeover costs and the costs of future maintenance and training must be evaluated and budgeted for. The development and implementation of **security measures** to prevent the misuse of corporate data, and to prevent fraud by unauthorised users (who may be employees or external to the organisation) have to be considered and costed. In addition, there may be a possible need to **recruit** specialised staff to implement the changes to the existing information system. All of these costs are foreseeable and can be planned.

(iii) **Changes**

Upgrading corporate information systems usually results in many unforeseen changes to the **culture** of the organisation and to the **working practices** of staff at all levels. For example, would greater efficiency be achieved by allowing staff to have more flexible hours of attendance? Can costs be reduced by allowing some staff to telecommute on a regular basis, thus allowing hot-desking to take place? Is it likely that morale will be adversely affected by staff who may be concerned about using new technology or staff who fear that they may lose their jobs through the changes?

The proposed changes are unlikely to change the **role and remit of management** in relation to the directing of staff, although it is likely that there will be some impact upon organising staff tasks as new needs arise. **Strategic and tactical planning** are likely to change in response to the improved, and more rapid, flow of information that the information system will provide.

Operational decisions can be taken at lower levels of the corporate hierarchy as information becomes available more rapidly and in an appropriate format. As well as providing a swift response to changes in the business environment, it is possible that the organisation will, in time, evolve into one with a **flatter hierarchy**. This would particularly suit the autonomous business unit structure in Story which already operates with devolved decision making. However, there is always the danger of '**information overload**' which can reduce efficiency and morale within the organisation.

(b) **Closed systems and open systems**

Closed system

A closed system is one that **does not react to external stimuli or allow communication from internal processes to interact with the outside environment**. They are seldom, if ever, found in naturally occurring situations. A typical example of a closed system would be a chemical reaction that takes place under controlled conditions within a laboratory. Closed systems can be created to eliminate external factors and then used to investigate the relationship between known variables in an experiment.

Open system

An open system is one that **interacts fully with its environment**. It accepts **inputs** from its surroundings, processes the inputs in some manner and then produces an **output**. The input parameters can be foreseen or be unpredictable. Similarly, outputs can either be predicted or unforeseen. For example, predictable inputs of a metal smelting works would include items like the raw materials and coal while the predictable outputs would be ash, smoke and the smelted metal. If the raw material to be smelted became contaminated in some way, it is likely that an undesirable product would be produced. These are examples of unforeseen inputs and outputs.

Examples in the question

Turning to the question, we can see that Story is clearly an **open system**. It reacts, albeit imperfectly, to inputs from its environment and produces outputs. Sales figures are collated and analysed and predictions are made based upon this information. Hence the organisation responds to external stimuli and reacts appropriately.

The question also provides instances of **sub-systems** within the organisation that are themselves open systems. For example, the information system, the corporate management team, the business units and retail outlets are examples of sub-systems within the business that are all open.

(c) **Three types of MIS and how they would be used in an organisation**

Type of MIS	Detail
Transaction processing systems (TPS)	Collect, store, modify and retrieve the transactions of an organisation. A **transaction** is an event that generates or modifies data that is eventually stored on an information system. There are two types of TPS: **Batch transaction processing** (BTP) collects transaction data as a group and processes it later, after a time delay, as batches of identical data. **Real time transaction processing** (RTTP) is the immediate processing of data. It involves using a terminal or workstation to enter data and display results and provides instant confirmation.
Executive information systems (EIS)	Give executives a straightforward means of access to **key internal and external data**. They provide summary-level data, captured from the organisation's main systems (which might involve integrating the executive's desk top PC with the organisation's mainframe), data manipulation facilities (such as comparison with budget or prior year data and trend analysis) and user-friendly presentation of data.
Enterprise resource planning systems (ERP)	Integrate the **key processes** in an organisation so that a single system can serve the information needs of all functional areas. They primarily support business operations including Finance, HR, Marketing and Accounting and work in real-time, meaning that the exact status of everything is always available to all users. ERP systems can be deployed at sites around the world, they can work in multiple languages and currencies. When they are, you can immediately see, for example, exactly how much of a particular part is on-hand at the warehouse in Japan and what its value is in yen or dollars.

282 Hammer

Text references. Transfer pricing is covered in Chapter 17.

Top tips. Do not forget to exclude fixed costs from your calculations in part (a). The question states that the current pricing policy is variable cost plus 30%.

Easy marks. Six marks are available in part (d) for discussing factors to consider when purchasing from outside suppliers.

Examiner's comments. The numerical parts to the question were quite well answered by most candidates. However, a disappointing number of answers included the fixed costs within part (a) and part (b) which defied the purpose of the whole question really. That having been said, most answers were good.

The quality of answers to part (c) was really poor. The question was looking for a couple of key points, for example, that including fixed costs guarantees a profit for the seller but invites manipulation of overheads and passes on inefficiencies from one part of the business to another. Also, that this strategy causes fixed costs of one division to be turned into a variable cost for another division.

Similarly, part (d) rarely produced answers scoring full marks. It asked whether retail stores should be allowed to buy in from outside suppliers. Key points in any answer should have been that the overall profitability of the company is key, as is goal congruence; these points were rarely made. Thankfully, many candidates did spot the more obvious points such as the fact that the quality and reliability of any external supplier would need to be assessed.

			Marks
(a)	Steel	1	
	Other material	1	
	Labour	1	
	Variable overhead	1	
	Delivery	1	
	Margin	1	
			6
(b)	Fixed cost	2	
	Margin	2	
			4
(c)	Covers all cost	1	
	Risk	1	
	Fixed cost accounting	1	
	Converts a FC to VC	2	
			max 4
(d)	Market price may be temporary	1	
	Brand	1	
	Profitability	1	
	Flexibility	1	
	Control	1	
	Motivation	1	
	Performance assessment	1	
			max 6
			20

(a) **Price Nail would charge under existing policy (cost plus 30%)**

	$
Steel (0.4kg/0.95 (5% steel loss)) × $4.00	1.68
Other materials ($3.00 × 0.9 × 0.1)	0.27
Labour ($10 × 0.25)	2.50
Variable overhead ($15 × 0.25)	3.75
Delivery	0.50
Total variable cost	8.70
Mark-up (30%)	2.61
Transfer price	11.31

(b) **Price Nail would charged under total cost plus 10%**

	$
Total variable cost from part (a)	8.70
Extra fixed cost (0.25 × $15 × 0.8)	3.00
Total cost	11.70
Mark up (10%)	1.17
Transfer price	12.87

The increase in price if the pricing policy switches to total cost plus 10% is $1.56 per unit ($12.87 - $11.31).

(c) Fixed costs can be accounted for in a number of ways. As such, including the fixed cost within the transfer price could lead to **manipulation of overhead treatment**. For example employing absorption costing or activity based costing.

Including the fixed costs in the transfer price will benefit the manufacturer who can ensure that **all costs** incurred during the manufacturing process are **covered**. Assuming the fixed overhead absorption calculations are accurate, the manufacturing division should be **guaranteed a profit**.

The main **problem** with this pricing strategy is **fixed costs** are **effectively treated as variable costs** from the perspective of the stores, as they are included within the variable buy-in price. This could lead to **poor decision-making** from a **group perspective**.

(d)   Managers of the retail stores are likely to be more **motivated** if they are given **freedom** in which to **operate** and are able to purchase from outside suppliers if prices are cheaper.

In addition, the performance of **store managers will be easier to assess** in an environment in which managers are able to control greater elements of the business.

Price differences are perhaps to be expected given that products are rarely identical. There is a **risk** that store managers purchase cheaper shears of **inferior quality** to those produced internally (whilst claiming they are comparable) in order to achieve a greater margin. Such scenarios jeopardise the **reputation** of the brand for the benefit of individual stores.

Allowing store managers to purchase from cheaper suppliers could result in Hammer **losing control** of its business as retail stores could potentially stock different shears and other products from a range of different suppliers. On the other hand **flexibility is increased** and profits could increase as store managers find bargain prices.

In a competitive market, it is unlikely that suppliers will offer products significantly cheaper to Hammer for a sustained period of time. Any cheap prices accessed by store managers are likely to be the result of a sale or special promotion. If this is the case, it would not be advisable for Hammer to grant store managers the power to purchase from cheaper external suppliers in the long term.

Overall profitability of the company is key. The retail stores and Nail should be working in a way that is best for the company overall. This is known as **goal congruence**.

283 Woodside

Text reference. Operating statements are covered in Chapter 12 and not-for-profit organisations in Chapter 18.

Top tips. In part (a), fixed costs do not relate to any particular activity of the charity and so a marginal costing approach has to be used in analysing the budgeted and actual information provided. Remember to apply your discussion to the specific entity. As the organisation is a charity, adverse variances do not necessarily equate to poor performance.

Part (b) is a straightforward discussion using knowledge that you should be familiar with for this exam but again, you must specifically refer to the issues that Woodside faces.

(a)   **Operating statement**

			$
Budgeted surplus (W1)			98,750
Funding shortfall (W3)			(80,000)
			18,750

	Favourable	*Adverse*	
	$	$	
Free meals (W4)			
Price variance		4,000	
Usage variance		8,750	
Overnight shelter (W5)			
Price variance		4,380	
Usage variance	31,000		
Advice centre (W6)			
Price variance		9,100	
Usage variance		7,500	
Campaigning and advertising (W7)			
Expenditure variance		15,000	
Fixed cost (W8)			
Expenditure variance		18,000	
	31,000	66,730	(35,730)
Actual shortfall (W2)			(16,980)

Workings

1 *Budgeted figures*

	$	
Free meals provision	91,250	(18,250 meals at $5 per meal)
Overnight shelter (variable)	250,000	(10,000 bed-nights at $30 – $5 per night)
Advice centre (variable)	45,000	(3,000 sessions at $20 – $5 per session)
Fixed costs	65,000	(10,000 × $5) + (3,000 × $5)
Campaigning and advertising	150,000	
	601,250	
Surplus for unexpected costs	98,750	
Fundraising target	700,000	

2 *Actual figures*

	$	
Free meals provision	104,000	(20,000 meals at $5.20 per meal)
Overnight shelter	223,380	(8,760 bed-nights $25.50 per night)
Advice centre	61,600	(3,500 sessions at $17.60 per session)
Fixed costs	83,000	
Campaigning and advertising	165,000	
	636,980	
Shortfall	16,980	
Funds raised	620,000	

3 Funding shortfall = 700,000 – 620,000 = $80,000 (A)

4 Free meals price variance = (5·00 – 5·20) × 20,000 = $4,000 (A)
   Free meals usage variance = (18,250 – 20,000) × 5·00 = $8,750 (A)

5 Overnight shelter price variance = (25·00 – 25·50) × 8,760 = $4,380 (A)
   Overnight shelter usage variance – (10,000 – 8,760) × 25 = $31,000 (F)

6 Advice centre price variance = (17·60 – 15·00) × 3,500 = $9,100 (A)
   Advice centre usage variance = (3,000 – 3,500) × 15·00 = $7,500 (A)

7 Campaigning and advertising expenditure variance = 150,000 – 165,000 = $15,000 (A)

8 Fixed cost expenditure variance = 65,000 – 83,000 = $18,000 (A)

There was a **fundraising shortfall** of $80,000 compared to the target and **costs were over budget** in all areas except overnight shelter provision.

Provision of free meals cost 14% (104,000 – 91,250/91,250) more than budgeted with most of the variance due to the extra 1,750 meals that were provided. However $4,000 of the variance was due to an increase of 20c (5.20 – 5.00) in the average cost of a meal.

Overnight shelter cost $26,620 (250,000 – 223,380) less than expected. $31,000 was saved because there were 1,240 bed nights less of the service used than expected, but the average unit cost of the provision increased by 50c, leading to an adverse price variance of $4,380.

Advice centre costs were also above budget by 37% (61,600 – 45,000/45,000). There were two factors contributing to this increase. **Usage of the service** increased by 17% (3,500 – 3,000/3,000) and **average costs** also increased by 17% (17.60 – 15/15).

Fixed costs of administration and centre maintenance were $18,000 (28%) above budget and **campaigning and advertising** were $15,000 (10%) above budget.

The shortfall identified in the operating statement may initially cause concern and individual adverse variances could be investigated to determine if **future cost increases could be controlled**. However, the **objective** of a charity such as Woodside is not to make money but to provide help to homeless people.

The figures demonstrate that this **objective was achieved** in terms of advice and free meals provided. It appears that the demand for overnight shelter has fallen so resources could be switched from this area if it is believed that this is a long-term trend. Further investigation of the reason for the fall in demand would be useful.

(b) Financial management and control in a not-for-profit organisation (NFPO) such as the Woodside charity needs to recognise that such organisations often have **multiple objectives** that can be **difficult to define** and are usually **non-financial**.

Performance of such organisations is judged in terms of inputs and outputs and hence the **value for money** criteria of economy, efficiency and effectiveness.

Economy means that inputs should be obtained at the lowest cost. **Efficiency** involves getting as much as possible for what goes in ie using the charity's resources as efficiently as possible to provide the services offered by the charity. **Effectiveness** means ensuring the outputs ie the services provided, have the desired impacts and achieve the charity's objectives.

Performance measures to determine whether objectives have been achieved can be difficult to formulate for an organisation such as Woodside.

Measures such as the number of free meals served, number of advice sessions given and number of bed-nights used, show that quantitative measures can be used to demonstrate that the charity is meeting a growing need.

Financial management and control in this organisation will primarily be concerned with preparing budgets and controlling costs.

Preparing budgets

Budgets rely on **forecasting** and accurate forecasts can be difficult to prepare for a charity such as Woodside. The level of activity is driven by the needs of the homeless and therefore **difficult to predict**. A high degree of **flexibility** is required to meet changing demand so provision needs to be built into budgets for this.

It is unlikely that Woodside has carried out a **detailed analysis of costs** and they have probably used an **incremental** approach to budgeting. This will limit the accuracy of their forecasts but staff may not have the necessary financial skills to use more advanced techniques.

Controlling costs

This is a key area of financial management due to the need for efficiency and economy. Inputs such as food, drink, bedding etc can be sourced as cheaply as possible and expenses such as electricity and telephone usage can be kept to an absolute minimum through careful use.

The responsibility for cost control would probably be the responsibility of the full-time members of staff but a culture of economy and efficiency can be encouraged amongst the volunteers.

Woodside will also need to provide **annual accounts** in order to retain charitable status and to show the providers of funds that their donations are being used as they intended.

284 Ties Only Co

Marking scheme

			Marks
(a)	Sales	2	
	Gross profit	2	
	Website development	2	
	Administration	2	
	Distribution	1	
	Launch marketing	2	
	Overall comment	2	
	Maximum		10
(b)	Future profits comment		3
(c)	Number of tie sales	1	
	Tie price calculation	2	
	On time delivery	2	
	Returns	2	
	System down time	1	
	Summary comment	1	
	Maximum		7
			20

(a)   **Financial performance**

Sales growth

Ties Only Co appear to have made an excellent start with initial sales of $420,000 growing by 62% ((680,000 – 420,000)/420,000 × 100%) to Quarter 2. This is particularly impressive given the acknowledged competitiveness of this business sector.

Gross profit

The gross profit margin in Quarter 1 was 52% (218,400/420,000 × 100%) and 50% (339,320/680,000 × 100%) in Quarter 2. The level of margin may be as expected for this business sector but we would need industry average data for comparison.

However, a **fall in margin** needs to be investigated. It could be that Ties Only was initially able to source cheaper ties but the rapid growth meant that alternative, more expensive suppliers had to be found. Alternatively, competitors quickly responded to this new entrant and lowered their prices in response. This pressure could have forced Ties Only to lower their prices.

BPP
LEARNING MEDIA

Website Development

All website development costs are being **written off as incurred** so we would expect costs to be higher in the initial quarters. The website costs are over a third of total expenses, so the initial loss is mostly explained by this write-off and does not therefore give any major cause for concern.

Administration costs

Although administration costs have risen in absolute terms, as a **percentage of sales** they have **fallen** from 23.9% (100,500/420,000 × 100%) to 22.2% (150,640/680,000 × 100%). Administration costs are the second biggest expense so very important to control.

This could indicate that administration costs are being **effectively controlled** which is good news. It could also be because fixed overheads are being **spread over a larger volume** and this will continue to improve as the business grows.

Distribution costs

These costs form the **smallest proportion** of total expenses (about 6%) and the proportion of distribution costs to sales has **remained constant** at 4.9% (20,763/420,000 × 100%). These costs will be subject to external influences such as a general rise in postage costs.

Launch marketing

This is similar to the website costs as it is expected to fall once the business is established. Ties Only will need to **continue to market** their website but this is likely to be cheaper than the initial big launch marketing campaign. The negative impact on profitability will therefore reduce over time.

Other variable expenses

These have again increased in line with the sales volume and are 11.9% of sales (50,000/420,000 × 100%).

(b) **Current and future profits**

An initial look at the accounts would identify a worrying total loss of $188,303 in the first two quarters.

However, much of this loss is due to the website development costs which will not be incurred again. Websites do need to be maintained and continually improved but this cost will be much lower. Launch marketing is another initial cost which will fall rapidly. If we deduct these expenses, the business made an **underlying profit** of $47,137 in Quarter 1 and $75,360 in Quarter 2, an encouraging **upward trend**.

The initial impact of the business has been very good. There is a threat from falling margins to consider but cost control looks effective so the future is promising.

These figures illustrate that a short-term view of a new business is not necessarily a good indicator of future performance.

(c) **Non-financial performance indicators**

Average price of ties

Quarter 1: $420,000/27,631 = $15.20
Quarter 2: $680,000/38,857 = $17.50

In part (a) it was suggested that **the fall in gross profit margin** might be due to a price reduction. This data provides evidence that this is **not** the case. There must therefore be an alternative explanation.

On time delivery

This has dropped significantly from 95% to 89% and this is worrying. The service provided to customers is a **key differentiator**, especially if the company is competing on quality not price. Customers will go elsewhere if their expectations are not met. Action will need to be taken to remedy this problem.

Sales returns

This is again a key indicator of **quality** and whether **customers' expectations** are being met. Returns have risen from 12% to 18% and are now above the industry average of 13%. Returns are to be expected on Internet sales where the product may look different in reality, but a higher than average rate means that the

internet is **not adequately describing and illustrating** the products. Again, quality may be less than customers expect.

Alternatively, the **pressure to dispatch orders** may be resulting in **errors** or packaging problems. Either of these reasons does not bode well for the business and action must be taken to remedy the problem.

System downtime

Customers who use shopping websites are usually **time pressured** individuals who will not react well to delays in loading pages. It is all too easy to immediately switch to a competitor's website so it is essential that system downtime is kept to an absolute minimum to **avoid lost sales**.

It would be useful to compare the figures with an **industry average** but the important point is that system downtime has **doubled**. This could be due to **pressure on the website** as a result of the volume of demand. As the website development has been such a costly and important part of the business set-up, the owners of Ties Only should have an urgent discussion with the website developers to come up with a solution.

Conclusion

Ties Only are doing well in terms of sales growth and potential profitability for a brand new business. However the owners need to focus their attention on the accuracy of order delivery, website reliability and the quality of the product. Further investigation needs to be made of the fall in gross profit margin.

285 The Accountancy Teaching Co

Text reference. Performance measurement is covered in Chapter 16.

Top tips. At first glance, you may not know where to begin with this question! Take care to structure your answer around the headings given in the requirement and set out your workings clearly to maximise your score in each area.

Be sure to explain what your calculations mean for AT Co, to add depth to your answer. Finally, do not forget to comment on each of the non-financial performance indicators.

Easy marks. There are easy marks available throughout this question (providing you spend enough time on each heading provided in the question requirement!)

Examiner's comments. This was a typical performance measurement question. There was quite a lot of information to absorb but I strongly believe that, unless you are given plenty of information to work with, it is only possible to make very generalised, insipid comments. This is not what F5 is all about. I want candidates to be able to handle information and make some quality analysis about it. It requires common sense and ability to link information. Needless to say, answers were poor. Anyone who had read my article on this area, or indeed my predecessor's article on this area, would know that insipid comments such as 'turnover decreased by 8.3%, which is poor' will score only a calculation mark, for working out the 8.3%. Is this decrease in turnover poor? Well, it depends on the market in which the company is operating. You have to read the scenario. When you take into account the fact that there has been a 20% decline in the demand for accountancy training, AT Co's 8.3% looks relatively good. You must link information; this is an essential skill for any accountant. Nothing is ever what it seems...ask any auditor!

Let me also take the opportunity to distinguish between an acceptable comment, which might earn one mark, compared to a good point, which might earn two marks. Cost of sales fell by $10.014m in the year. Part of this reduction was down to a fall in freelance lecture costs. A good candidate would have commented that, whilst the company requested that freelance lecturers reduce their fees by 10%, the actual fee reduction gained was 15%, a strong performance. A comment such as this would have earned two marks. A less observant comment, earning one mark, would have been that the reduction in cost of sales was partly due to the fact that the company requested freelance lecturers to reduce their fees by 10%.

I hope that this question will serve as a good revision question to future examinees of F5. The information given is there to help you make worthwhile comments. When planning the question, you should annotate it carefully, cross-referencing different parts of the question, linking financial and non-financial information etc.

	Marks
Turnover:	
8.3% decrease	½
Actual turnover 14.6% higher	½
Performed well CF market conditions	1
Transfer of students	1
	3
Cost of sales:	
19.2% decrease	½
63.7% of turnover	½
15% fee reduction from freelance staff	2
Other costs of sale fell by $3.555m	2
Online marking did not save as much as planned	1
	Max 5
Gross profit – numbers and comment	1
Indirect expenses:	
Marketing costs:	
42.1% increase	½
Increase necessary to reap benefits of developments	1
Benefits may take more than one year to be felt	½
Property costs – stayed the same	½
Staff training:	
163.9% increase	½
Necessary for staff retention	1
Necessary to train staff on new website etc	1
Without training, staff would have left	1
Less student complaints	1
Interactive website and student helpline:	
Attracted new students	1
Increase in pass rate	1
Enrolment costs:	
Fall of 80.9%	½
Result of electronic system being introduced	1
Reduced number of late enrolments	1
	Max 9
Net operating profit:	
Fallen to $2.106	½
Difficult market	1
Staff training costs should decrease in the future	1
Future increase in market share	1
Lower advertising cost in future	1
Charge for website	1
	Max 3
	20

Turnover

Turnover has decreased by 8.3% from $72·025 million in 20X9 to $66·028 million in 20Y0. Given the 20% **decline in demand for accountancy training**, AT Co's turnover would have been expected to fall to $57·62m in line with market conditions. As such, it would appear that **AT has performed well in a tough market as it's actual turnover is 14·6% higher than expected.**

Non-financial performance indicators show that the number of students who transferred to AT from an alternative training provider in has increased to 20% in 20Y0 (from 8% in 20X9). This **increase in market share** is likely to be directly linked to **the improved service provided to students** as a result of the new student helpline and interactive website as well as other developments.

Cost of sales

Cost of sales has decreased by 19·2% from $52.078m in 20X9 to $42.056m in 20Y0. In 20X9, cost of sales represented 72·3% of turnover and in 20Y0 this figure was 63·7%. The reasons for this substantial decrease are considered below.

Freelance costs in 20X9 were $14·582m. Given that a minimum 10% reduction in fees had been requested to freelance lecturers and the number of courses run by them was the same year on year, the expected cost for freelance lecturers in 20Y0 was $13·124m. The **reduction in costs was successful** as actual costs were $12·394m (a reduction of 15%).

Prior to any cost cuts and **assuming a consistent cost of sales to turnover ratio**, costs of sales for 20Y0 were expected to be $47·738m. The actual cost of sales was $5·682m lower at $42.056m. Freelance lecturer costs fell by $2·188m, meaning that the remaining $3.494m is made up of decreases in other costs of sale.

Employees were told they would not receive a pay rise for at least one year and the average number of employees hardly changed year on year. As such, **the decreased costs are unlikely to be related to staff costs**.

The introduction of the **electronic marking system was expected to save the company $4m**. It is possible that the system did not save as much as predicted, hence the $3.494m fall. Alternatively, the saved marking costs may have been partially counteracted by an increase in another cost included in cost of sales.

Gross profit

As a result of the increased market share and cost savings discussed above, the **gross profit margin has increased** in 20Y0 from 27·7% to 36·3%.

Indirect expenses

Marketing costs

AT Co has increased spend on marketing campaigns to make students aware of the improved service and the range of facilities that the company offer. As such, marketing costs have increased by 42·1% in 20Y0. It would appear that the marketing campaigns have been a success, with higher student numbers relative to the competition in 20Y0. It is important to recognise the time lag between the cost outlay and the benefit received from such campaigns. It is likely that many of the benefits will not be felt until 20Y1.

Property costs

Property costs have remained in line with 20X9, indicating no significant investment in company premises.

Staff training

Training costs have increased dramatically from $1.287m in 20X9 to $3.396m in 20Y0, an increase of 163.9%. In 20X9 and before, AT Co had experienced problems with staff retention which resulted in a lower quality service being provided to students.

Considerable time and money is likely to have been spent on training staff to use the new interactive website as well as the electronic enrolment and marking systems. If the company had not spent this money on essential training, the quality of service would have deteriorated further and more staff would have left as they became increasingly dissatisfied with their jobs.

The number of student complaints has fallen dramatically in 20Y0 to 84 from 315, indicating that the staff training appears to have improved the quality of service being provided to students.

Interactive website and the student helpline

Interactive website and student helpline costs have not been incurred in previous years and have arisen from the drive towards providing students with an improved service and to increase pass rates. The percentage of students passing exams first time increased from 48% in 20X9 to 66% in 20Y0 which would suggest that the developments have improved the student learning environment.

Enrolment costs

Enrolment costs have fallen by $4.072m (80·9%), largely due to the new electronic enrolment system that was launched in 20Y0. It is likely that the new system has contributed to the reduction in late enrolments from 297 in 20X9 to 106 in 20Y0.

Net operating profit

Net operating profit has fallen from $3·635m to $2·106m (42%). Whilst this is a significant decrease, AT Co has been operating in tough market conditions in 20Y0. The company may have considered charging students a fee to use the interactive website in order to recoup some of the funds invested. This would have increased net operating profit.

Going forward, staff training costs are likely to decrease as staff become familiar with the new developments and staff retention improves. Higher pass rates are likely to attract more students in the coming years which will further increase market share.

As the AT brand becomes established in the market, it is likely that fewer advertising campaigns will take place, resulting in lower marketing costs.

Workings (**Note.** All workings are in $'000)

1   *Turnover*

Decrease in turnover = $72,025 – $66,028/$72,025 = 8.3%

Expected 20Y0 turnover given 20% decline in market = $72,025 × 80% = $57,620

Actual 20Y0 turnover CF expected = $66,028 – $57,620/$57,620 = 14.6% higher

2   *Cost of sales*

Decrease in cost of sales = $42,056 – $52,078/$52,078 = 19.2%

Cost of sales as percentage of turnover: 20X9 = $52,078/$72,025 = 72.3%

20Y0 = $42,056/$66,028 = 63.7%

3   *Freelance staff costs*

In 20X9 = $41,663 × 35% = $14,582

Expected cost for 2010 = $14,582 × 90% = $13,124

Actual 20Y0 cost = $12,394

$12,394 – $14,582 = $2,188 decrease

$2,188/$14,582 = 15% decrease in freelancer costs

4   *Expected cost of sales for 20Y0*

Before costs cuts, = $66,028 × 72.3% = $47,738

Actual cost of sales = $42,056

Difference = $5,682, of which $2,188 relates to freelancer savings and $3,494 relates to other savings.

5   *Gross profit margin*

20X9: $19,947/$72,025 = 27.7%

20Y0: $23,972/$66,028 = 36.3%

6   *Increase in marketing costs*

$4,678 – $3,291/$3,291 = 42.1%

7   *Increase in staff training costs*

   $3,396 – $1,287/$1,287 = 163.9%

8   *Decrease in enrolment costs*

   $960 – 5,032/5,032 = 80.9%

9   *Net operating profit*

   Decreased from $3,635 to $2,106. This is fall of 1,529/3,635 = 42.1%

286 Jump

Text references. Performance measurement is covered in Chapter 16.

Top tips. Ensure that your answer to part (b) supports both arguments. Use headings in your answer, one for each target.

Easy marks. Part (c) is relatively straight forward and is worth five marks.

Examiner's comments. Answers to part (a) were good on the whole. For a narrative requirement, part (b) was fairly well answered overall. Part (c) asked for a description of ways in which the manager could manipulate the situation in order to make sure he gets his bonus.

Again, there were some good answers here, with only a minority of candidates talking about manipulating profits, which wasn't relevant to a business where profit based targets weren't being used.

Marking scheme

			Marks
(a)	Per target	2	
			6
(b)	For each target – supporting controllability	1½	
	For each target – denying controllability	1½	
			9
(c)	For each idea of manipulation	2½	
			5
			20

(a)   Bonus calculation

	Qtr to 30 June 20X9	Qtr to 30 September 20X9	Qtr to 31 December 20X9	Qtr to 31 March 20Y0	Bonus hits
Staff on time?					
On-time %	95.5%	94.2%	94.0%	95.8%	
	(430/450)	(452/480)	(442/470)	(460/480)	
Bonus earned?	Yes	No	No	Yes	2

	Qtr to 30 June 20X9	Qtr to 30 September 20X9	Qtr to 31 December 20X9	Qtr to 31 March 20Y0	Bonus hits
Member visits					
Target visits	21,600	23,040	23,760	24,480	
	(60% × 3,000 × 12)	(60% × 3,200 ×12)	(60% × 3,300 × 12)	(60% × 3,400 × 12)	
Actual visits	20,000	24,000	26,000	24,000	
Bonus earned?	No	Yes	Yes	No	2

	Qtr to 30 June 20X9	Qtr to 30 September 20X9	Qtr to 31 December 20X9	Qtr to 31 March 20Y0	Bonus hits
Personal training					
Target visits	300	320	330	340	
	(10% × 3,000)	(10% × 3,200)	(10% × 3,300)	(10% × 3,400)	
Actual visits	310	325	310	339	
Bonus earned?	Yes	Yes	No	No	2

Total number of bonus hits from table above = 6

The earned by the manager is 6 × $400 = $2,400. This represents 50% of the total bonus available.

(b)   It is essential that the targets set are based on elements of the job that the local managers are able to control. Targets that are based on elements that local managers are unable to influence will be seen as pointless and unrealistic and could **demotivate staff** at the local manager level.

Staff on time

Individual members of staff may be late for work as a result of external factors including home pressures or delayed public transport. Such factors cannot be controlled by the local manager. However if such problems occur on a regular basis to certain members of staff, the local manager does have the power **to amend their contract of employment**.

The way in which the local manager manages staff will impact upon how **motivated** they are to work and to arrive on time. The **local manager** has the power to **devise shift patterns** that best their team and can **reward** them accordingly through their ability to amend employment contracts.

In summary, **lateness** to work **can be controlled** by the local manager.

Personal training sessions

The local manager has control over prices charged to customers. If demand for personal training sessions falls he/she can reduce prices or make special offers in a bid to increase customer numbers.

A number of potential customers may view personal training sessions as a luxury, particularly in the current economic climate. Also, the personal training market is particularly competitive which may make it difficult for the local managers to increase sales. Local managers can take steps to improve the service offered by the sports club but any significant expenditure requires approval at Board level.

In summary, the local manager can only **partly control** the number of **personal training sessions** that are booked.

Member use of facilities

The local manager controls the staff and hence the level of customer service. It is likely that a **high level of customer service** could encourage some **members to use** the facilities **more often**. The local manager also has the ability to influence member numbers by **adjusting membership prices**.

However, external factors such as **work pressures** and level of **health** may prevent some members from visiting the club as often as they would like.

In summary, the local manager can only **partly control** the **number of member visits**.

(c)   **Reduce prices**

The targets are largely volume driven and local managers have the power to **adjust membership fees** and **prices for personal training sessions**. Local managers could therefore reduce prices to ensure that they meet the targets and therefore obtain their bonus. Such a scenario would **harm** Jump's **overall profitability**.

Recording of transactions

A local manager with access to the accounting records could deliberately record visits to the club in the **incorrect period** in order to ensure that he/she achieves a bonus. For example, in Q2 the target for personal training sessions was not met by 5 sessions. The manager could record the first 5 transactions of Q3 in Q2 to ensure that he/she obtains an extra $400 bonus.

287 Bridgewater Co

Marking scheme

		Marks	
(a)	Per target discussed	2	
			8
(b)	Revised forecasts		
	Voucher sales effect	1	
	Vista sales effect	2	
	Extra trainer cost	1	
	Extra room hire cost	1	
	Staff training increase	½	
	Software cost	½	
	Overall revised profit calculation	1	
	Maximum		6
(c)	Per idea commented on	2	
			Max 6
			20

(a)   **Each quarter, sales should grow and annual sales should exceed budget**

In the Northwest division, sales are forecasted to fall by 10% ($4/40 \times 100\%$) from Quarter 1 to Quarter 2 but then start to grow. Average growth per quarter over the year is 14.5% ($\sqrt[3]{(60/40)} - 1$). Annual sales are forecast to exceed the sales budget by $6,000 (186 – 180).

It would therefore appear that the annual **target will be met**. However, the promotion decision is to be taken in Quarter 3 and the **slow start** to the year may not reflect well on the manager of the Northwest division.

Trainer costs should not exceed $180 per teaching day

The manager is paying $200 (8,000/40) per teaching day in trainer costs which **exceeds the target**. He believes in quality and therefore appears to be paying more to attract better teaching staff. This may well

BPP
LEARNING MEDIA

improve sales in the long-term as the reputation for quality delivery becomes known, but it is at the expense of increased costs in the short-term.

Room hire costs should not exceed $90 per teaching day

The manager of this division is also **spending more** on room hire costs than the target. He is spending $100 per teaching day rather than $90. This could be again part of his quality improvement policy as he is hiring better facilities, but it could also be due to poor negotiation and buying strategy.

Each division should meet its budget for profit per quarter and annually

The achievement of this target suffers from the same problem as the sales target. The manager will meet the target for the year by $2,500, but is **below target** in the first two quarters.

This again will impact on his promotion prospects which overall are not looking good. He is failing to meet any of the targets in the first two quarters and will have to hope that the senior managers agree with his **long-term** rather than **short-termist** approach.

(b) **Revised forecasts**

	Q1 $'000	Q2 $'000	Q3 $'000	Q4 $'000	Total $'000
Existing sales	40.0	36.0	50.0	60.0	186.0
Voucher sales ($125 × 80/4)	2.5	2.5	2.5	2.5	10.0
Software training			10.0	12.0	22.0
	42.5	38.5	62.5	74.5	218.0
Less:					
Existing trainer costs	8.0	7.2	10.0	12.0	37.2
Additional training costs ($200 × teaching days)			2.0	2.4	4.4
Room hire	4.0	3.6	5.0	6.0	18.6
Additional room hire ($100 × teaching days)			1.0	1.2	2.2
Staff training	1.0	1.0	1.0	1.0	4.0
Additional staff training	0.5	0.5			1
Other costs	3.0	1.7	6.0	7.0	17.7
Software	1.8				1.8
Forecast net profit	24.2	24.5	37.5	44.9	131.1
Original budget profit	25.0	26.0	27.0	28.0	106.0

(c) **Voucher scheme**

The voucher scheme looks like a good idea as the manager is confident that the take-up would be good and customers would follow his advice to attend one session per quarter. This will **increase revenue** without incurring additional costs as customers would attend existing planned courses. However, some additional unforeseen costs may still be incurred.

The additional revenue and profit will help, but targets for Quarters 1 and 2 will still not be met so the voucher scheme will not necessarily improve the manager's promotion prospects.

There is always the danger with offering a discount that **existing customers** will be disgruntled, particularly if they have already paid a higher price for a course that is now being offered at a discount. The vouchers are however only being offered to **new** customers so the manager should be able to offer this promotion without upsetting existing customers.

Software upgrade

It is essential that a software training company uses the **latest software technology** on its courses. The investment in software and staff training is therefore a **necessity** and cannot be avoided.

The courses will generate **extra revenue** but not until Quarters 3 and 4. This software upgrade will therefore further damage the achievement of targets in Quarters 1 and 2, as costs will rise but the extra revenue will be too late for the promotion assessment.

It is to be hoped that the senior managers will recognise the essential long-term planning being undertaken.

Delaying payments to trainers

This is not a good idea. None of the performance targets will be affected, as the plan will not affect costs or profits. The only positive impact will be on **cash flow**. The worrying aspect is the negative impact it may have on **relationships with trainers**. Software training is a competitive market and good trainers will be in demand by a number of training providers. If the company is to offer quality training, it must have the best trainers and this is not the way to retain them.

In conclusion, if all the proposals were taken together, they will **not improve** the manager's chance of promotion as any benefits will accrue after Quarter 2.

288 Oliver's Salon

Text references. Performance measurement is covered in Chapter 16.

Top tips. This is quite a long scenario with lots of information to deal with. In part (a) you need to use the sales value and the number of client visits to calculate the average price. Part (b) relates only to financial performance so a range of ratios need to be calculated and explained. The approach to use is to calculate a ratio (½ mark), make a qualitative statement (1 mark) and suggest a cause or some other comment (1 mark).

Part (c) gives you the headings to give a structure to your answer. Quality and resource utilisation are two of the dimensions in the Building Block Model. The question does not ask for recommendations for Oliver so make sure you stick to the requirements of the question.

Easy marks. The ratio analysis in part (b) has plenty of easy marks available but make sure you do more than just calculate the ratios.

Examiner's comments. A significant number of candidates could not calculate the prices for female and male clients in the two years in question. In part (b) there was some improvement in candidate's ability to assess performance. There were problems however: Mathematical descriptions are not performance assessments; simply stating the % increases in numbers is not enough; indicating the absolute change in a cost is rarely that useful; too narrow a range of figures considered, virtually all the numbers in the question carry marks.

In part (c) answers on quality dealt with the complaints issue well, but very few talked about the new members of staff and how their performance might be suspect. The lack of a pay rise can be de-motivating and so quality might suffer, this too was rarely picked up.

On resource utilisation candidates had a mixed result. The male throughput per specialist was very high but this was perhaps due to the fact that male hair tends to be easier (quicker) to cut. The female situation was different, with fewer clients for more staff. Many candidates recognised this. Very few talked about the property utilisation at all.

Marks

(a)	Average price for male customers	1
	Average price for female customers	2
		3
(b)	Sales growth	3
	Gross margin	3
	Rent	1½
	Advertising spend	1
	Staff costs	1½
	Electricity	1
		11
(c)	Quality – single gender	1
	Quality – wage levels	1
	Quality – other	1
	Resource utilisation – property	1
	Resource utilisation – staff	1
	Resource utilisation – other	1
		6
		20

(a) **Average price for hair services per female client**

20X8: Sales = $200,000
Number of female client visits = 8,000
Average price = 200,000/8,000
= $25

20X9: Prices were not increased so average price is still $25

Average price for hair services per male client

20X8: No male clients

20X9: Sales = $238,500

Female sales = $25 × 6,800 visits
= $170,000

Male sales = 238,500 – 170,000
= $68,500

Average price = 68,500/3,425
= $20

(b) **Financial performance**

Sales growth

Sales have grown by 19.25% ((238,500 – 200,000)/200,000 × 100%) from 20X8 to 20X9. This is particularly impressive as Oliver's Salon experiences high levels of competition.

This growth has come from the new **male hairdressing** part of the business as female sales have fallen by 15% ((200,000 – 170,000)/200,000 × 100%). There was **no price increase** during this time so this fall is due to less female client visits.

Gross profit

The gross profit margin in 20X8 was 53% (106,000/200,000 × 100%) and in 20X9 had **fallen** to 47.2% (112,500/238,500 × 100%). This is predominantly due to a 40% ((91,000 – 65,000)/65,000 × 100%) in **staff costs** as a result of the recruitment of two new staff.

The new specialist hairdresser for male clients is on a salary of $17,000 (91,000 – 65,000 – 9,000) whereas the female hairdressers were paid an average of $16,250 (65,000/4) in 20X8.

However it is the **female client** business which has been responsible for the drop in gross profit margin.

	20X8 Female $	20X9 Female $	20X9 Male $
Sales	200,000	170,000	68,500
Less cost of sales:			
Hairdressing staff	(65,000)	(74,000)	(17,000)
Hair products – female	(29,000)	(27,000)	
Hair products – male			(8,000)
Gross profit	106,000	69,000	43,500
Gross profit margin	106/200 × 100% = 53%	69/170 × 100% = 40.6%	43.5/68.5 × 100% = 63.5%

The gross profit margin from male clients is higher than for female clients.

Rent

This has not changed so is a **fixed cost** at the moment.

Administration salaries

These have increased by only 5.6% ((9,500 – 9,000)/9,000 × 100%) which is impressive given the expansion in the business.

Electricity

This has increased by 14.3% ((8,000 – 7,000)/7,000 × 100%. More clients would involve more electricity so it is a **semi-variable cost**. There may also have been a **general increase** in electricity prices which would be beyond the control of Oliver.

Advertising

This has increased by 150%((5,000 – 2,000)/2,000 × 100%) which could be expected at the **launch of a new service**. Provided the advertising has generated new clients, it should not be a cause for concern.

Net profit

Net profit has only increased by 2.6% ((80,000 – 78,000/78,000 × 100%) which is disappointing compared to a 19.25% increase in sales.

(c) **Non-financial performance**

Quality

The number of complaints has increased significantly by 283% ((46 – 12)/12 × 100%). This is not just due to the increase in client numbers.

Complaints per customer visit have increased from 0.15% (12/8,000 × 100%) to 0.44%. This is a cause for concern in a service business, especially as many customers will not actually complain but will just not come back.

The complaints could be from the new male clients who are not happy with the new hairdresser, or they could be from female clients who do not like having men in the salon. More information is needed and action to be taken to reduce the complaints.

Resource utilisation

The resources in Oliver's Salon are the **salon** itself and the **staff**. The salon is being utilised more as a result of the increase in clients from 8,000 in 20X8 to 10,225 (6,800 + 3,425) in 20X9. This is a 27.8% ((10,225 – 8,000)/8,000 × 100%) increase. This increase in utilisation has not however resulted in a proportionate increase in profit.

The **female specialist hairdressers** served 2,000 (8,000/4) clients per specialist in 20X8 and this fell to 1,360 (6,800/50) in 20X9, following the recruitment of two new staff. Oliver may be prepared to accept this reduction in resource utilisation in order to boost service levels and reduce complaints.

This contrasts with the higher figure of 3,425 clients per **male specialist** in 20X9. The time taken per male client is much less so this should be expected.

Mock exams

ACCA

Paper F5

Performance Management

Mock Examination 1

Question Paper: 3 hours 15 minutes
ALL questions are compulsory and MUST be attempted

DO NOT OPEN THIS PAPER UNTIL YOU ARE READY TO START UNDER EXAMINATION CONDITIONS

Section A – ALL FIFTEEN questions are compulsory and MUST be attempted

Each question is worth 2 marks.

1 X Co uses rolling budgeting, updating its budgets on a quarterly basis. After carrying out the last quarter's update to the cash budget, it projected a forecast cash deficit of $400,000 at the end of the year. Consequently, the planned purchase of new capital equipment has been postponed.

Which of the following types of control is the sales manager's actions an example of?

A   Feedforward control
B   Negative feedback control
C   Positive feedback control
D   Double loop feedback control

2 A company makes a single product which it sells for $2 per unit.

Fixed costs are $13,000 per month.

The contribution/sales ratio is 40%.

Sales revenue is $62,500.

What is the margin of safety (in units)?

A   15,000
B   16,250
C   30,000
D   31,250

3 The following statements have been made about different types of standards in standard costing systems.

(1)   Basic standards provide the best basis for budgeting because they represent an achievable level of productivity.

(2)   Ideal standards are short-term targets and useful for day-to-day control purposes.

Which of the above statements is/are true?

A   1 only
B   2 only
C   Neither 1 nor 2
D   Both 1 and 2

4 A budget that is continuously updated by adding a further accounting period (a month or quarter) when the earlier accounting period has expired is known as a:

A   Zero base budget
B   Rolling budget
C   Periodic budget
D   Flexible budget

5   Division X and Division Y are profit centres in the same company. Division X makes a single component product. It has a fixed contract to supply an external customer with 5,000 units each month at a price of $35 per unit. All other sales are to Division Y at $30 per unit. Budgeted monthly profits for Division X are as follows:

	$
Sales: External	350,000
Sales to Division Y	150,000
	500,000
Variable costs	(270,000)
Fixed costs	(170,000
Profit	60,000

An external supplier offers to sell 4,000 units of the component to Division Y at a price of $25 per unit, for one month only. Division X would not be able to sell additional components externally.

If Division Y chooses to buy the components from the external supplier, how will profits for the month be affected?

A   Division X profit will be $0. The company's profit will be $20,000 lower
B   Division X profit will be $0. The company's profit will be $28,000 lower
C   Division X profit will be $12,000. The company's profit will be $20,000 lower
D   Division X profit will be $12,000. The company's profit will be $28,000 lower

6   The following are types of management accounting techniques.

(i)   Flow cost accounting
(ii)   Input/output analysis
(iii) Life cycle costing
(iv)   Activity based costing

Which of the above techniques could be used by a company to account for its environmental costs?

A   i only
B   i and ii only
C   i, ii and iii only
D   All of the above

7   A business makes two components which it uses to produce one of its products. Details are:

	Component A	Component B
Per unit information:	$	$
Buy in price	14	17
Material	2	5
Labour	4	6
Variable overheads	6	7
General fixed overheads	4	3
Total absorption cost	16	21

The business wishes to maximise contribution and is considering whether to continue making the components internally or buy in from outside.

Which components should the company buy in from outside in order to maximise its contribution?

A   A only
B   B only
C   Both A and B
D   Neither A nor B

8   The following circumstances may arise in relation to the launch of a new product:

(i)   Demand is relatively inelastic
(ii)   There are significant economies of scale
(iii)   The firm wishes to discourage new entrants to the market
(iv)   The product life cycle is particularly short

Which of the above circumstances favour a penetration pricing policy?

A   (ii) and (iii) only
B   (ii) and (iv)
C   (i), (ii) and (iii)
D   (ii), (iii) and (iv) only

9   Tree Co is considering employing a sales manager. Market research has shown that a good sales manager can increase profit by 30%, an average one by 20% and a poor one by 10%. Experience has shown that the company has attracted a good sales manager 35% of the time, an average one 45% of the time and a poor one 20% of the time. The company's normal profits are $180,000 per annum and the sales manager's salary would be $40,000 per annum.

Based on the expected value criterion, which of the following represents the correct advice which Tree Co should be given?

A   Do not employ a sales manager as profits would be expected to fall by $1,300
B   Employ a sales manager as profits will increase by $38,700
C   Employ a sales manager as profits are expected to increase by $100
D   Do not employ a sales manager as profits are expected to fall by $39,900

10   Which one of the following may be used to study possible future outcomes when there are many different variables in the situation and the relationships between variables are not predictable?

A   Sensitivity analysis
B   Stress testing
C   Pay-off table
D   Simulation model

11   The following costs arise in relation to production of a new product.

(i)   Research and development costs
(ii)   Design costs
(iii)   Testing costs
(iv)   Advertising costs
(v)   Production costs

In calculating the lifetime costs of the product, which of the above items would be **excluded**?

A   i, ii, and iii only
B   ii and iii only
C   iv and v only
D   None of the above

12   The following statements have been made about zero based budgeting.

(1)   Employees will focus on eliminating wasteful expenditure.
(2)   Short-term benefits could be emphasised over long-term benefits.

Which of the above statements is/are true?

A   1 only
B   2 only
C   Neither 1 nor 2
D   Both 1 and 2

13   Which of the following is the best definition of a traceable divisional cost?

A   A variable cost incurred in a division

B   A cost incurred in a division over which the divisional manager has control

C   A cost attributable directly to a division over which the manager may or may not have control

D   Costs charged to a division, including both directly attributable costs and a share of general overheads

14   A company makes and sells Product P. At the current selling price of $6 per unit, weekly demand is 4,000 units. It is estimated that for every $0.50 increase in price, sales demand will fall by 200 units, and for every $0.50 reduction in price, sales demand will increase by 200 units.

What is the formula for the sales demand curve for this product, where P is the sales price and Q is the quantity demanded?

A $P = 6 - 0.0025Q$
B $P = 16 - 0.0025Q$
C $P = 6 - 0.005Q$
D $P = 16 - 0.005Q$

15   The following statements have been made about activity based costing.

(1)   There may be more than one cost driver for an activity.
(2)   ABC involves some arbitrary allocation or apportionment of overhead costs.

Which of the above statements is/are true?

A   1 only
B   2 only
C   Neither 1 nor 2
D   Both 1 and 2

Section B – All 15 questions are compulsory and MUST be attempted

The following scenario relates to questions 16-20.

Linacre Co

Linacre Co operates an activity-based costing system and has forecast the following information for next year.

Cost Pool	Cost	Cost Driver	Number of Drivers
Production set-ups	$105,000	Set-ups	300
Product testing	$300,000	Tests	1,500
Component supply and storage	$25,000	Component orders	500
Customer orders and delivery	$112,500	Customer orders	1,000

General fixed overheads such as lighting and heating, which cannot be linked to any specific activity, are expected to be $900,000 and these overheads are absorbed on a direct labour hour basis. Total direct labour hours for next year are expected to be 300,000 hours.

Linacre Co expects orders for Product ZT3 next year to be 100 orders of 60 units per order and 60 orders of 50 units per order. The company holds no inventories of Product ZT3 and will need to produce the order requirement in production runs of 900 units. One order for components is placed prior to each production run. Four tests are made during each production run to ensure that quality standards are maintained. The following additional cost and profit information relates to product ZT3:

Component cost:	$1.00 per unit
Direct labour:	10 minutes per unit at $7.80 per hour
Profit mark up:	40% of total unit cost

Required

16 Calculate the activity-based recovery rates for production set ups and product testing.

    A   Production set up $350 per set up, product testing $600 per test
    B   Production set up $350 per set up, product testing $200 per test
    C   Production set up $210 per set up, product testing $200 per test
    D   Production set up $210 per set up, product testing $1,000 per test   **(2 marks)**

17 Calculate the activity-based recovery rates for component supply and storage, and customer orders and delivery.

    A   Component supply and storage $50 per order, customer orders and delivery $112.50 per order.
    B   Component supply and storage $50 per order, customer orders and delivery $225 per order.
    C   Component supply and storage $25 per order, customer orders and delivery $225 per order.
    D   Component supply and storage $25 per order, customer orders and delivery $112.50 per order.   **(2 marks)**

18 Calculate the general overhead per unit and the direct labour cost per unit of Product ZT3.

    A   General overhead $0.50 per unit, Direct labour cost $7.80 per unit.
    B   General overhead $3 per unit, Direct labour cost $1.30 per unit.
    C   General overhead $3 per unit, Direct labour cost $7.80 per unit.
    D   General overhead $0.50 per unit, Direct labour cost $1.30 per unit.   **(2 marks)**

19   The following statements have been made about Linacre.

   (1)   The use of a mark up to determine the price and profit per unit of ZT3 may lead to the incorporation of components which are not valued by the customer.

   (2)   A target costing approach would place an emphasis on the planning and design stage of products in Linacre.

   Which of the above statements is/are true?

   A   1 only
   B   2 only
   C   Neither 1 nor 2
   D   Both 1 and 2   (2 marks)

20   The following statements have been made about Linacre.

   (1)   Unlike traditional absorption costing, ABC identifies variable overhead costs in the production of ZT3, for allocation to product costs.

   (2)   ABC can be used as an information source for budget planning based on activity rather than incremental budgeting.

   Which of the above statements is/are true?

   A   1 only
   B   2 only
   C   Neither 1 nor 2
   D   Both 1 and 2   (2 marks)

                                                                              (Total = 10 marks)

The following scenario relates to questions 21-25.

SH (12/08, amended)

Shifters Haulage (SH) is considering changing some of the vans it uses to transport crates for customers. The new vans come in three sizes; small, medium and large. SH is unsure about which type to buy. The capacity is 100 crates for the small van, 150 for the medium van and 200 for the large van.

Demand for crates varies and can be either 120 or 190 crates per period, with the probability of the higher demand figure being 0·6.

SH has in the past been very aggressive in its decision-making, pressing ahead with rapid growth strategies. However, its managers have recently grown more cautious as the business has become more competitive.

Profits table

	Small van	Medium van	Large van
Capacity	**100**	**150**	**200**
Low demand (120 crates) 0·4	300	468	368
High demand (190 crates) 0·6	300	500	816

Required

21   Using the profit table, state which van SH should buy if the management is risk averse.

   A   Small van
   B   Medium van
   C   Large van
   D   Small van and medium van gives the same result.   (2 marks)

22   Using the profit table, state which van SH should buy if the management is risk taking.

    A   Small van
    B   Medium van
    C   Large van
    D   Small van and large van gives the same result   **(2 marks)**

23   Using the profit table, state which van SH should buy if the management is risk neutral.

    A   Small van
    B   Medium van
    C   Large van
    D   Medium van and large van gives the same result   **(2 marks)**

24   The following statements have been made about SH.

    (1)   If the managers in SH are optimistic about the future the will choose the van using the maximin criteria.

    (2)   If the managers in SH are pessimistic and becoming more cautious, they will use expected values to make this decision.

    Which of the above statements is/are true?

    A   1 only
    B   2 only
    C   Neither 1 nor 2
    D   Both 1 and 2   **(2 marks)**

25   Which one of the following would reduce the level of uncertainty for SH in their decision making process?

    A   Expected value analysis
    B   Market research
    C   Sensitivity analysis
    D   Relevant costing   **(2 marks)**

(Total = 10 marks)

The following scenario relates to questions 26-30.

Spinster Co

Spinster Co has developed a new product. The first batch of 10 units will take 300 labour hours to produce. There will be an 80% learning curve that will continue until 540 units have been produced. Batches after this level will each take the same amount of time as the 54th batch. The batch size will always be 10 units.

Note: The learning index for an 80% learning curve is -0.3219

Ignore the time value of money.

26   Calculate the cumulative average time per batch for the first 54 batches

    A   4485.78 hours
    B   83.57 hours
    C   83.07 hours
    D   82.58 hours   **(2 marks)**

27   The total time for the first 16 batches of units was 3,300 hours. What was the actual learning rate closest to the nearest %?

    A   85%
    B   91%
    C   90%
    D   87%   **(2 marks)**

28 Once a 'steady state' was reached in production, Spinster Co set the standard costs for the new product. Which of the following best describes an attainable standard?

   A   A standard which can be attained under perfect operating conditions

   B   A standard based on current working conditions

   C   A long term standard which remains unchanged over the years and is used to show trends.

   D   A standard which can be achieved if production is carried out efficiently, machines are properly operated and/or materials are properly used.   **(2 marks)**

29 The staff at Spinster Co received incentives based on monthly variance analysis. Six months after setting the standards for the new product, the operating manager reported back to the board to say that despite unfavourable variances being reported each month, staff seemed less motivated to improve the situation in month six, than they were after the first couple of months.

   Based on this information, which of the following standards do you think was applied to the new product.

   A   Ideal
   B   Attainable
   C   Current
   D   Basic   **(2 marks)**

30 Spinster Co wish to improve their standard costing system by holding managers accountable for the costs over which they have some influence. Which of the following costs are not controllable by a production department manager?

   A   Variable production overheads

   B   Direct labour rate

   C   Increases in overall material costs due to high levels of wastage caused by poor supervision of production workers

   D   An increase in the level of idle time because of poorly maintained machines by the production department   **(2 marks)**

                                                                                    (Total = 10 marks)

Section C – Both questions are compulsory and MUST be attempted

31 PC Co (12/11)

You have recently been appointed as an assistant management accountant in a large company, PC Co. When you meet the production manager, you overhear him speaking to one of his staff, saying:

'Budgeting is a waste of time. I don't see the point of it. It tells us what we can't afford but it doesn't keep us from buying it. It simply makes us invent new ways of manipulating figures. If all levels of management aren't involved in the setting of the budget, they might as well not bother preparing one.'

Required

(a) Identify and explain SIX objectives of a budgetary control system.   **(9 marks)**

(b) Discuss the concept of a participative style of budgeting in terms of the six objectives identified in part (a).   **(11 marks)**

                                                                                    (Total = 20 marks)

32 Rotech group (6/14)

The Rotech group comprises two companies, W Co and C Co.

W Co is a trading company with two divisions: The Design division, which designs wind turbines and supplies the designs to customers under licences and the Gearbox division, which manufactures gearboxes for the car industry.

C Co manufactures components for gearboxes. It sells the components globally and also supplies W Co with components for its Gearbox manufacturing division.

The financial results for the two companies for the year ended 31 May 20X4 are as follows:

| | W Co | | C Co |
| | Design division | Gearbox division | |
	$'000	$'000	$'000
External sales	14,300	25,535	8,010
Sales to Gearbox division			7,550
			15,560
Cost of sales	(4,900)	(16,200)*	(5,280)
Administration costs	(3,400)	(4,200)	(2,600)
Distribution costs	–	(1,260)	(670)
Operating profit	6,000	3,875	7,010
Capital employed	23,540	32,320	82,975

* Includes cost of components purchased from C Co.

Required

(a)   Discuss the performance of C Co and each division of W Co, calculating and using the following three performance measures:

   (i)   Return on capital employed (ROCE)
   (ii)   Asset turnover
   (iii)   Operating profit margin

   Note. There are 4.5 marks available for calculations and 5.5 marks available for discussion.   **(10 marks)**

(b)   C Co is currently working to full capacity. The Rotech group's policy is that group companies and divisions must always make internal sales first before selling outside the group. Similarly, purchases must be made from within the group wherever possible. However, the group divisions and companies are allowed to negotiate their own transfer prices without interference from Head Office.

   C Co has always charged the same price to the Gearbox division as it does to its external customers. However, after being offered a 5% lower price for similar components from an external supplier, the manager of the Gearbox division feels strongly that the transfer price is too high and should be reduced. C Co currently satisfies 60% of the external demand for its components. Its variable costs represent 40% of revenue.

   Required

   Advise, using suitable calculations, the total transfer price or prices at which the components should be supplied to the Gearbox division from C Co.   **(10 marks)**

   (Total = 20 marks)

Answers

**DO NOT TURN THIS PAGE UNTIL YOU HAVE
COMPLETED THE MOCK EXAM**

A PLAN OF ATTACK

Managing your nerves

As you turn the pages to start this mock exam a number of thoughts are likely to cross your mind. At best, examinations cause anxiety so it is important to stay focused on your task for the next three hours! Developing an awareness of what is going on emotionally within you may help you manage your nerves. Remember, you are unlikely to banish the flow of adrenaline, but the key is to harness it to help you work steadily and quickly through your answers.

Working through this mock exam will help you develop the exam stamina you will need to keep going for three hours.

Managing your time

Planning and time management are two of the key skills which complement the technical knowledge you need to succeed. To keep yourself on time, do not be afraid to jot down your target completion times for each question, perhaps next to the title of the question on the paper. As all the questions are **compulsory**, you do not have to spend time wondering which question to answer!

Doing the exam

Actually doing the exam is a personal experience. There is not a single **right way**. As long as you submit complete answers to all questions after the three hours are up, then your approach obviously works.

Looking through the paper

Section A has 15 MCQs. This is the section of the paper where ACCA examination team can test knowledge across the breadth of the syllabus. Make sure you read these questions carefully. The distractors are designed to present plausible, but incorrect, answers. Don't let them mislead you. If you really have no idea – guess. You may even be right.

Section B has three questions, each with a scenario and five objective test questions.

Section C has two longer questions:

- Question 31 is about the objectives of budgetary control. Use the objectives identified in part (a) to structure your answer to part (b). Address each objective under a separate heading.

- Question 32 looks at performance measurement. Use a clear layout for your calculations and headings to give a structure to your discussions and explanations. Each part of the question can be answered separately so if you get stuck of are unsure what is required, move on.

Allocating your time

BPP's advice is to always allocate your time **according to the marks for the question**. However, **use common sense**. If you're doing a question but haven't a clue how to do part (b), you might be better off re-allocating your time and getting more marks on another question, where you can add something you didn't have time for earlier on. Make sure you leave time to recheck the MCQs and make sure you have answered them all.

Section A

1   A   Feedforward control is control based on forecast results. In other words if the forecast is bad, control action is taken well in advance of actual results.

           Negative feedback indicates that results or activities must be brought back on course, as they are deviating from the plan.

           Positive feedback results in control action continuing the current course.

           Double loop feedback is information used to change the plan itself. For example, if sales targets are not reached, the company may need to change the plan.

2   A   Sales = $62,500

           Break even sales = $13,000/0.40 = $32,500

           Margin of safety (sales revenue) = $62,500 – $32,500 = $30,000
           Margin of safety (units) $30,000/$2 =15,000 units

3   C   A basic standard is a historical standard, and will often no longer represent current levels of productivity. Ideal standards are not achievable in the short term, but may be longer-term targets.

4   B   A rolling budget is also known as a continuous budget.

5   D   External sales are 10,000 units and internal transfers are 5,000 units. The marginal cost per unit produced in Division X is $270,000/(10,000 + 5,000) = $18.

           The marginal cost of making the units is $18 and the cost of external purchase would be $25. By purchasing externally, the company as a whole would incur additional costs of $(25 – 18) × 4,000 units = $28,000.

Division profit	$
Sales: External	350,000
Sales to Division Y (1,000 units)	30,000
	380,000
Variable costs (11,000 × $18)	(198,000)
Fixed costs	(170,000)
Profit	12,000

           Division Y profits would increase by $20,000, Division X profits would fall be $48,000 and the company as a whole would suffer a fall in profit of $28,000.

6   D   Material flow cost accounting (MFCA) and input-output analysis are environmental management accounting techniques. Life cycle costing is concerned with analysing costs of a product over its entire life cycle from initial development to eventual withdrawal from the market. However, as long as you are aware that activity based costing is a management accounting technique, the answer to this question is straightforward. Only Option D includes ABC.

7   B   For a make-or-buy decision, we compare the marginal cost (relevant cost) of in-house production with the cost of buying in the item. Profit is maximised by selecting the lower cost.

           Component A: Relevant cost = $(2 + 6 + 4) = $12. Buy in cost = $14. Therefore produce in-house.

           Component B: Relevant cost = $(5 + 6 + 7) = $18. Buy in cost = $17. Therefore buy in from an external supplier.

8   A   (i) is incorrect because a penetration policy is favourable in circumstances where demand is relatively **elastic**. The circumstance in (iv) favours a market skimming policy.

9	A	Expected value of increase in profit of hiring a sales manager:		

Good manager:	$180,000 × 30% × 35% =	$18,900
Average manager:	$180,000 × 20% × 45% =	$16,200
Poor manager:	$180,000 × 10% × 20% =	$3,600
Expected value		$38,700
Less the sales manager's salary		($40,000)
Effect on profit of hiring sales manager		($1,300)

10   D   Sensitivity analysis is a term used to describe any technique whereby decision options are tested for their vulnerability to changes in any 'variable' such as expected sales volume, sales price per unit, material costs, or labour costs. It can be used in any situation so long as the relationships between the key variables can be established. Stress tests are used to test for extreme possible circumstances and what the outcome might then be.

Simulation models can be used to deal with decision problems involving a large number of uncertain variables, when the relationship between the variables is uncertain or unpredictable. In practice, simulation modelling is carried out using a computer model.

11   D   All the costs are included in the lifetime costs of a product.

12   D   Zero based budgeting begins by looking at the minimum budgeted expenditure, and building a budget from this zero base. This encourages employees to focus on wasteful and unnecessary spending.

However the focus is on short-term savings and may give insufficient consideration to longer-term benefits of current spending.

13   C   A distinction can be made between controllable fixed costs of a division, which are fixed costs over which the divisional manager has some control or influence, and traceable fixed costs which are costs attributable to a division but over which the manager has no control. For example, if a division is located in separate premises, the rental cost or depreciation cost of the premises is a traceable cost to the division, but the divisional manager may have no control over the amount of the expense.

14   B   If $P = a - bQ$, a is the price when $Q = 0$

$Q = 0$ when $P = 6 + [(4,000/200) \times 0.50] = 16$

Demand falls by 200 for every $0.5 change in the price, so the demand curve formula is:

$P = 16 - (0.5/200) \times Q$

$P = 16 - 0.0025Q$

15   D   There may be more than one cost driver for an activity, but in order to simplify the ABC system, it is usual to use just one cost driver per activity. ABC does involve some arbitrary apportionment of overhead costs to activities, such as factory rental and heating costs. Alternatively, general overheads are absorbed into costs on a direct labour hour or machine hour basis: this too is an arbitrary method of charging overheads.

Section B

Linacre Co

16   B   **The correct answer is:**

Production set ups: **350 per set up**

Product testing: **200 per test**

ABC recovery rates for production set ups and product testing

Cost Pool	Cost ($)	Cost driver	Number of drivers	ABC recovery rate ($)
Production set ups	105,000	Set-ups	300	350 per set –up
Product testing	300,000	Tests	1,500	200 per test

17   A   **The correct answer is:**

Component supply and storage: **50 per order**

Customer orders and delivery: **112.50 per order**

ABC recovery rates for component supply and storage, and customer orders and delivery

Cost Pool	Cost ($)	Cost driver	Number of drivers	ABC recovery rate ($)
Component supply and storage	25,000	Component orders	500	50 per order
Customer orders and delivery	112,500	Customer orders	1,000	112.50 per order

18   D   **The correct answer is:**

General overhead: $0.50 per unit

Direct labour cost $1.30 per unit

General overhead per unit of Product ZT3

General overhead = 0.50 per unit

$900,000/300,000 = $3/direct labour hour

9,000/6 or 1,500 direct labour hours spent on manufacture (10 minutes per unit)

1,500 hours/9,000 units $\times$ $3/unit = $0.50/unit

Direct labour per unit of Product ZT3

10 minutes per unit at $7.80 per hour = 10/60 □ 7.80 = $1.30 per unit

19   D   **Both 1 and 2**

Statement 1 is true. This is one of the main flaws associated with a mark up approach to costing. The product's price is based on its cost, but no one might want to buy at that price.

Statement 2 is true. There is an emphasis on the planning and design stage with target costing. This becomes very important to the cost of the product because if something is designed such that it is needlessly expensive to make, it does not matter how efficient the production process is, it will always be a struggle to make satisfactory profits.

20   B   ABC is a method of absorption costing that uses cost drivers to calculate absorption rates per unit of overhead activity, and then apportion overhead costs to products. It is not a technique for identifying variable overhead costs.

ABC can be used as a basis for preparing budgets. This approach to budgeting is called activity based budgeting (ABB).

SH

21   B   **Risk averse** – Medium van

If the managers are pessimistic and becoming more cautious, they will choose the van with the least unattractive worst outcome (the maximin criterion). This is the medium van with a profit of $468.

22   C   **Risk taker – Large van**

If the managers are **optimistic** about the future, they would choose the van with the best possible outcome (the maximax criteria). This is the large van as this has the highest profit of $816.

23   C   **Risk neutral – Large van**

Expected values support a **risk neutral attitude** and are used when a decision is being made more than once.

The expected values for this situation are:

Small van: $300
Medium van: ($468 × 0.4) + ($500 × 0.6) = $487
Large van: ($368 × 0.4) + (816 × 0.6) = $637

The large van therefore has the highest expected value.

24   C   Neither 1 nor 2

Statement 1 is false. If the managers in SH are optimistic about the future the will choose the van using the maximax criterion.

Statement 2 is false. If the managers in SH are pessimistic and becoming more cautious, they will the maximin criterion.

25   B   Market research

Market research could be used to obtain data about customer/consumer attitudes. This could help reduce the uncertainty for some elements of decision making.

Spinster Co

26   C   **The correct answer is 83.07 hours**

Cumulative average time per batch for the first 54 batches

$Y = ax^b$

Where Y = the cumulative average time per unit to produce x units
x = the cumulative number of units
a = the time taken for the first unit of output
b = the index of learning (logLR/log2)

The cumulative average time per batch, with a learning curve of 80% is therefore

$Y = aX^{-0.3219}$

where a = the time for the first batch (300 hours) and X is the number of the batch. For the 54th batch, X = 54.

$Y = 300 \times 54^{-0.3219}$

$= 300 \times 0.2769 = 83.07$

The cumulative average time per batch for the first 54 batches is 83.07 hours.

27   B

Batches	Total time	Average time/unit
1	300	
2		$300 \times r$
4		$300 \times r^2$
8		$300 \times r^3$
16	3,300	$300 \times r^4$

$3,300 = 16 \times 300\, r^4$

$3,300/(16 \times 300) = r^4$

$r = 0.91$ or 91%

28   D   A standard which can be achieved if production is carried out efficiently, machines are properly operated and/or materials are properly used.

Distractors:

A   This is an ideal standard
B   This is a current standard
C   This is a basic standard

29   A   Ideal

It is likely that management at Spinster Co have applied an ideal standard. Their view may have been that this created an incentive to be more efficient, even though it is highly unlikely that the standard will be achieved. However, the differences between standards and actual results will always be adverse. It appears that the employees feel that the goals are unattainable so they are unmotivated to improve their performance.

30   B   Direct labour rate

This rate will be governed by legislation and market conditions. It is therefore out of the control of the production department manager.

Section C

31 PC Co

Text reference. Objectives of budgetary control are covered in Chapter 8. Budgetary systems are covered in Chapter 9.

Top tips. Use the objectives identified in part (a) to structure your answer to part (b). Address each objective under a separate heading.

Easy marks. There are plenty of easy marks available in part (a).

Examiner's comments. Part (a) was where the bulk of the easy marks were on this paper and a good number of answers scored full marks.

Part (b) was a little more challenging: a requirement to discuss the concept of participative budgeting in terms of the objectives identified in part (a). Answers to this were mixed, with some good attempts but some poor ones too. A small number of candidates didn't know what participative budgeting was (the clue is in the title) so they scored nothing. Others managed to score marks by making some valid observations about it, even if they didn't necessarily tackle it in the best way, which was by using the objectives in part (a) as headings in order to give the answer some structure.

Marking scheme

		Marks
(a)	Objectives:	
	Each objective - 1½ marks per objective	max 9
(b)	Participative style of budgeting:	
	Explanation of participative budgeting	2
	Each objective discussed in relation to it – 1½ marks per objective	9
		11
		20

(a) Objectives of a budgetary control system

To compel planning

Budgeting forces management to look ahead and to set out detailed plans for **achieving targets** for each department, operation and (ideally) each manager within the organisation. It thus prevents management from relying on ad hoc or uncoordinated planning which may be detrimental to the performance of the organisation.

To communicate ideas and plans

A formal budgeting system is necessary to ensure that each person affected by management plans is aware of what he or she is supposed to be doing. Communication might be **one-way** with managers giving orders to subordinates, or there may be a **two-way dialogue** and exchange of ideas (participative budgeting).

To coordinate activities

Budgetary control systems help to coordinate the activities of different departments or sub-units of the organisation, ensuring **maximum integration** of effort towards common goals. The concept of coordination implies, for example, that the purchasing department should base its budget on production requirements and that the production budget should in turn be based on sales expectations. Coordination is difficult to achieve and there is often **conflict** between departmental plans in the budget so that the efforts of each department are not fully integrated into a combined plan to achieve the company's **best targets**.

To provide a framework for responsibility accounting

Budgetary planning and control systems require that managers of **budget centres** are made responsible for the achievement of **budget targets** for the operations under their personal control.

To establish a system of control

A budget is a **benchmark** against which actual performance is **measured** and **assessed**. Control over actual performance is provided by the comparisons of actual results against the budget plan. Departures from budget can then be **investigated** and the reasons for the departures can be divided into controllable and uncontrollable factors.

To motivate employees to improve their performance

Employees can be motivated via a system of **feedback** of actual results, which lets them know how well or badly they are performing. The identification of controllable reasons for departures from budget with managers responsible provides an incentive for **improving future performance**.

Top tips. The question asks you to identify and explain SIX objectives of a budgetary control system. Other possible objectives include the following.

To ensure the achievement of the organisation's objectives

Objectives can be set for individual departments and operations as well as the organisation as a whole. Quantified expressions of these objectives are then drawn up as **targets** to be achieved within the timescale of the **budget plan**.

To evaluate performance

Performance can be evaluated by **comparing actual results against the budget**. Employees are often rewarded with bonuses if performance **exceeds budget**. This makes more sense than simply comparing actual results against the previous year as economic conditions can change and events happen that may not be expected to reoccur.

(b)   **Participative budgeting**

Under a participative style of budgeting budgets are developed by **lower-level managers** who then submit the budgets to their superiors. The budgets are based on the lower-level managers' perceptions of what is achievable and the associated necessary resources.

Each of the objectives from part (a) is addressed below, considering the extent to which participate budgeting hopes to achieve this.

To compel planning

Participative budgeting (bottom-up budgeting) will compel planning. Under this style of budgeting, participation starts at the **lowest level of management** and goes all the way up to the top. In this way, planning takes place at **all levels** within the organisation. As a result, plans should be **more accurate** as they will be based on information from employees who are most familiar with day-to-day operations.

To communicate ideas and plans

Communication of **ideas and plans** will be particularly effective with participative budgeting. If all levels of management actively participate in the budgeting process then they will all know what the plan is. However, budgets may be updated during the **review process** to conform with the expectations of top level management. If this happens, lower-level management will have to work towards budgets that differ from those that were originally submitted.

To coordinate activities

Co-ordination of activities is likely to take **significantly longer** under a style of participative budgeting. For everyone to know what the plan is, not only does there need to be co-ordination between departments but there also has to be co-ordination between the **different levels of management** within each department.

To provide a framework for responsibility accounting

Participative budgeting is likely to **improve morale** amongst lower-level management and motivate them to work towards the budget targets under their control. However, there is a risk that lower-level management will introduce **budgetary slack** to make targets more achievable.

To establish a system of control

As stated above, budgets are likely to be more accurate if a participative style of budgeting is used, thus providing a solid **benchmark** against which to monitor actual results. However, the type of budgeting style used is largely irrelevant in establishing an effective **system of control**. Actual results should be compared against budget on a regular basis and any significant differences should be investigated, regardless of the budgetary system in place.

To motivate employees to improve their performance

Managers are more likely to think that a budget is **realistic** if they have been involved in the budget-setting process. They will therefore work harder to achieve the targets set. However, lower-level management may become disillusioned if top management make **significant changes** to the budget. They may be deliberately unproductive so that the final budget is not achieved and to prove that the budget they initially submitted was **more realistic / accurate**.

32 Rotech Group

Text reference. Performance measurement is covered in Chapters 16 and 17.

Top tips. Use a clear layout for your calculations and headings to give a structure to your discussions and explanations. Each part of the question can be answered separately so if you get stuck or are unsure what is required, move on.

Easy marks. The calculations are straightforward and there are plenty of marks available for common sense explanations.

Examiner's comments. The calculations in the first part of the question were done quite well, although a common mistake was to combine the two divisions of W Co an calculate the ratios for W Co as a whole. This was presumably caused by insufficient reading of the requirement. Students had difficulty dealing with the discussion that followed the calculations with candidates failing to identify the difficulty comparing a design business to a manufacturing business.

Marking scheme

		Marks
Ratios		
Calculating ROCE	1.5	
Calculating asset turnover	1.5	
Calculating operating profit margin	1.5	
Marks per valid comment (max 5.5)	5.5	
Transfer pricing		10
Each valid comment/calculation	1/2	
		10
		20

(a) **Financial ratios**

		W Co Design	W Co Gearbox	C Co
Return on capital employed	$\dfrac{\text{Profit before interest and tax}}{\text{Capital employed}}\%$	$6,000/$23,540 = 25.49%	$3,875/$32,320 = 11.99%	$7,010/82,975 = 8.45%
Asset turnover	$\dfrac{\text{Sales}}{\text{Capital employed}}$	$14,300/$23,540 = 0.61 times	$25,535/$32,320 = 0.79 times	$15,560/$82,975 = 0.19 times
Operating profit margin	$\dfrac{\text{Profit before interest and tax}}{\text{Sales}}\%$	$6,000/$14,300 = 41.96%	$3,875/$25,535 = 15.18%	$7,010/$15,560 = 45.05%

Return on capital employed:

ROCE shows how much profit has been made in relation to the amount of resources invested. C Co and both divisions of W Co are profitable. The Design division of W Co has the highest ROCE at over 25% while the Gearbox division and C Co are significantly lower at 11.99% and 8.45% respectively. This is primarily due to the nature of the design business which derives its profits from personnel rather than physical assets. Employees generate profits by designing products, rather than using expensive machinery. Therefore the Design divisions capital employed (asset) figure is significantly lower.

C Co has the largest asset base, and this is reflected in a relatively low ROCE. The Gearbox division is closer to this than to the design division but this is as a result of similarities in the nature of the business rather than division performance alone.

Asset turnover:

Asset turnover is a measure of how well the assets of a business are being used to generate sales. The Gearbox division has the highest level at 79%, while C Co has the lowest at 19%. This is probably due in part to the fact that the Gearbox division buys from C Co, therefore C Co must hold a large asset base to produce the relevant components. Both divisions of W Co do not have the same requirement and this is reflected in the higher asset turnover figures.

Operating profit margin:

C Co comes out on top in the final profitability measure, which is he operating profit margin at just over 45%, while the Gearbox division is the lowest at 15.18%. The Design division performs well at 41.96%, as it did in asset turnover. This was to be expected from the ROCE of 25%, which is a combination of the other two ratios. The Design division has both high unit profitability and generates sales at a high lever compared to its asset base.

There are limitations to these types of comparisons due to the differing nature of the businesses. It would be more useful to compare each business unit to an industry average for similar businesses, as well as comparing year on year figures to monitor the units on an ongoing basis.

(b) **Transfer prices**

From C Co's perspective

C Co transfers components to the Gearbox division at the same price as it sells components to the external market. However, if C Co were not making internal sales then, given that it already satisfies 60% of external demand, it would not be able to sell all of its current production to the external market. External sales are $8,010,000, therefore unsatisfied external demand is ([$8,010,000/0·6] – $8,010,000) = $5,340,000.

From C Co's perspective, of the current internal sales of $7,550,000, $5,340,000 could be sold externally if they were not sold to the Gearbox division. Therefore, in order for C Co not to be any worse off from selling internally, these sales should be made at the current price of $5,340,000, less any reduction in costs which C Co saves from not having to sell outside the group (perhaps lower administrative and distribution costs).

As regards the remaining internal sales of $2,210,000 ($7,550,000 – $5,340,000), C Co effectively has spare capacity to meet these sales. Therefore, the minimum transfer price should be the marginal cost of producing these goods. Given that variable costs represent 40% of revenue, this means that the marginal cost for these sales is $884,000. This is therefore the minimum price which C Co should charge for these sales.

In total, therefore, C Co will want to charge at least $6,224,000 for its sales to the Gearbox division.

From the Gearbox division's perspective

The Gearbox division will not want to pay more for the components than it could purchase them for externally. Given that it can purchase them all for 95% of the current price, this means a maximum purchase price of $7,172,500.

Overall

Taking into account all of the above, the transfer price for the sales should be somewhere between $6,224,000 and $7,172,500.

ACCA

Paper F5

Performance Management

Mock Examination 2

Question Paper: 3 hours 15 minutes
ALL FIVE questions are compulsory and MUST be attempted

DO NOT OPEN THIS PAPER UNTIL YOU ARE READY TO START UNDER EXAMINATION CONDITIONS

Section A – ALL FIFTEEN questions are compulsory and MUST be attempted

Each question is worth 2 marks.

1 The following statements have been made when making comparisons between traditional absorption costing and activity-based costing.

(1) ABC has evolved as a response to the increase in support activities in modern organisations.

(2) Absorption costing uses volume as a basis for cost allocation, and so tends to allocate too great a proportion of overheads to low volume products.

Which of the above statements is/are true?

☐ 1 only
☐ 2 only
☐ Neither 1 nor 2
☐ Both 1 and 2

2 Highfly Co manufactures two products, X and Y, and any quantities produced can be sold for $60 per unit and $25 per unit respectively.

Variable costs per unit of the two products are as follows:

	Product X	Product Y
	$	$
Materials (at $5 per kg)	15	5
Labour (at $6 per hour)	24	3
Other variable costs	6	5
Total	45	13

Next month, only 4,200 kg of material and 3,000 labour hours will be available. The company aims to maximise its profits each month.

The company wants to use the linear programming model to establish an optimum production plan. The model considers 'x' to be number of units of product X and 'y' to be the number of units of product Y.

Which of the following objective functions and constraint statements (relating to material and labour respectively) is correct?

Objective function	Material constraint	Labour constraint
☐ 60x + 25y	3x + y ≤ 4,200	4x + 0.5y ≤ 3,000
☐ 15x + 12y	3x + y ≥ 4,200	4x + 0.5y ≥ 3,000
☐ 15x + 12y	3x + y ≤ 4,200	4x + 0.5y ≤ 3,000
☐ 60x + 25y	3x + y ≥ 4,200	4x + 0.5y ≥ 3,000

3 The following statements have been made about the balanced scorecard.

(1) It focuses solely on non-financial performance measures.
(2) It looks at both internal and external matters concerning the organisation.

Which of the above statements is/are true?

☐ 1 only
☐ 2 only
☐ Neither 1 nor 2
☐ Both 1 and 2

4   The following statements have been made about changing budgetary systems.

      (1)   The costs of implementation may outweigh the benefits.

      (2)   Employees will always welcome any new system which improves planning and control within the
            organisation.

      Which of the above statements is/are true?

      ☐   1 only
      ☐   2 only
      ☐   Neither 1 nor 2
      ☐   Both 1 and 2

5   A manufacturing company uses throughput accounting. It manufactures two products, X and Y, using the
      same types of machine (Machine M and Machine T) for both products. Machine time on Machine Type M is
      a production bottleneck. The following information is available.

	Product X	Product Y
Throughput accounting ratio	2.4	3.0
Machine M time per unit produced	15 minutes	30 minutes
Machine T time per unit produced	30 minutes	20 minutes

      There is unlimited sales demand for both products.

      If extra production capacity is made available, amounting to 10 extra machine M hours and 10 extra machine
      T hours, how many additional units of output would be produced in order to maximise profit?

      ☐   units of Product Y
      ☐   units of Product X

      ☐   10 units of Product Y and 20 units of Product X
      ☐   20 units of Product Y and 40 units of Product X
      ☐   20 units of Product Y
      ☐   40 units of Product X

6   A company has entered two different new markets.

      In market A, it is initially charging low prices so as to gain rapid market share while demand is relatively
      elastic.

      In market B, it is initially charging high prices so as to earn maximum profits while demand is relatively
      inelastic.

      Which price strategy is the company using in each market?

      ☐   Penetration pricing in market A and price skimming in market B
      ☐   Price discrimination in market A and penetration pricing in market B
      ☐   Price skimming in market A and penetration pricing in market B
      ☐   Price skimming in market A and price discrimination in market B

7   The following are all types of control within an organisation.

(i)   Logical access controls
(ii)   Database controls
(iii)   Hierarchical passwords
(iv)   Range checks

Which of the above controls help to ensure the security of highly confidential information?

☐   i and ii only

☐   i and iii only

☐   i, ii and iii only

☐   All of the above

8   Total production costs for 900 units of output are $58,200 and total production costs for 1,200 units are $66,600.

The variable cost per unit is constant up to a production level of 2,000 units per month but a step up of $6,000 in the monthly total fixed cost occurs when production reaches 1,100 units per month.

What is the total cost for a month when 1,000 units are produced?

$ [   ]

9   S Company is a manufacturer of multiple products and uses target costing. It has been noted that Product P currently has a target cost gap and the company wishes to close this gap.

Which of the following may be used to close the target cost gap for product P?

☐   Use overtime to complete work ahead of schedule

☐   Substitute current raw materials with cheaper versions

☐   Raise the selling price of P

☐   Negotiate cheaper rent for S Company's premises

10   The following statements have been made about management information systems.

(1)   They are designed to report on existing operations.
(2)   They have an external focus.

Which of the above statements is/are true?

☐   1 only

☐   2 only

☐   Neither 1 nor 2

☐   Both 1 and 2

11   The following are some of the areas which require control within a division.

(i)   Generation of revenues
(ii)   Investment in non-current assets
(iii)   Investment in working capital
(iv)   Apportioned head office costs

Which of the above does the manager have control over in an investment centre?

☐   i, ii and iii only

☐   ii, iii and iv only

☐   i, ii and iv only

☐   All of the above

12   An investment centre in a manufacturing group produced the following results in the previous financial year:

	£'000
Operating profit	360
Capital employed: non-current assets	1,500
current assets	100

For the purpose of performance measurement, non-current assets are valued at cost. The investment centre is considering a new investment that will increase annual operating profit by £25,000, and will require an investment of £100,000 in a non-current asset and an additional £30,000 in working capital.

Will the performance measurement criteria of (1) Return on Investment (ROI) and (2) residual income (RI) motivate the centre manager to undertake the investment? Assume a notional capital charge of 18% on divisional capital.

ROI	RI
☐ Yes	Yes
☐ Yes	No
☐ No	Yes
☐ No	No

13   For a charitable organisation providing relief services to underdeveloped economies, which one of the following performance measurements would be the most suitable measurement of the effectiveness in the use of the charity's aid funds?

☐ Percentage of funds spent on frontline activities

☐ Ratio of volunteer helpers to full-time employees in the organisation

☐ Size of operating surplus (fund income less expenditure)

☐ Total spending by the charity on its operations

14   A company introduced Product C to the market 12 months ago and is now about to enter the maturity stage of its life cycle. The maturity stage is expected to last for three months. The Director of Sales and Marketing has suggested four possible prices that the company could charge during the next three months. The following table shows the results of some market research into the level of weekly demand at alternative prices:

Selling price per unit	$300	$255	$240	$225
Weekly demand (units)	1,800	2,400	3,600	4,200

Each unit of product C has a variable cost of $114 and takes one standard hour to produce.

Which selling price will maximise the weekly profit during this stage of the product life cycle?

$ ☐

15   A company has received a special order for which it is considering the use of material B which it has held in its inventory for some time. This inventory of 945 kg was bought at $4.50 per kg. The special order requires 1,500 kg of material B. If the inventory is not used for this order, it would be sold for $2.75 per kg. The current price of material B is $4.25 per kg.

What is the total relevant cost of material B for the special order?

$ ☐

Section B – All 15 questions are compulsory and MUST be attempted

The following scenario relates to questions 16-20.

Yam Co

Yam Co is involved in the processing of sheet metal into products A, B and C using three processes, pressing, stretching and rolling. The factory has many production lines each of which contain the three processes: Raw material for the sheet metal is first pressed then stretched and finally rolled. The processing capacity varies for each process and the factory manager has provided the following data:

| | Processing time per metre in hours | | |
	Product A	Product B	Product C
Pressing	0·50	0·50	0·40

The total annual processing hours for the factory is 225,000. On average one hour of labour is needed for each of the 225,000 hours of factory time. Labour is paid $10 per hour.

The raw materials cost per metre is $2·50 for product B. Other factory costs (excluding labour and raw materials) are $18,000,000 per year. Selling prices per metre are $60 for product B. The return per factory hour of product A is $134.

Yam carries very little inventory. Pressing has been identified as the bottleneck.

Required

16   What is the maximum output capacity per year for the bottleneck 'pressing' for each product?

Product A

metres

Product B

metres

Product C

metres

(2 marks)

17   What is the conversion cost per factory hour?

$

(2 marks)

18   What is the return per factory hour of product B?

$

(2 marks)

19   Yam Co is considering increasing the labour rate per hour. This would result in a conversion cost per factory hour of $95.

What is the throughput accounting ratio (TPAR) for product A assuming that this change occurs and the bottleneck process is fully utilised? (to 2 dp)

(2 marks)

20   The following statements have been made about throughput accounting in Yam Co:

(1)   When the bottleneck 'pressing' is overcome ('elevated'), a new bottleneck will appear.
(2)   It should be expected that the throughput accounting ratio for any product in Yam Co will exceed 1.

Which of the above statements is/are correct?

☐   Neither 1 nor 2
☐   2 only
☐   1 only
☐   Both 1 and 2   **(2 marks)**

(Total = 10 marks)

The following scenario relates to questions 21-25.

Willow Co

An investment centre with capital employed of $600,000 is budgeted to earn a profit of $100,000 next year. A proposed fixed asset investment of $150,000, not included in the budget at present, will earn a profit next year of $23,000 after depreciation. The company's cost of capital is 13%.

Required

21   What is the budgeted Return on Investment (ROI) for next year, both before and after the investment is made (to the nearest %)?

☐ ____   % before investment

☐ ____   % after investment   **(2 marks)**

22   What is the residual income (RI) for next year, both before and after the investment is made?

☐ ____ $ before investment

☐ ____ $ after investment   **(2 marks)**

23   Due to its size, Willow Co operates a divisionalised structure. One of manager's area of responsibility is "decisions over costs, revenues, and assets". The typical financial performance measures used by this manager is return on investment and residual income. Which of the following centre's best describes the manager's responsibility area?

☐   Profit centre
☐   Responsibility centre
☐   Cost centre
☑   Investment centre   **(2 marks)**

24   Two of the divisional managers in Willow Co disagree on the performance measure which should be used to determine their bonus for the year. Manager 1 is the manager of a large division, while manager 2 is manager of a small division. Manager 1 prefers to use residual income and has given the following examples of limitations of ROI to support this decision. Which of the following is a valid reason for Willow Co choosing to use RI and not ROI?

   ☐   ROI requires an estimate of the cost of capital, a figure which can be difficult to calculate

   ☐   ROI can overemphasise short-term performance at the expense of long-term performance

   ☐   If assets are valued at net book value, ROI figures generally improve as assets get older. This can encourage managers to retain outdated plant and machinery.

   ☑   ROI is a relative measure, therefore small investments with a high rate of return, may appear preferable to a larger investment with lower ROI. However, the larger investment may be worth more in absolute terms. **(2 marks)**

25   Manager 2 wishes to use ROI as a performance measure. Which of the following reasons is a valid reason for Willow Co choosing to use ROI and not RI?

   ☐   Identifying controllable (traceable) profits and investment can be difficult

   ☐   RI attempts to measure divisional performance in a single figure.

   ☐   ROI ties in with NPV, theoretically the best way to make investment decisions.

   ☑   Manager 1 will show a higher RI because of the size of the division rather than superior managerial performance. **(2 marks)**

   (Total = 10 marks)

The following scenario relates to questions 26-30.

Kiss Co

Kiss Co has developed a new product. The first batch of 200 units will take 3,500 labour hours to produce. There will be an 75% learning curve that will continue until 4,800 units have been produced. Batches after this level will each take the same amount of time as the 24th batch. The batch size will always be 200 units.

Note. The learning index for an 75% learning curve is -0.415

Ignore the time value of money.

26   Calculate the time taken for the 24th batch (to the nearest hour). [   ] **(2 marks)**

27   The total time for the first 16 batches of units was 22,000 hours. What was the actual learning rate closest to the nearest %? [   ] **(2 marks)**

28   Kiss Co makes another product, the Lyco. The learning effect stopped after the 16th batch of product, and a 'steady state' was reached. Workers in Kiss Co received $15 per hour. The first batch of Lyco took 0.75 hours to produce. The 16th batch of Lyco took 0.5 hours, and the standard cost was revised to this figure once the 'steady state' was reached. Kiss Co produced 10,000 batches of Lyco during the year.

   Calculate the favourable labour efficiency planning variance. [   ] **(2 marks)**

29 The following statements have been made about Kiss Co.

(1) Because of the learning effect, the labour efficiency planning variance of Lyco will always be favourable.

(2) A standard labour cost should only be established when a 'steady state' is reached.

☐ 1 only
☐ 2 only
☐ Both 1 and 2
☐ Neither 1 nor 2   (2 marks)

30 In which one of the following ways might an operational manager in Kiss Co try to improve labour efficiency and achieve favourable labour efficiency variances?

☐ Increase output volumes
☐ Increase inspection and testing of products
☐ Provide workers with training
☐ Arrange for overtime working   (2 marks)

(Total = 10 marks)

Section C – Both questions are compulsory and MUST be attempted

31 Sauce Co (6/12 / 12/09, amended)

Sauce Co manufactures and sells cartons of cooking sauces, which deteriorate over time and must be used within three months. Over the last two years, Sauce Co has experienced all kinds of problems. The financial and sales directors believe these to be a result of persistently unrealistic sales targets imposed by the managing director, who makes forecasts based on his own subjective and overly optimistic views about future sales. Production volumes are currently based on anticipated sales rather than actual orders.

Whilst an incentive scheme is in place for employees, the company has not hit its targets for the last three years, so no bonuses have been paid out.

Required

(a) Discuss the likely impact that the budgeting style and inaccurate sales forecasts have had on the staff and business of Sauce Co.   (10 marks)

(b) Explain what is meant by the controllability principle and its implications for a company such as Sauce Co.   (4 marks)

Incremental budgets take a previous period's actual figures, adjust for any known changes to operations and then add a % for expected inflation in order to set the next period's budget.

Required

(c) Describe two advantages and two disadvantages of Sauce Co using incremental budgeting as its main forecasting technique.   (6 marks)

(Total = 20 marks)

32 Brace Co (6/11)

(a) Brace Co is an electronics company specialising in the manufacture of home audio equipment. Historically, the company has used solely financial performance measures to assess the performance of the company as a whole. The company's Managing Director has recently heard of the 'balanced scorecard approach' and is keen to learn more.

Required

Describe the balanced scorecard approach to performance measurement. **(10 marks)**

(b) Brace Co is split into two divisions, A and B, each with their own cost and revenue streams. Each of the divisions is managed by a divisional manager who has the power to make all investment decisions within the division. The cost of capital for both divisions is 12%. Historically, investment decisions have been made by calculating the return on investment (ROI) of any opportunities and at present, the return on investment of each division is 16%.

A new manager who has recently been appointed in division A has argued that using residual income (RI) to make investment decisions would result in 'better goal congruence' throughout the company.

Each division is currently considering the following separate investments:

	Project for Division A	Project for Division B
Capital required for investment	$82.8 million	$40.6 million
Sales generated by investment	$44.6 million	$21.8 million
Net profit margin	28%	33%

The company is seeking to maximise shareholder wealth.

Required

Calculate both the return on investment and residual income of the new investment for each of the two divisions. Comment on these results, taking into consideration the manager's views about residual income.

(10 marks)

(Total = 20 marks)

Answers

**DO NOT TURN THIS PAGE UNTIL YOU HAVE
COMPLETED THE MOCK EXAM**

A PLAN OF ATTACK

Managing your nerves

As you turn the pages to start this mock exam a number of thoughts are likely to cross your mind. At best, examinations cause anxiety so it is important to stay focused on your task for the next three hours! Developing an awareness of what is going on emotionally within you may help you manage your nerves. Remember, you are unlikely to banish the flow of adrenaline, but the key is to harness it to help you work steadily and quickly through your answers.

Working through this mock exam will help you develop the exam stamina you will need to keep going for three hours.

Managing your time

Planning and time management are two of the key skills which complement the technical knowledge you need to succeed. To keep yourself on time, do not be afraid to jot down your target completion times for each question, perhaps next to the title of the question on the paper. As all the questions are **compulsory**, you do not have to spend time wondering which question to answer!

Doing the exam

Actually doing the exam is a personal experience. There is not a single **right way**. As long as you submit complete answers to all questions after the three hours are up, then your approach obviously works.

Looking through the paper

Section A has 15 MCQs. This is the section of the paper where ACCA examination team can test knowledge across the breadth of the syllabus. Make sure you read these questions carefully. The distractors are designed to present plausible, but incorrect, answers. Don't let them mislead you. If you really have no idea – guess. You may even be right.

Section B has three questions, each with a scenario and five objective test questions.

Section C has two longer questions:

*   Question 31 is about budgeting styles. There are plenty of easy marks available throughout this question. Remember to relate your answer to the scenario.
*   Question 32 looks at the balanced scorecard. Make your answer to part (a) easy to mark. Start with a short introduction then write a little bit about each perspective under separate headings.

Allocating your time

BPP's advice is to always allocate your time **according to the marks for the question**. However, **use common sense**. If you're doing a question but haven't a clue how to do part (b), you might be better off re-allocating your time and getting more marks on another question, where you can add something you didn't have time for earlier on. Make sure you leave time to recheck the MCQs and make sure you have answered them all.

Section A

1   1 only

ABC involves the identification of factors known as cost drivers, which drive the costs of an organisation's major activities. Support Overhead costs of support services are then charged to   products on the basis of their usage of an activity.

Absorption costing uses volume as a basis for cost allocation, and so tends to allocate too great a proportion of overheads to high volume products and too low a proportion of overheads to low volume products.

2      $15x + 12y$ $3x + y \leq 4{,}200$ $4x + 0.5y \leq 3{,}000$

Contribution for X = \$15 (\$60 − \$45)

Contribution for Y = \$12 (\$25 − \$13)

Objective function is to maximise: $15x + 12y$

Constraints:

Material = $3x + y \leq 4{,}200$ (as X uses 3 kg of material (15/5), Y uses 1 kg (5/5))

Labour = $4x + 0.5y \leq 3{,}000$ (as X uses 4 labour hrs (24/6), Y uses 0.5 hrs (3/6))

3   2 only

The balanced scorecard includes a financial perspective. It also has a customer perspective, which means that it is concerned with external as well as internal matters.

4   1 only

The costs of introducing a new system may exceed the benefits. Employees are often inclined to resist change, even though the planned changes may improve planning and control within the organisation.

5   The correct answer is: 20 units of Product Y

C   Priority for production, in order to maximise profit, should be given to the product with the higher throughput accounting ratio. This is Product Y. With Machine M as a bottleneck, extra Machine T hours could not be utilised. With the additional 10 machine M hours, it would be possible to make and sell 20 units of Product Y (10 hours at 30 minutes per unit).

6   Penetration pricing in market A and price skimming in market B

Charging low prices initially to gain a large market share is market penetration pricing. Charging high prices in order to maximise unit profits is market skimming. Market penetration pricing is most effective when demand for the product is elastic (sensitive to price) and market skimming can maximise profitability when demand is inelastic (fairly insensitive to price).

Price elasticity of demand can be reduced by trying to persuade customers to buy products for reasons other than price, such as quality or design features. Advertising and sales promotion can also have the effect of reducing price elasticity.

7   i, ii and iii only

A range check is a control within specific IT applications to check that an input item of data has a value within an acceptable range, and any input items with a value outside the range are reported as errors.

8   The correct answer is: \$59,000

	\$
Total cost at 1,200 units	66,600
Deduct step increase in fixed costs	(6,000)
Total cost at 1,200 units excluding step cost increase	60,600
Total cost of 900 units	58,200
Therefore variable cost of 300 units	2,400

Variable cost per unit = $8

	$
Total cost of 900 units	58,200
Variable cost of 900 units (at 8 each)	7,200
Therefore fixed costs at this level of output	51,000

Total costs of 1,000 units = $51,000 + $(8 × 1,000) = $59,000

9   Substitute current raw materials with cheaper versions

Reducing the target cost gap should focus on ways of reducing the direct or variable costs of the product. This can be achieved by using a substitute cheaper raw material, but without affecting product quality. Reducing fixed overhead costs is not a way of reducing the gap. Using overtime is likely to increase costs and the target cost gap. Raising the selling price does not affect the cost gap directly, although it may lead to a reassessment of the target cost.

10   1 only

Management information systems provide information to management about existing operations, and have an internal focus.

11   i, ii and iii only

The manager of an investment centre should have control over costs, revenues, and non-current assets and working capital of the centre, but does not have control over general head office costs.

12   ROI: No   RI: Yes

Current ROI 360/1,600 = 22.5% Residual income (in $'000) = 360 − (18% × 1,600) = $72,000

The new project: ROI = 25,000/130,000 = 19.2%. This is less than 22.5%; therefore ROI will fall.

New project RI = 25,000 − (18% × 130,000) = + £1,600. RI would increase.

13   Percentage of funds spent on frontline activities

Effectiveness is a measure of the way in which resources (inputs) are used to create desired outputs, which in the case of the charity is the provision of relief services. Of the four measures, the percentage of funds spent on front-line activities, rather than on the organisation's administration, is the most appropriate measure of resource inputs to outputs.

14   The correct answer is: $225

Selling price/unit ($)	300	255	240	225
Contribution/unit ($)	186	141	126	111
Demand (units)	1,800	2,400	3,600	4,200
	$334,800	$338,400	$453,600	$466,200

15   The correct answer is: $4,957.50

Incremental purchases = (1,500 − 945)kg × $4.25 per kg = $2,358.75

Opportunity cost of materials already purchased = 945 kg × $2.75 = $2,598.75

Total relevant cost = $2,358.75 + $2,358.75 = $4,957.50

Section B

Yam Co

16 **The correct answer is:**

Product A: 450,000 metres
Product B: 450,000 metres
Product C: 562,500 metres

Output capacity for each process

Total processing hours for the factory = 225,000

	Product A Metres	Product B Metres	Product C Metres
Pressing	225,000/0.50 = 450,000	225,000/0.50 = 450,000	225,000/0.40 = 562,500

17 **The correct answer is $90**

Conversion cost = Labour costs + factory costs
= (225,000 hours × $10) + $18,000,000
= $20,250,000

Conversion cost per factory hour = $20,250,000/225,000 hours = $90

18 **The correct answer is $115**

Return per factory hour = Sales − direct costs/usage of bottleneck resource in hours

	Product B $
Selling price per metre	60.00
Raw material cost per metre	2.50
Return	57.50
Usage of bottleneck resource in hours	0.50
Return per factory hour	115.00

19 The correct answer is: **1.41**

Throughput accounting ratios

TPAR = Return per factory hour/total conversion cost per factory hour

Return per factory hour = Sales − direct costs/usage of bottleneck resource in hours

	Product A $
Return per factory hour	134.00
Conversion cost per factory hour	95.00
TPAR	1.41

20 Both 1 and 2

The theory of constraints is based on the view that the focus should be on elevating a bottleneck resource to the level where it ceases to be a bottleneck, and at this time a new bottleneck will 'take over'. The throughput accounting ratio is the ratio of return per factory hour divided by cost per factory hour. If this ratio is less than 1, the commercial viability of Yam Co's product should be questioned.

Willow Co

21 The answer is: **Before investment: 17%, After investment 16%.**

	Before investment $	After investment $
Divisional profit	100,000	123,000
Capital employed	600,000	750,000
ROI	17%	16%

22 The answer is: **Before investment: $22,000, After investment $25,500.**

	Before investment $	After investment $
Divisional profit	100,000	123,000
Imputed interest		
$(600,000 \times 0.13)$	78,000	
$(750,000 \times 0.13)$		97,500
Residual income	22,000	25,500

23 Investment centre

Distractors:

- Profit centre. The manager's area of responsibility is: 'Decisions over costs and revenues', and a typical financial performance measure is 'Controllable profit'.

- Responsibility centre. This is the overall name of the categories of centre or accounting unit that can exist within a divisionalised company.

- Cost centre. The manager's area of responsibility is: 'Decisions over costs', and a typical financial performance measure is 'Standard cost variances'.

24 ROI is a relative measure, therefore small investments with a high rate of return, may appear preferable to a larger investment with lower ROI. However, the larger investment may be worth more in absolute terms.

The distractors are all examples of limitations which are common to both ROI and RI

25 Manager 1 will show a higher RI because of the size of the division rather than superior managerial performance.

The first two distractors are examples of limitations which are common to both ROI and RI. Distractor 3 is false, RI ties in with NPV.

Kiss Co

26 The correct answer is **552 hours**

Time taken for the 24th batch

Cumulative average time per batch for the first 24 batches

$Y = ax^b$

Where Y = the cumulative average time per unit to produce x units
x = the cumulative number of units
a = the time taken for the first unit of output
b = the index of learning (logLR/log2)

The cumulative average time per batch, with a learning curve of 75% is therefore

$Y = aX^{-0.415}$

where a = the time for the first batch (3,500 hours) and X is the number of the batch. For the 24th batch, X = 24.

$Y = 3,500 \times 24^{-0.415}$

$= 3,500 \times 0.2674 = 936$

The cumulative average time per batch for the first 24 batches is 936 hours.

The cumulative average time per batch for the first 23 batches is $Y = 3,500 \times 23^{-0.415} = 3,500 \times 0.2722 = 952.7$

	Hours
Total time for 1st 24 batches (24 × 936)	22,464.0
Total time for 1st 23 batches (23 × 952.7)	21,912.1
Time for the 24th batch	551.9

27 The correct answer is **79%**

Batches	Total time	Average time/unit
1	3,500	
2		$3,500 \times r$
4		$3,500 \times r^2$
8		$3,500 \times r^3$
16	22,000	$3,500 \times r^4$

$22,000 = 16 \times 3,500\ r^4$

$22,000/(16 \times 3,500) = r^4$

$r = 0.79$ or 79%

28 The correct answer is: $37,500

Labour efficiency planning variance

	Hours
10,000 batches of product should take: original standard (× 0.75)	7,500
10,000 batches of product should take: revised standard (× 0.5)	5,000
Labour efficiency planning variance in hours	2,500 (F)
Original standard rate per hour	$15
Labour efficiency planning variance in $	$37,500 (F)

29 Both 1 and 2

The learning effect has the effect of reducing the labour time per unit. Therefore, the labour efficiency planning variance will always be favourable.

Standards should be as accurate as possible. Therefore, it is not advisable to set standards before 'steady state' production is reached. However, it is possible to combine standard costing with the learning curve to calculate planning and operational variances.

30 Provide workers with training

Training may help employees to improve their efficiency in a job. Overtime working should increase output, but there is no reason why it should improve efficiency (output per hour worked). Extra inspection and testing may reduce efficiency by taking up more time: they will not improve efficiency, because they do not test efficiency, only quality. Output capacity relates to potential output volume, not efficiency of working: for example output capacity may be increased by hiring extra workers, but this does not affect productivity.

Section C

31 Sauce Co

Marking scheme

			Marks
(a)	Likely impact – 2 marks per point discussed		10
(b)	Explanation of controllability principle	2	
	Likely implications for company	2	
			4
(c)	1½ marks per advantage/disadvantage		Max 6
			20

(a) **Business**

Production volumes are currently based on **anticipated sales** rather than actual orders. As the managing director has overestimated sales, it is likely that Sauce Co has a large inventory of **perishable products**. Both inventory holding costs and the cost of disposing waste are likely to be high.

Sauce Co is likely to have too many staff, assuming **staffing levels** are based on forecast production volumes. Production is likely to slow down when it becomes apparent that sales of the sauces are lower than expected, resulting in **idle time** within the workforce. As well as being costly to the company, workers are likely to become de-motivated.

If inventory is held for some time (due to sales being lower than forecast), customers may receive goods that are close to the **expiry date** (the sauces must be used within three months). This could result in **poor customer feedback** and be damaging for the company's reputation.

Staff

Budgets at Sauce Co are **imposed by the managing director**. As such, operational managers are unlikely to voice their ideas and will not feel **valued**.

The absence of a participative style of budgeting is likely to adversely impact **staff morale** as they have not been involved in the budgeting process and have not had a chance to express their views.

Staff have not received a bonus for three years due to **unachievable sales targets**. This is likely to create a feeling amongst employees that 'all targets are unachievable' and that the bonus scheme is pointless. Team spirit is likely to be low and staff will not be motivated to work at an optimum level – many will do the bare minimum.

(b)   **Controllability principle**

The **controllability principle** is that managers of responsibility centres should only be held accountable for costs over which they have some influence. From a **motivation** point of view this is important because it can be very demoralising for managers who feel that their performance is being judged on the basis of something over which they have no influence. It is also important from a **control** point of view in that control reports should ensure that information on costs is reported to the manager who is able to take action to control them.

The controllability principle can be **implemented** either by removing the uncontrollable items from the areas that managers are accountable for, or producing reports which calculate and distinguish between controllable and uncontrollable items.

For Sauce Co, the controllability principle means that operational managers should only be held responsible for **excess** idle time, above that which is expected, based on realistic forecasts.

In a further example, the order processing department may have handled **fewer orders than expected** and this could be due to inefficiency within this department or a lower level of sales, both of which would not be under the control of operational/production managers.

(c)   **Advantages of incremental budgeting**

Incremental budgeting is a **simple approach** to a budget that everyone in the organisation should be able to understand. This simplicity may be attractive to Sauce Co through enabling other directors and operational managers to become more involved in the budgeting process.

Incremental budgeting is **less time consuming** than many other budget processes and is based on prior year **actual** figures. Forecasts using this technique are likely to be far more accurate that the current top-down approach imposed by the managing director of Sauce Co.

Disadvantages of incremental budgeting

Incremental budgeting encourages **slack** and **wasteful spending** to creep into budgets. Operational managers involved in the budgeting process may use up all of this year's budget in order to ensure that next year's budget will be as high as possible.

Uneconomic activities may be continued. For example, Sauce Co may continue to produce cooking sources in-house when it may be cheaper to outsource.

32 Brace Co

Text references. The balanced scorecard approach to performance measurement is covered in Chapter 16. Return on investment and residual income are covered in Chapter 17.

Top tips. Make your answer to part (a) easy to mark. Start with a short introduction then write a little bit about each perspective under separate headings.

Easy marks. Although it is based in the context of a company, the requirement in part (a) is really generic. You should score highly providing your answer covers all four perspectives of the balanced scorecard.

Examiner's comments. There were some really good answers to part (a), although the structure of answers could have been better. It is really hard to mark a question like this where candidates' answers include no headings and often not even any paragraphs.

About 50% of candidates scored full marks on the calculations in part (b) but some had no idea how to calculate ROI/RI. As for the commentary, most answers were poor, showing that there is little understanding of what these figures actually mean.

Marks

(a)   Balanced scorecard approach:
        Stating what it is   2
        Financial perspective   2
        Customer perspective   2
        Internal perspective   2
        Learning and growth perspective   2
                                                                          10

(b)   ROI/RI:
        ROI for A   1
        ROI for B   1
        RI for A   2
        RI for B   2
        Comments:
        A rejects, B accepts under ROI   1
        Both accept under RI   1
        ROI produces wrong decision for company   1
        RI produces right decision   1
        Manager right   1
        Other factors to consider   1
                                                              Max 10
                                                                  20

(a)   **Balanced scorecard**

The **balanced scorecard** approach to performance measurement emphasises the need to provide management with a set of information which covers all relevant areas of performance in an objective and unbiased fashion.

The information provided may be both financial and non-financial and cover areas such as profitability, customer satisfaction, internal efficiency and innovation.

The balanced scorecard focuses on **four different perspectives**, as follows.

Customer perspective

The customer perspective considers how new and existing customers view the organisation. This perspective should identify targets that matter to customers such as cost, quality, delivery, inspection and so on.

The customer perspective is linked to revenue/profit objectives in the financial perspective. If customer objectives are achieved, it is likely that revenue/profit objectives will also be achieved.

Internal perspective

The internal perspective makes an organisation consider what processes it must excel at in order to achieve financial and customer objectives.

The perspective aims to improve internal processes and decision making.

Innovation and learning perspective

The innovation and learning perspective requires the organisation to consider how it can continue to improve and create value.

Organisations must seek to acquire new skills and develop new products in order to maintain a competitive position in their respective market(s) and provide a basis from which the other perspectives of the balanced scorecard can be accomplished.

Financial perspective

The financial perspective considers whether the organisation meets the expectations of its shareholders and how it creates value for them.

This perspective focuses on traditional measures such as growth, profitability and cost reduction.

(b) **Division A**

Return on investment (ROI):
Net profit = $44.6m × 28% = $12.488m
ROI = (profit / capital employed) × 100%
    = $12.488m / $82.8m = 15.08%

Residual income (RI):
Net profit = $12.488m
Capital employed = $82.8m
Imputed interest charge = $82.8m × 12% (cost of capital for both divisions) = $9.936m
RI = net profit − imputed interest charge
    = $12.488m − $9.936m = $2.552m

Division B

Return on investment (ROI):
Net profit = $21.8m × 33% = $7.194m
ROI = $7.194m / $40.6m = 17.72%

Residual income (RI):
Net profit = $7.194m
Capital employed = $40.6m
Imputed interest charge = $40.6m × 12% = $4.872m
RI = $7.194m − $4.872m = $2.322m

Comments

The current return on investment (ROI) of each division is 16%. It is likely that the manager of Division A will reject any proposal based solely on ROI as the Division A investment only has a ROI of 15.08%. The proposed investment would reduce Division A's ROI by 0.92 percentage points.

In contrast, the manager of Division B is likely to accept the proposal as the Division B investment has an ROI of 17.72%. The proposed investment would increase Division B's ROI by 1.72 percentage points.

Both divisions are likely to accept the proposal based on residual income as both have a healthy RI ($2.552m and $2.322m respectively).

The views of the new manager of Division A are correct. The use of ROI as the sole decision tool in the past has led to a lack of goal congruence between Division A and the company as a whole.

It is clear that the use of RI as an investment measure will help the divisions to make decisions that are in the best interests of the company.

ACCA

Paper F5

Performance Management

Mock Examination 3
Specimen exam

Question Paper: 3 hours 15 minutes
This paper is divided into three sections:
Section A – **ALL FIFTEEN** questions are compulsory and **MUST** be attempted
Section B – **ALL FIFTEEN** questions are compulsory and **MUST** be attempted
Section C – Both questions are compulsory and **MUST** be attempted

DO NOT OPEN THIS PAPER UNTIL YOU ARE READY TO START UNDER EXAMINATION CONDITIONS

Section A – All FIFTEEN questions are compulsory and MUST be attempted

Each question is worth 2 marks.

1   A company manufactures two products, C and D, for which the following information is available:

	Product C	Product D	Total
Budgeted production (units)	1,000	4,000	5,000
Labour hours per unit/in total	8	10	48,000
Number of production runs required	13	15	28
Number of inspections during production	5	3	8
Total production set up costs	$140,000		
Total inspection costs	$80,000		
Other overhead costs	$96,000		

Other overhead costs are absorbed on a labour hour basis.

Using activity-based costing, what is the budgeted overhead cost per unit of Product D?

A $43.84
B $46.25
C $131.00
D $140.64

2   The selling price of Product X is set at $550 for each unit and sales for the coming year are expected to be 800 units.

A return of 30% on the investment of $500,000 in Product X will be required in the coming year.

What is the target cost for each unit of Product X?

A $385.00
B $165.00
C $187.50
D $362.50

3   P Co makes two products, P1 and P2. The budgeted details for each product are as follows:

	P1	P2
	$	$
Selling price	10.00	8.00
Cost per unit:		
Direct materials	3.50	4.00
Direct labour	1.50	1.00
Variable overhead	0.60	0.40
Fixed overhead	1.20	1.00
Profit per unit	3.20	1.60

Budgeted production and sales for the year ended 30 November 20X5 are:

Product P1   10,000 units
Product P2   12,500 units

The fixed overhead costs included in P1 relate to apportionment of general overhead costs only. However, P2 also included specific fixed overheads totalling $2,500.

If only product P1 were to be made, how many units (to the nearest whole unit) would need to be sold in order to achieve a profit of $60,000 each year?

- A   25,625 units
- B   19,205 units
- C   18,636 units
- D   26,406 units

4   Which of the following statements regarding environmental cost accounting are true?

    (1)   The majority of environmental costs are already captured within a typical organisation's accounting system. The difficulty lies in identifying them

    (2)   Input/output analysis divides material flows within an organisation into three categories: material flows; system flows; and delivery and disposal flows

    (3)   One of the cost categories used in environmental activity-based costing is environment-driven costs which is used for costs which can be directly traced to a cost centre

    (4)   Environmental life-cycle costing enables environmental costs from the design stage of the product right through to decommissioning at the end of its life to be considered

- A   (1), (2) and (4)
- B   (1) and (4) only
- C   (2), (3) and (4)
- D   (2) and (3) only

5   To produce 19 litres of Product X, a standard input mix of 8 litres of chemical A and 12 litres of chemical B is required.

Chemical A has a standard cost of $20 per litre and chemical B has a standard cost of $25 per litre.

During September, the actual results showed that 1,850 litres of Product X were produced, using a total input of 900 litres of chemical A and 1,100 litres of chemical B.

The actual costs of chemicals A and B were at the standard cost of $20 and $25 per litre respectively.

Based on the above information, which of the following statements is true?

- A   Both variances were adverse
- B   Both variances were favourable
- C   The total mix variance was adverse and the total yield variance was favourable
- D   The total mix variance was favourable and the total yield variance was adverse

6   A budget is a quantified plan of action for a forthcoming period. Budgets can be prepared using a variety of different approaches.

Which of the following statements regarding approaches to budgeting are correct?

    (1)   Incremental budgeting builds previous inefficiencies into the budget whereas zero-based budgeting encourages employees to avoid wasteful expenditure

    (2)   Beyond budgeting uses adaptive management processes and plans on a rolling basis

    (3)   Activity-based budgeting ensures that the budget is continually updated by adding a new budget period once the most recent budget period has ended

    (4)   Flexible budgeting recognises different cost behaviour patterns and so takes into account the organisation's overall strategy during the budget process

- A   (1) and (2) only
- B   (1), (2) and (4)
- C   (3) and (4)
- D   (1) and (3)

7   A leisure company owns a number of large health and fitness resorts, but one is suffering from declining sales and is predicted to make a loss in the next year. As a result management have identified a number of possible actions:

(1)   Shut down the resort and sell off the assets
(2)   Undertake a major upgrade to facilities costing $4.5m
(3)   Undertake a minor upgrade to facilities costing $2m

The upgrades are predicted to have variable results and the probability of good results after a major upgrade is 0.8, whereas the probability of good results after a minor upgrade is 0.7.

The company is risk neutral and has prepared the following decision tree.

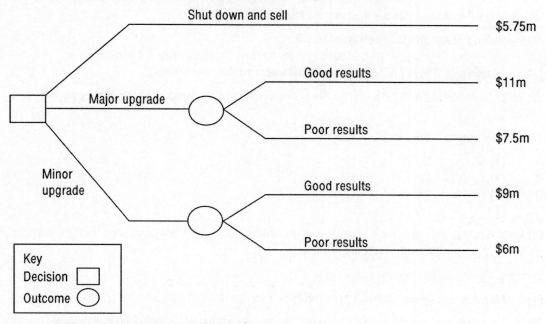

Which decision should the company make?

A   Shutdown and sell
B   Undertake the major upgrade
C   Undertake the minor upgrade
D   Undertake the major upgrade if results are good

8   A company has the following production planned for the next four weeks. The figures reflect the full capacity level of operations. Planned output is equal to the maximum demand per product.

Product	A	B	C	D
	$ per unit	$ per unit	$ per unit	$ per unit
Selling price	160	214	100	140
Raw material cost	24	56	22	40
Direct labour cost	66	88	33	22
Variable overhead cost	24	18	24	18
Fixed overhead cost	16	10	8	12
Profit	30	42	13	48
Planned output	300	125	240	400
Direct labour hours per unit	6	8	3	2

It has now been identified that labour hours available in the next four weeks will be limited to 4,000 hours.

In what order should the products be manufactured, assuming that the company wants to maximise profits in the next four weeks?

A   D, A, C, B
B   D, B, A, C
C   B, A, D, C
D   D, C, A, B

9   Def Co provides accounting services to government departments. On average, each staff member works six chargeable hours per day, with the rest of their working day being spent on non-chargeable administrative work. One of the company's main objectives is to produce a high level of quality and customer satisfaction.

Def Co has set its targets for the next year as follows:

(1)   Cutting departmental expenditure by 5%
(2)   Increasing the number of chargeable hours handled by advisers to 6.2 per day
(3)   Obtaining a score of 4.7 or above on customer satisfaction surveys

Which of the following options allocates the above targets to the correct value for money performance category?

	Economy	Efficiency	Effectiveness
A	(1)	(3)	(2)
B	(2)	(1)	(3)
C	(3)	(2)	(1)
D	(1)	(2)	(3)

10   Different types of information systems provide the information which organisations need for strategic planning, management and operational control.

Which of the following statements are correct?

(1)   Management information systems (MIS) summarise internal data into periodic reports

(2)   Transaction processing systems (TPS) facilitate the immediate processing of data

(3)   Executive information systems (EIS) utilise dashboard facilities and interactive graphics

(4)   Enterprise resource planning systems (ERPS) can be set up with extranet links to suppliers and customers

A   (1), (2) and (3) only
B   (1) and (3) only
C   (2) and (4) only
D   (1), (2), (3) and (4)

11   The following are all types of costs associated with management information:

(1)   Use of bar coding and scanners
(2)   Payroll department's processing of personnel costs
(3)   Completion of timesheets by employees
(4)   Input of data into the production system

Which of the above are examples of direct data capture costs?

A   (1) and (3) only
B   (1), (3) and (4)
C   (2) and (3)
D   (1) and (4) only

12   Which of the following statements regarding life-cycle costing are correct?

     (1)   It can be applied not only to products but also to an organisation's customers
     (2)   It includes any opportunity costs associated with production
     (3)   The maturity phase is characterised by a rapid build-up in demand
     (4)   Often between 70% to 90% of costs are determined early in the product life cycle

     A   (1), (2) and (4)
     B   (3) and (4)
     C   (1) and (4) only
     D   (2) and (3)

13   A company manufactures a product which requires four hours per unit of machine time. Machine time is a bottleneck resource as there are only ten machines which are available for 12 hours per day, five days per week. The product has a selling price of $130 per unit, direct material costs of $50 per unit, labour costs of $40 per unit and factory overhead costs of $20 per unit. These costs are based on weekly production and sales of 150 units.

   What is the throughput accounting ratio?

     A   1.33
     B   2.00
     C   0.75
     D   0.31

14   Ox Co has two divisions, A and B. Division A makes a component for air conditioning units which it can only sell to Division B. It has no other outlet for sales.

   Current information relating to Division A is as follows:

Marginal cost per unit	$100
Transfer price of the component	$165
Total production and sales of the component each year	2,200 units
Specific fixed costs of Division A per year	$10,000

   Cold Co has offered to sell the component to Division B for $140 per unit. If Division B accepts this offer, Division A will be closed.

   If Division B accepts Cold Co's offer, what will be the impact on profits per year for the group as a whole?

     A   Increase of $65,000
     B   Decrease of $78,000
     C   Decrease of $88,000
     D   Increase of $55,000

15   Which of the following statements regarding Fitzgerald and Moon's Building Blocks model are correct?

     (1)   The determinants of performance are quality, innovation, resource utilisation and competitiveness

     (2)   Standards are targets for performance and should be fair, achievable and controllable

     (3)   Rewards encourage staff to work towards the standards and should be clear, motivating and controllable

     (4)   It is a performance measurement framework particularly suitable for service organisations

     A   (1), (2) and (3)
     B   (2) and (3) only
     C   (3) and (4)
     D   (1), (2) and (4)

(Total = 30 marks)

Section B – All FIFTEEN questions are compulsory and MUST be attempted

Each question is worth 2 marks.

The following scenario relates to questions 16–20.

Glam Co is a hairdressing salon which provides both 'cuts' and 'treatments' to clients. All cuts and treatments at the salon are carried out by one of the salon's three senior stylists. The salon also has two salon assistants and two junior stylists.

Every customer attending the salon is first seen by a salon assistant, who washes their hair; next, by a senior stylist, who cuts or treats the hair depending on which service the customer wants; then finally, a junior stylist who dries their hair. The average length of time spent with each member of staff is as follows:

	Cut Hours	Treatment Hours
Assistant	0.1	0.3
Senior stylist	1.0	1.5
Junior stylist	0.6	0.5

labour is fixed cost

The salon is open for eight hours each day for six days per week. It is only closed for two weeks each year. Staff salaries are $40,000 each year for each senior stylist, $28,000 each year for each junior stylist and $12,000 each year for each of the assistants. The cost of cleaning products applied when washing the hair is $1.50 per client. The cost of all additional products applied during a 'treatment' is $7.40 per client. Other salon costs (excluding labour and raw materials) amount to $106,400 each year. *VC — other fixed cost*

Glam Co charges $60 for each cut and $110 for each treatment.

The senior stylists' time has been correctly identified as the bottleneck activity.

16   What is the annual capacity of the bottleneck activity?

	Cuts	Treatments
A	2,400	1,600
B	4,800	4,800
C	7,200	4,800
D	9,600	9,600

17   The salon has calculated the cost per hour to be $42.56.

What is the throughput accounting ratio (TPAR) for both services?

	Cuts	Treatments
A	1.37	1.58
B	1.41	2.38
C	1.37	1.61
D	1.41	2.41

18   Which of the following activities could the salon use to improve the TPAR?

(1)   Increase the time spent by the bottleneck activity on each service ✗
(2)   Identify ways to reduce the material costs for the services ✓
(3)   Increase the level of inventory to prevent stock-outs ?
(4)   Increase the productivity of the stage prior to the bottleneck ✓
(5)   Improve the control of the salon's total operating expenses ✓
(6)   Apply an increase to the selling price of the services ✓

A   (1), (2) and (4)
B   (2), (3) and (5)
C   (2), (5) and (6)
D   (1), (4) and (6)

19   What would be the effect on the bottleneck if the salon employed another senior stylist?

    A   The senior stylists' time will be a bottleneck for cuts only
    B   The senior stylists' time will be a bottleneck for treatments only
    C   The senior stylists' time will remain the bottleneck for both cuts and treatments
    D   There will no longer be a bottleneck

20   Which of the following statements regarding the theory of constraints are correct?

    (1)   It focuses on identifying stages of congestion in a process when production arrives more quickly ✓ than the next stage can handle

    (2)   It is based on the concept that organisations manage three key factors – throughput, operating expenses and inventory *nur* JIT

    (3)   It uses a sequence of focusing steps to overcome a single bottleneck, at which point the improvement process is complete

    (4)   It can be applied to the management of all limiting factors, both internal and external, which can affect an organisation

    (A)   (1) and (2) only
    B   (1), (2) and (3)
    C   (2), (3) and (4)
    D   (1), (3) and (4)

The following scenario relates to questions 21–25.

Chair Co has in development several new products. One of them is a new type of luxury car seat. The estimated labour time for the first unit is 12 hours but a learning curve of 75% is expected to apply for the first eight units produced. The cost of labour is $15 per hour.

The cost of materials and other variable overheads is expected to total $230 per unit. Chair Co plans on pricing the seat by adding a 50% mark-up to the total variable cost per seat, with the labour cost being based on the incremental time taken to produce the 8th unit.

21   What is the labour cost of the 8th unit?

    A $45.65
    B $75.94
    C $4.32
    D $3.04

22   The first phase of production has now been completed for the new car seat. The first unit actually took 12.5 hours to make and the total time for the first eight units was 34.3 hours, at which point the learning effect came to an end. Chair Co are planning on adjusting the price to reflect the actual time it took to complete the 8th unit.

    What was the actual rate of learning which occurred?

    A   65.7%
    B   58.6%
    C   70.0%
    D   76.5%

23   Another product which Chair Co has in development is a new design of high chair for feeding young children. Based on previous experience of producing similar products, Chair Co had assumed that a learning rate of 85% would apply to the manufacture of this new design but after the first phase of production had been completed, management realised that a learning rate of 80% had been achieved.

Which of the following statements could explain why the actual rate of learning differed from the rate which was expected?

(1)   Staffing levels were stable during the first manufacturing phase
(2)   There were machine breakdowns during production
(3)   Assembly of the chairs was manual and very repetitive
(4)   There was high staff turnover during this period
(5)   There were minimal stoppages in the production process
(6)   The design of the chair was changed several times at this early phase

A   (2), (3) and (4)
B   (1), (3) and (5)
C   (1), (5) and (6)
D   (2), (4) and (6)

24   Chair Co uses cost-plus pricing.

Which of the following statements regarding cost-plus pricing strategies are correct?

(1)   Marginal cost-plus pricing is easier where there is a readily identifiable variable cost
(2)   Full cost-plus pricing requires the budgeted level of output to be determined at the outset
(3)   Cost-plus pricing is a strategically focused approach as it accounts for external factors
(4)   Cost-plus pricing requires that the profit mark-up applied by an organisation is fixed

A   (1), (2) and (4)
B   (1) and (2) only
C   (3) and (4)
D   (1) and (3)

25   Chair Co has also developed a new type of office chair and management is trying to formulate a budget for this product. They have decided to match the production level to demand, however, demand for this chair is uncertain.

Management have collected the following information:

	Demand units	Probability
Worst possible outcome	10,000	0.3
Most likely outcome	22,000	0.5
Best possible outcome	35,000	0.2

The selling price per unit is $25. The variable cost per unit is $8 for any production level up to 25,000 units. If the production level is higher than 25,000 units, then the variable cost per unit will decrease by 10% and this reduction will apply to all the units produced at that level.

Total fixed costs are estimated to be $75,000.

Using probabilistic budgeting, what is the expected budgeted contribution of the product?

A $282,000
B $357,000
C $287,600
D $362,600

The following scenario relates to questions 26–30.

The Hi Life Co (HL Co) makes sofas. It has recently received a request from a customer to provide a one-off order of sofas, in excess of normal budgeted production. The order would need to be completed within two weeks. The following cost estimate has already been prepared:

		$
Direct materials:		
Fabric	200 m² at $17 per m²	3,400
Wood	50 m² at $8·20 per m²	410
Direct labour:		
Skilled	200 hours at $16 per hour	3,200
Semi-skilled	300 hours at $12 per hour	3,600
Factory overheads	500 hours at $3 per hour	1,500
Total production cost		12,110
General fixed overheads as 10% of total production cost		1,211
Total cost		13,321

A quotation now needs to be prepared on a relevant cost basis so that HL Co can offer as competitive a price as possible for the order.

26   The fabric is regularly used by HL Co. There are currently 300 m² in inventory, which cost $17 per m². The current purchase price of the fabric is $17.50 per m².

The wood is regularly used by HL Co and usually costs $8.20 per m². However, the company's current supplier's earliest delivery time for the wood is in three weeks' time. An alternative supplier could deliver immediately but they would charge $8.50 per m². HL Co already has 500 m² in inventory but 480 m² of this is needed to complete other existing orders in the next two weeks. The remaining 20 m² is not going to be needed until four weeks' time.

What is the cost of the fabric and the wood which should be included in the quotation?

	Fabric	Wood
A	$3,500	$419
B	$3,400	$419
C	$3,500	$255
D	$0	$255

27.   The skilled labour force is employed under permanent contracts of employment under which they must be paid for 40 hours per week's labour, even if their time is idle due to absence of orders. Their rate of pay is $16 per hour, although any overtime is paid at time and a half. In the next two weeks, there is spare capacity of 150 labour hours.

There is no spare capacity for semi-skilled workers. They are currently paid $12 per hour or time and a half for overtime. However, a local agency can provide additional semi-skilled workers for $14 per hour.

What cost should be included in the quotation for skilled labour and semi-skilled labour?

	Skilled	Semi-skilled
A	$3,600	$4,200
B	$1,200	$4,200
C	$3,600	$5,400
D	$1,200	$5,400

28   Of the $3 per hour factory overheads costs, $1.50 per hour reflects the electricity costs of running the cutting machine which will be used to cut the fabric and wood for the sofas. The other $1.50 per hour reflects the cost of the factory supervisor's salary. The supervisor is paid an annual salary and is also paid $15 per hour for any overtime he works.

He will need to work 20 hours overtime if this order is accepted.

What is the cost which should be included in the quotation for factory overheads?

A $1,050
B $1,800
C $750
D $300

29   Which statement correctly describes the treatment of the general fixed overheads when preparing the quotation?

A   The overheads should be excluded because they are a sunk cost
B   The overheads should be excluded because they are not incremental costs
C   The overheads should be included because they relate to production costs
D   The overheads should be included because all expenses should be recovered

30   Which of the following statements about relevant costing are true?

(1)   An opportunity cost will always be a relevant cost even if it is a past cost
(2)   Fixed costs are always general in nature and are therefore never relevant
(3)   Committed costs are never considered to be relevant costs
(4)   An opportunity cost represents the cost of the best alternative forgone
(5)   Notional costs are always relevant as they make the estimate more realistic
(6)   Avoidable costs would be saved if an activity did not happen and so are relevant
(7)   Common costs are only relevant if the viability of the whole process is being assessed
(8)   Differential costs in a make or buy decision are not considered to be relevant

A   (2), (3), (4) and (6)
B   (1), (2), (5) and (7)
C   (3), (4), (6) and (7)
D   (1), (5), (6) and (8)

(Total = 30 marks)

Section C – Both questions are compulsory and MUST be attempted

31 Carad Co is an electronics company which makes two types of television – plasma screen TVs and LCD TVs. It operates within a highly competitive market and is constantly under pressure to reduce prices. Carad Co operates a standard costing system and performs a detailed variance analysis of both products on a monthly basis. Extracts from the management information for the month of November are shown below:

		Note
Total number of units made and sold	1,400	1
Material price variance	$28,000 A	2
Total labour variance	$6,050 A	3

Notes

(1) The budgeted total sales volume for TVs was 1,180 units, consisting of an equal mix of plasma screen TVs and LCD screen TVs. Actual sales volume was 750 plasma TVs and 650 LCD TVs. Standard sales prices are $350 per unit for the plasma TVs and $300 per unit for the LCD TVs. The actual sales prices achieved during November were $330 per unit for plasma TVs and $290 per unit for LCD TVs. The standard contributions for plasma TVs and LCD TVs are $190 and $180 per unit respectively.

(2) The sole reason for this variance was an increase in the purchase price of one of its key components, X. Each plasma TV made and each LCD TV made requires one unit of component X, for which Carad Co's standard cost is $60 per unit. Due to a shortage of components in the market place, the market price for November went up to $85 per unit for X. Carad Co actually paid $80 per unit for it.

(3) Each plasma TV uses 2 standard hours of labour and each LCD TV uses 1.5 standard hours of labour. The standard cost for labour is $14 per hour and this also reflects the actual cost per labour hour for the company's permanent staff in November. However, because of the increase in sales and production volumes in November, the company also had to use additional temporary labour at the higher cost of $18 per hour. The total capacity of Carad's permanent workforce is 2,200 hours production per month, assuming full efficiency. In the month of November, the permanent workforce were wholly efficient, taking exactly 2 hours to complete each plasma TV and exactly 1.5 hours to produce each LCD TV. The total labour variance therefore relates solely to the temporary workers, who took twice as long as the permanent workers to complete their production.

Required

(a) Calculate the following for the month of November, showing all workings clearly:

   (i) The sales price variance and sales volume contribution variance; **(4 marks)**
   (ii) The material price planning variance and material price operational variance; **(2 marks)**
   (iii) The labour rate variance and the labour efficiency variance. **(5 marks)**

(b) Explain the reasons why Carad Co would be interested in the material price planning variance and the material price operational variance. **(9 marks)**

(Total = 20 marks)

32   Thatcher International Park (TIP) is a theme park and has for many years been a successful business, which has traded profitably. About three years ago the directors decided to capitalise on their success and reduced the expenditure made on new thrill rides, reduced routine maintenance where possible (deciding instead to repair equipment when it broke down) and made a commitment to regularly increase admission prices. Once an admission price is paid customers can use any of the facilities and rides for free.

These steps increased profits considerably, enabling good dividends to be paid to the owners and bonuses to the directors. The last two years of financial results are shown below.

	20X4	20X5
	$	$
① Sales	5,250,000	5,320,000
② Less expenses:		
A Wages	2,500,000	2,200,000
B Maintenance – routine	80,000	70,000
Repairs	260,000	320,000
Directors' salaries	150,000	160,000
C Directors' bonuses	15,000	18,000
D Other costs (including depreciation)	1,200,000	1,180,000
③ Net profit	1,045,000	1,372,000
Book value of assets at start of year	13,000,000	12,000,000
Dividend paid	500,000	650,000
Number of visitors	150,000	140,000

Handwritten annotations: costs (next to Less expenses); profit, profit margin, ROCE; ? next to Other costs; "– Investor" next to Dividend paid; "– connect to sales" next to Number of visitors; "@sales" in text.

TIP operates in a country where the average rate of inflation is around 1% per annum.

Required   *(handwritten: sales, costs, profits   6 numbers   8 words)*

(a)   Assess the financial performance of TIP using the information given above.   **(14 marks)**

During the early part of 20X4 TIP employed a newly qualified management accountant. He quickly became concerned about the potential performance of TIP and to investigate his concerns, he started to gather data to measure some non-financial measures of success. The data he has gathered is shown below:

Table 1

	20X4	20X5
Hours lost due to breakdown of rides (see note 1)	9,000 hours	32,000 hours
Average waiting time per ride	20 minutes	30 minutes

Note 1. TIP has 50 rides of different types. It is open 360 days of the year for 10 hours each day

Required

(b)   Assess the QUALITY of the service which TIP provides to its customers using Table 1 and any other relevant data and indicate the RISKS it is likely to face if it continues with its current policies.

(6 marks)

(Total = 20 marks)

Formulae Sheet

Learning curve

$Y = ax^b$

Where

Y = cumulative average time per unit to produce x units
a = the time taken for the first unit of output
x = the cumulative number of units produced
b = the index of learning (log LR/log2)
LR = the learning rate as a decimal

Demand curve

$P = a - bQ$

$$B = \frac{\text{change in price}}{\text{change in quantity}}$$

A = price when Q = 0

$MR = a - 2bQ$

End of Question Paper

Answers

DO NOT TURN THIS PAGE UNTIL YOU HAVE
COMPLETED THE MOCK EXAM

CANDIDATE ANSWER BOOKLET

SAMPLE PAGE ONLY

USE THIS PAGE TO RECORD ANSWERS TO MULTIPLE CHOICE QUESTIONS

- If your question paper has less than 60 questions, fill in the relevant answers only.

- Each multiple choice question has only one correct answer. Fill in one bubble only (A, B, C, or D) to indicate your choice of answer.

- The mark available for each question is indicated on your question paper. There is no penalty for incorrect answers or unanswered questions.

- No marks are awarded if you do not clearly indicate your final choice or if more than one bubble per question is filled in.

- To void a selected answer, place a cross (X) over the bubble.

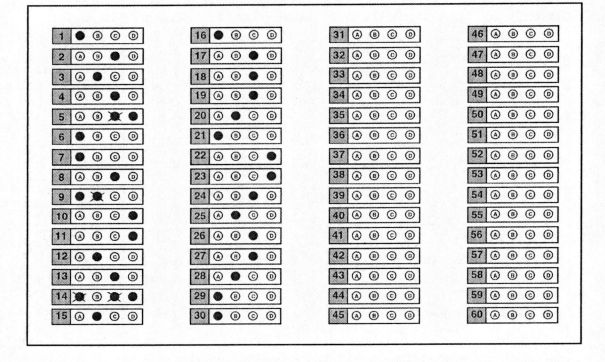

A PLAN OF ATTACK

Managing your nerves

As you turn the pages to start this mock exam a number of thoughts are likely to cross your mind. At best, examinations cause anxiety so it is important to stay focused on your task for the next three hours! Developing an awareness of what is going on emotionally within you may help you manage your nerves. Remember, you are unlikely to banish the flow of adrenaline, but the key is to harness it to help you work steadily and quickly through your answers.

Working through this mock exam will help you develop the exam stamina you will need to keep going for three hours.

Managing your time

Planning and time management are two of the key skills which complement the technical knowledge you need to succeed. To keep yourself on time, do not be afraid to jot down your target completion times for each question, perhaps next to the title of the question on the paper. As all the questions are **compulsory**, you do not have to spend time wondering which question to answer!

Doing the exam

Actually doing the exam is a personal experience. There is not a single **right way**. As long as you submit complete answers to all questions after the three hours are up, then your approach obviously works.

Looking through the paper

Section A has 15 MCQs. This is the section of the paper where ACCA examination team can test knowledge across the breadth of the syllabus. Make sure you read these questions carefully. The distractors are designed to present plausible, but incorrect, answers. Don't let them mislead you. If you really have no idea – guess. You may even be right.

Section B has three questions, each with a scenario and five objective test questions.

Section C has two longer questions:

- Question 31 requires you to calculate sales variances. There are plenty of easy marks in the question. If you get stuck on the details of which numbers to use where, make an attempt at something sensible and move on.

- Question 32 looks at performance measurement. This is a classic performance measurement question with a contrast between the picture painted by financial indicators and that given by non-financial indicators. Start with the ratio calculations and then make sure that you fully analyse what the numbers are telling you.

Allocating your time

BPP's advice is to always allocate your time **according to the marks for the question**. However, **use common sense**. If you're doing a question but haven't a clue how to do part (b), you might be better off re-allocating your time and getting more marks on another question, where you can add something you didn't have time for earlier on. Make sure you leave time to recheck the MCQs and make sure you have answered them all.

Section A

1   B   Set-up costs per production run = $140,000/28 = $5,000
Cost per inspection = $80,000/8 = $10,000
Other overhead costs per labour hour = $96,000/48,000 = $2

Overhead costs of product D:

	$
Set-up costs (15 × $5,000)	75,000
Inspection costs (3 × $10,000)	30,000
Other overheads (40,000 × $2)	80,000
	185,000

Overhead cost per unit = $185,000/4,000 units = $46.25

2   D   Return: $500,000 × 30% = $150,000
Total sales revenue = $550 × 800 = $440,000
Therefore total cost = $440,000 − $150,000 = $290,000
Unit cost = $290,000/800 = $362·50

3   C   The number of units required to make a target profit = (fixed costs + target profit)/contribution per unit of P1.

Fixed costs = ($1.20 × 10,000) + ($1.00 × 12,500) − $2,500 = $22,000

Contribution per unit of P = $3.20 + $1.20 = $4·40

($22,000 + $60,000)/$4.40 = 18,636 units

4   B   Most organisations do collect data about environmental costs but find it difficult to split them out and categorise them effectively.

Life-cycle costing does allow the organisation to collect information about a product's environmental costs throughout its life cycle.

The technique which divides material flows into three categories is material flow cost accounting, not input/output analysis.

ABC does categorise some costs as environment-driven costs, however, these are costs which are normally hidden within total

overheads in a conventional costing system. It is environment-related costs which can be allocated directly to a cost centre.

5   D   Mix variance:

Material	AQSM	AQAM	Difference litres	Standard cost $/litre	Variance $
A	800	900	100 A	20	2,000 A
B	1,200	1,100	100 F	25	2,500 F
	2,000	2,000			500 F

Yield variance:

Material	SQSM	AQSM	Difference litres	Standard cost $/litre	Variance $
A	779	800	21 A	20	420 A
B	1,168	1,200	32 A	25	800 A
	(W1) 1,947	2,000			1,220 A

(W1) 1,850 litres of output should use 1,947 litres of input (1,850/0.95)

6	A	An incremental budget builds from the previous year's figures and so any inefficiencies will be carried forward and zero-based budgeting starts from scratch with each item justified for its inclusion in the budget and so should encourage the identification of waste and non-value adding activities, so Statement 1 is correct.

Beyond budgeting attempts to move away from conforming to a rigid annual budget and uses adaptive processes to encourage management to be responsive to current situations which facilitates the use of rolling forecasts, so Statement 2 is correct.

Rolling budgeting are budgets which are continuously updated throughout the year and so forces managers to reassess plans more regularly, whereas activity-based budgeting involves defining the activities which underpin the financial figures and using the activity to allocate resources for the budget, so Statement 3 is incorrect.

Flexible budgets are designed to show the changes in financial figures based on different activity levels and so will recognize different cost behaviour patterns, however, it is activity-based budgeting which ensures that the overall strategy is taken into account because it attempts to manage the business as interrelated parts, not separate activities, so Statement 4 is incorrect.

7   C   EV for major upgrade = $(0.80 \times \$11m) + (0.2 \times \$7.5m) = \$10.3m$

EV for minor upgrade = $(0.70 \times \$9m) + (0.3 \times \$6m) = \$8.1m$

Decision

Shutdown and sell	$5.75m
Major upgrade (10.3m – 4.5m)	$5.8m
Minor upgrade ($8.1m – $2m)	$6.1m

As the minor upgrade has the highest expected return that should be the option chosen.

8   A   In a single limiting factor situation products should be ranked based on their contribution per unit of limiting factor, which in this case is labour hours.

Product	A	B	C	D
Contribution per unit ($)	46	52	21	60
Number of labour hours required per unit	6	8	3	2
Contribution per labour hour ($)	7.67	6.50	7.00	30.00
Ranking	2nd	4th	3rd	1st

9   D   Target 1 is a financial target and so assesses economy factors. Target 2 is measuring the rate of work handled by staff which is an efficiency measure. Target 3 is assessing output, so is a measure of effectiveness.

10   D   Management information systems do summarise data from TPS into periodic reports for management to use for decision-making.

Transaction processing systems do facilitate the immediate processing of data.

Executive information systems draw data from the MIS and support senior managers to make strategic decisions. They usually have dashboard and interactive graphics so that the big picture can be seen.

Enterprise resource planning systems can have extranet links set up with customers and suppliers.

11   A   Direct data capture costs is a type of data input in which there is no data entry but instead it is captured for a specific purpose.

Therefore the use of bar coding and scanners and the completion of timesheets are examples of direct data capture costs.

Time spent by the payroll department processing personnel costs and the input of data into the production system are examples of process costs.

12	C	Customer life-cycle costing can be used by organisations.

It has been reported that the majority of a product's costs are determined early on, i.e. at the design phase.

Life-cycle costing does not include any opportunity costs associated with production.

The growth phase is characterised by a rapid increase in demand.

13	A	Return per factory hour = ($130 − $50)/4 hours = $20

Factory costs per hour = $20 + ($40/4) = $15
TPAR = $20/$15 = 1.33

14	B	Increase in variable costs per unit from buying in ($140 − $100) =$40

Therefore total increase in variable costs (2,200 units × $40) = $88,000
Less the specific fixed costs saved if A is shut down = ($10,000)
Decrease in profit = $78,000

15	C	The determinants of performance are quality, innovation, resource utilisation and flexibility. Competitiveness is a result of the determinants.

Standards should be fair, achievable and staff should have ownership of them. Controllability is a feature of the rewards block.

Rewards should be clear, motivating and controllable, so this is correct.

It is a framework designed to attempt to overcome the problems associated with performance management in service companies.

Section B

16 C Total salon hours = $8 \times 6 \times 50 = 2{,}400$ each year.

There are three senior stylists, therefore total hours available = 7,200.

Based on the time taken for each activity, they can perform 7,200 cuts (7,200 hours/1 hour per cut) or 4,800 treatments (7,200 hours/1.5 hours per treatment).

17 A

Cuts

Return per hour = (Selling price – materials)/time taken on the bottleneck = $(60 - 1.50)/1 = 58.50$
TPAR = Return per hour/cost per hour = $58.50/42.56 = 1.37$ (to two decimal places)

Treatments

Return per hour = (Selling price – materials)/time taken on the bottleneck = $(110 - 8.90)/1.5 = 67.40$
TPAR = Return per hour/cost per hour = $67.40/42.56 = 1.58$ (to two decimal places)

18 C The factors which are included in the TPAR are selling price, material costs, operating expenses and bottleneck time. Increasing the selling price and reducing costs will improve the TPAR.

Increasing the time which each service takes on the bottleneck (the senior stylists' time) will only reduce the number of services they can provide, so this will not improve throughput.

Throughput accounting does not advocate the building of inventory as it is often used in a just-in-time environment and there is no point increasing the activity prior to the bottleneck as it will just create a build-up of work-in-progress. Neither of these will improve the rate of throughput through the process.

19 B The existing capacity for each activity is:

	Cut	Treatment
Assistants	48,000	16,000
Senior stylists	7,200	4,800
Junior stylists	8,000	9,600

If another senior stylist is employed, this will mean that their available hours will be $(4 \times 2{,}400) = 9{,}600$.

This will give them capacity to now do 9,600 cuts (9,600 hours/1 hour per cut) and 6,400 treatments (9,600 hours/1.5 hours per treatment).

As a result, the senior stylists will still be the bottleneck activity for treatments but for cuts the bottleneck will now be the junior stylists as they can only do 8,000 cuts compared to the senior stylists of 9,600.

20 A The theory of constraints is focused on identifying restrictions in a process and how to manage that restriction (commonly termed a bottleneck).

It is based on the concept of managing throughput, operating expenses and inventory.

It does use a series of focusing steps but it is not complete once the bottleneck has been overcome. In fact it is an ongoing process of improvement, as once the bottleneck has been elevated it is probable that another bottleneck will appear and the process will continue.

It cannot be applied to all limiting factors as some, particularly those external to the organisation, may be out of the organisation's control.

21 A Learning curve formula = $y = ax^b$

Cumulative average time per unit for 8 units: $Y = 12 \times 8^{-415} = 5.0628948$ hours.
Therefore cumulative total time for 8 units = 40.503158 hours.
Cumulative average time per unit for 7 units: $Y = 12 \times 7^{-415} = 5.3513771$ hours.
Therefore cumulative total time for 7 units = 37.45964 hours.
Therefore incremental time for 8th unit = 40.503158 hours – 37.45964 hours = 3.043518 hours.
Total labour cost for 8th unit = $3.043518 \times \$15 = \$45.65277$

22 C Actual learning rate

Cumulative number of seats produced	Cumulative total hours	Cumulative average hours per unit
1	12.5	12.5
2	?	$12.5 \times r$
4	?	$12.5 \times r^2$
8	34.3	$12.5 \times r^3$

Using algebra:
$$34.3 = 8 \times (12.5 \times r^3)$$
$$4.2875 = (12.5 \times r^3)$$
$$0.343 = r^3$$
$$r = 0.70$$

Therefore the learning rate was 70%.

23 B An 80% learning rate means that the learning was faster than expected.

Factors which are present for a learning curve to take effect are a highly manual and repetitive process (so staff can become quicker the more they perform the same series of tasks), no stoppages to production (so the learning rate will not be lost whilst staff are idle) and a stable workforce (so the learning process does not have to keep restarting).

If there is high staff turnover, stoppages in production and continual design changes, then the learning rate will not be effective and should be slower.

24 B As marginal costing is based on variable costs, it is easier when a readily identifiable variable cost has been established.

The budgeted volume of output does need to be determined for full cost-plus pricing as it would be used to calculate the overhead absorption rate for the calculation of the full cost per unit.

Cost-plus pricing is internally focused and a drawback of the technique is that it fails to consider external influences, like competitor pricing strategies.

The mark-up percentage does not have to be fixed; it can vary and be adjusted to reflect market conditions.

25 D As the variable cost per unit is changing depending on the production level, contribution for each level needs to be calculated and then the probabilities applied to the outcomes.

Demand (units)	Contribution (per unit)	Total contribution	Probability	Expected budgeted contribution
10,000	17.00	170,000	0.3	51,000
22,000	17.00	374,000	0.5	187,000
35,000	17.80	623,000	0.2	124,600
				362,600

26 A Fabric is in regular use, so the replacement cost is the relevant cost (200 m^2 × $17.50) = $3,500.

30 m^2 of wood will have to be ordered in from the alternative supplier but the remaining 20 m^2 which is in inventory and not needed for other work can be used and then replaced by an order from the usual supplier (30 m^2 × $8.50) + (20 m^2 × $8.20) = $419.

27   B

Skilled labour:

There is no cost for the first 150 hours as there is spare capacity. The remaining 50 hours required will be paid at time and a half, which is $16 \times 1.5 = $24.

50 hours $\times$ $24 = $1,200

Semi-skilled labour:

There is no spare capacity, so the company will either need to pay overtime or hire in additional staff. The cost of paying overtime would be $18 per hour, so it would be cheaper to hire in the additional staff for $14 per hour.

300 hours $\times$ $14 = $4,200

28   A   The electricity costs are incremental as the machine will be used more to produce the new order (500 hours $\times$ $1.50) = $750.

The supervisor's salary is not relevant as it is paid anyway; however, the overtime is relevant (20 hours $\times$ $15) = $300.

29   B   The general fixed overheads should be excluded as they are not incremental, i.e. they are not arising specifically as a result of this order. They are not sunk as they are not past costs. This is a common misconception.

30   C   An opportunity cost does represent the cost of the best alternative forgone, however, if it is an historic (past) cost, it would not be relevant.

Fixed costs can be incremental to a decision and in those circumstances would be relevant.

Committed costs are costs the organisation has already agreed to and can no longer influence and so are not relevant.

Notional costs are used to make cost estimates more realistic; however, they are not real cash flows and are not considered to be relevant.

Avoidable costs are saved if an activity is not undertaken and if this occurs as a result of the decision, then they are relevant.

Common costs are relevant if the whole process is being evaluated; however, they are not relevant to a further processing decision.

Differential costs are relevant in a make or buy decision as the organisation is trying to choose between two options.

Section C

31 (a) (i) **Sales price variance and sales volume variance**

Sales price variance = (actual price − standard price) × actual volume

	Actual price $	Standard price $	Difference $	Actual volume	Sales price variance $
Plasma TVs	330	350	−20	750	15,000 A
LCD TVs	290	300	−10	650	6,500 A
					21,500 A

Sales volume contribution variance = (actual sales volume − budgeted sales volume) × standard margin

	Actual sales volume $	Budgeted Sales volume $	Difference	Standard margin $	Sales volume variance $
Plasma TVs	750	590	160	190	30,400 F
LCD TVs	650	590	60	180	10,800 F
	1,400	1,180			41,200 F

(ii) **Material price planning and purchasing operational variances**

Material planning variance
= (original target price − general market price at time of purchase) × quantity purchased

($60 − $85) × 1,400 = $35,000 A

Material price operational variance
= (general market price at time of purchase − actual price paid) × quantity purchased

($85 − $80) × 1,400 = $7,000 F

(iii) **Labour rate and labour efficiency variances**

Labour rate variance
= (standard labour rate per hour − actual labour rate per hour) × actual hours worked

Actual hours worked by temporary workers:

Total hours needed if staff were fully efficient = (750 × 2) + (650 × 1.5) = 2,475.
Permanent staff provide 2,200 hours, therefore excess = 2,475 − 2,200 = 275.
However, temporary workers take twice as long, therefore hours worked = 275 × 2 = 550.

Labour rate variance relates solely to temporary workers, therefore ignore permanent staff in the calculation.

Labour rate variance = ($14 − $18) × 550 = $2,200 A

Labour efficiency variance
= (standard labour hours for actual production − actual labour hours worked) × standard rate

(275 − 550) × $14 = $3,850 A

(b) **Explanation of planning and operational variances**

Before the material price planning and operational variances were calculated, the only information available as regards material purchasing was that there was an adverse material price variance of $28,000. The purchasing department will be assessed on the basis of this variance, yet, on its own, it is not a reliable indicator of the purchasing department's efficiency. The reason it is not a reliable indicator is because market conditions can change, leading to an increase in price, and this change in market conditions is not within the control of the purchasing department.

By analysing the materials price variance further and breaking it down into its two components – planning and operational – the variance actually becomes a more useful assessment tool. The planning variance represents the uncontrollable element and the operational variance represents the controllable element.

The planning variance is really useful for providing feedback on just how skilled management is in estimating future prices. This can be very easy in some businesses and very difficult in others. Giving this detail could help to improve planning and standard setting in the future, as management will be increasingly aware of factors which could create volatility in their forecasts.

The operational variance is more meaningful in that it measures the purchasing department's efficiency given the market conditions which prevailed at the time. As can be seen in Carad, the material price operational variance is favourable which demonstrates that the purchasing department managed to acquire the component which was in short supply at a better price than expected. Without this breakdown in the variance, the purchasing department could have been held accountable for the overall adverse variance which was not indicative of their actual performance. This is then a fairer method of assessing performance and will, in turn, stop staff from becoming demotivated.

32   (a)   TIP's financial performance can be assessed in a number of ways:

Sales growth

Sales are up about 1.3% (W1) which is a little above the rate of inflation and therefore a move in the right direction. However, with average admission prices jumping about 8.6% (W2) and numbers of visitors falling, there are clearly problems. Large increases in admission prices reduce the value proposition for the customer, it is unlikely that the rate of increase is sustainable or even justifiable. Indeed with volumes falling (down by 6.7% (W6)), it appears that some customers are being put off and price could be one of the reasons.

Maintenance and repairs

There appears to be a continuing drift away from routine maintenance with management preferring to repair equipment as required. This does not appear to be saving any money as the combined cost of maintenance and repair is higher in 20X5 than in 20X4 (possible risks are dealt with in part (b)).

Directors' pay

Absolute salary levels are up 6.7% (W3), well above the modest inflation rate. It appears that the shareholders are happy with the financial performance of the business and are prepared to reward the directors accordingly. Bonus levels are also well up. It may be that the directors have some form of profit related pay scheme and are being rewarded for the improved profit performance. The directors are likely to be very pleased with the increases to pay.

Wages

Wages are down by 12% (W5). This may partly reflect the loss of customers (down by 6.7% (W6)) if it is assumed that at least part of the wages cost is variable. It could also be that the directors are reducing staff levels beyond the fall in the level of customers to enhance short-term profit and personal bonus. Customer service and indeed safety could be compromised here.

Net profit

Net profit is up a huge 31.3% (W7) and most shareholders would be pleased with that. Net profit is a very traditional measure of performance and most would say this was a sign of good performance.

Return on assets

The profitability can be measured relative to the asset base which is being used to generate it. This is sometimes referred to as ROI or return on investment. The return on assets is up considerably to 11.4% from 8% (W8). This is partly due to the significant rise in profit and partly due to the fall in asset value. We are told that TIP has cut back on new development, so the fall in asset value is probably due to depreciation being charged with little being spent during the year on assets. In this regard it is inevitable that return on assets is up but it is more questionable whether this is a good performance. A theme park (and thrill rides in particular) must be updated to keep customers coming back. The directors of TIP are risking the future of the park.

(b)   Quality provision

Reliability of the rides

The hours lost has increased significantly. Equally the percentage of capacity lost due to breakdowns is now approaching 17.8% (W9). This would appear to be a very high number of hours lost. This would surely increase the risk that customers are disappointed being unable to ride. Given the fixed admission price system, this is bound to irritate some customers as they have effectively already paid to ride.

Average queuing time

Queuing will be seen by customers as dead time. They may see some waiting as inevitable and hence acceptable. However, TIP should be careful to maintain waiting times at a minimum. An increase of 10 minutes (or 50%) is likely to be noticeable by customers and is unlikely to enhance the quality of the TIP experience for them. The increase in waiting times is probably due to the high number of hours lost due to breakdown with customers being forced to queue for a fewer number of ride options.

Safety

The clear reduction in maintenance could easily damage the safety record of the park and is an obvious quality issue.

Risks

If TIP continues with current policies, then they will expose themselves to the following risks:

- The lack of routine maintenance could easily lead to an accident or injury to a customer. This could lead to compensation being paid or reputational damage.

- Increased competition. The continuous raising of admission prices increases the likelihood of a new competitor entering the market (although there are significant barriers to entry in this market, e.g. capital cost, land and so on).

- Loss of customers. The value for money which customers see when coming to TIP is clearly reducing (higher prices, less reliability of rides and longer queues). Regardless of the existence of competition, customers could simply choose not to come, substituting another leisure activity instead.

- Profit fall. In the end if customers' numbers fall, then so will profit. The shareholders, although well rewarded at the moment, could suffer a loss of dividend. Directors' job security could then be threatened.

Workings

1   Sales growth is $5,320,000/$5,250,000 = 1.01333 or 1.3%.

2   Average admission prices were:

   20X4: $5,250,000/150,000 = $35 per person
   20X5: $5,320,000/140,000 = $38 per person
   An increase of $38/$35 = 1.0857 or 8.57%.

3   Directors' pay up by $160,000/$150,000 = 1.0667 or 6.7%.

4   Directors' bonuses levels up from $15,000/$150,000 or 10% to $18,000/$160,000 or 12.5% of turnover. This is an increase of 3/15 or 20%.

5   Wages are down by (1 – $2,200,000/$2,500,000) or 12%.

6   Loss of customers is (1 – 140,000/150,000) or 6.7%.

7   Profits up by $1,372,000/$1,045,000 = 1.3129 or 31.3%.

8   Return on assets:

   20X4: $1,045,000/$13,000,000 = 1.0803 or 8.03%
   20X5: $1,372,000/$12,000,000 = 1.114 or 11.4%

9   Capacity of rides in hours is 360 days × 50 rides × 10 hours per day = 180,000.

20X4 lost capacity is 9,000/180,000 = 0.05 or 5%.
20X5 lost capacity is 32,000/180,000 = 0.177 or 17.8%.

Review Form – Paper F5 Performance Management (02/16)

Name: _____   **Address:** _____

_____

_____

How have you used this Kit?
(Tick one box only)

☐ Home study (book only)

☐ On a course: college _____

☐ With 'correspondence' package

☐ Other _____

Why did you decide to purchase this Kit?
(Tick one box only)

☐ Have used the complementary Study text

☐ Have used other BPP products in the past

☐ Recommendation by friend/colleague

☐ Recommendation by a lecturer at college

☐ Saw advertising

☐ Other _____

During the past six months do you recall seeing/receiving any of the following?
(Tick as many boxes as are relevant)

☐ Our advertisement in *Student Accountant*

☐ Our advertisement in *Pass*

☐ Our advertisement in *PQ*

☐ Our brochure with a letter through the post

☐ Our website www.bpp.com

Which (if any) aspects of our advertising do you find useful?
(Tick as many boxes as are relevant)

☐ Prices and publication dates of new editions

☐ Information on product content

☐ Facility to order books off-the-page

☐ None of the above

Which BPP products have you used?

| Text | ☐ | Passcards | ☐ | Home Study Package | ☐ |
| Practice & Revision Kit | ☑ | i-Pass | ☐ | | |

Your ratings, comments and suggestions would be appreciated on the following areas.

	Very useful	Useful	Not useful
Passing F5	☐	☐	☐
Questions	☐	☐	☐
Top Tips etc in answers	☐	☐	☐
Content and structure of answers	☐	☐	☐
Mock exam answers	☐	☐	☐

| Overall opinion of this Practice & Revision Kit | Excellent ☐ | Good ☐ | Adequate ☐ | Poor ☐ |

Do you intend to continue using BPP products?   Yes ☐   No ☐

The BPP author of this edition can be emailed at: accaqueries@bpp.com

Please return this form to: Head of ACCA & FIA Programmes, BPP Learning Media Ltd, FREEPOST, London, W12 8AA

Review Form (continued)

TELL US WHAT YOU THINK

Please note any further comments and suggestions/errors below.